The Fiction of
Martin Amis

EDITED BY NICOLAS TREDELL

Consultant editor: Nicolas Tredell

macmillan

Published by
PALGRAVE MACMILLAN
Houndmills, Basingstoke, Hampshire RG21 6XS and
175 Fifth Avenue, New York, N.Y. 10010
Companies and representatives throughout the world

PALGRAVE MACMILLAN is the global academic imprint of the Palgrave
Macmillan division of St. Martin's Press, LLC and of Palgrave Macmillan Ltd.
Macmillan® is a registered trademark in the United States, United Kingdom
and other countries. Palgrave is a registered trademark in the European
Union and other countries.

First published 2000 by Icon Books Ltd

ISBN 1–84046–135–7

This book is printed on paper suitable for recycling and made from fully
managed and sustained forest sources.

A catalogue record for this book is available from the British Library.

Transferred to digital printing 2003

Printed and bound in Great Britain by
Antony Rowe Ltd, Chippenham and Eastbourne

Contents

INTRODUCTION   7

Summarises Amis's current critical reputation, provides a brief biography,
and outlines the criticism in the rest of the Guide.

CHAPTER ONE   13

Postmodern Prurience: *The Rachel Papers* (1973)

Perceptive reviews by Peter Prince and Peter Ackroyd; Amis's comments
on his first novel from a 1980s perspective; James Diedrick's exploration
of *The Rachel Papers*, a 'comedy of self-consciousness'; David Hawkes's
view of the novel's protagonist as a postmodern character; Richard
Brown on how the USA figures in the book.

CHAPTER TWO   23

Country-House Carnage: *Dead Babies* (1975)

Insightful reviews by John Mellors, Elaine Feinstein and Peter Ackroyd;
Richard Brown on the novel's trio of Americans; Neil Powell on its literary allusions and grotesque characters; James Diedrick's informed
assessment of *Dead Babies* as a satire.

CHAPTER THREE   34

Snakes and Ladders: *Success* (1978)

Challenging reviews by Blake Morrison and Paul Ableman; James
Diedrick's valuable analysis of the intertextual references of *Success* and
his suggestion that it is a prophecy of Thatcherism; Neil Powell's considered assessment of Amis's first three novels.

CHAPTER FOUR   44

Descent into Hell: *Other People: A Mystery Story* (1981)

The perplexity this novel caused; Blake Morrison's thorough review; Martin Amis's illuminating explications of the novel's mysteries; Brian Finney's intriguing account of the central character's descent into hell.

CHAPTER FIVE   55

Self's the Man: *Money: A Suicide Note* (1984)

Eric Korn's lively and percipient review; Richard Brown on Amis in the USA and England; Bernard Bergonzi's significant remarks on the fusion of English and American fiction in Amis's fifth novel; Amis's own extensive observations on this work, including his response to charges of writing pornographic scenes; Richard Todd's exploration of its intrusive author; Laura L. Doan's challenging critique of its sexism and class bias.

CHAPTER SIX   80

Writing the Unthinkable: *Einstein's Monsters* (1987)

David Profumo's helpful review/Amis interview, combining Profumo's own responses to this collection of short stories with Amis's own comments; Adam Mars-Jones's account of the book in *Venus Envy* (1990), which mounts a powerful general assault on Amis's style; Rachel Falconer's sustained and productive close reading of the stories.

CHAPTER SEVEN   97

Pity the Planet: *London Fields* (1989)

The controversy over this novel's exclusion from the Booker Prize shortlist, allegedly for sexism, followed by four subtle and complex interpretations; Penny Smith's reading of *London Fields* in relation to millennial concerns; Brian Finney's account of its links between murder and narrative; Frederick Holmes on its parody and literalisation of the 'death of the author'; Peter Stokes on the novel's concern with authorship and apocalypse.

CHAPTER EIGHT   126

Wrong in Time: *Time's Arrow* (1991)

Amis's anxieties in writing about the Holocaust; Roger Scruton's surprising endorsement; Donald E. Morse's judicious and sensitive analysis of its themes and techniques; Neil Easterbrook's investigation of the way *Time's Arrow* implicates the reader and of Amis's use of *The Nazi Doctors*; Richard Menke's fascinating account of the novel's thermodynamic metaphors.

CHAPTER NINE   154

That Comes at Night: *The Information* (1995)

The publicity surrounding this novel; thoughtful reviews by Adam Mars-Jones and Julian Loose; and an informed and responsible essay by John Nash which links the themes of the novel to the situation of the modern writer and the debate about the literary canon.

CHAPTER TEN   173

Cops and Slobs: *Night Train* (1997) and *Heavy Water and Other Stories* (1998)

John Updike and Anita Brookner denounce *Night Train*; Russell Celyn Jones dislikes it and Natasha Walter applauds it; Adam Phillips provides a critically sophisticated view. When it comes to *Heavy Water*, Jones and Walter reverse their responses, Jones liking it, Walter hating it, thus demonstrating Amis's continued power to provoke.

NOTES   184

SELECT BIBLIOGRAPHY   193

ACKNOWLEDGEMENTS   203

INDEX   204

A NOTE ON REFERENCES AND QUOTATIONS

Cross-references to the extracts in this Guide, and page references to Martin Amis's fiction, are given in brackets in the main text of the Guide.

All other references are in the endnotes. The Amis texts used are UK hardback or paperback editions; full details can be found in the Bibliography (see p. 193).

In the extracts in this Guide, insertions by the editor are in square brackets and standard type. Definitions of words, where provided by the editor, are taken from the *Concise Oxford Dictionary*, unless otherwise stated in the endnotes. Insertions in square brackets and bold type in the extracts are by the authors of the extracts themselves.

In any quotation, unless otherwise stated, a row of three dots indicates an editorial ellipse within a sentence or paragraph, and a row of six dots (that is, two ellipses) indicates an editorial omission of a paragraph break, or of one or more paragraphs.

INTRODUCTION

MARTIN AMIS is a major writer of our time, and his best work is likely to endure, if the human race is not wiped out by that nuclear apocalypse which is one of the dark figures of his fiction. But his status has not been universally acknowledged. In that respect, of course, he is in good company: Dickens was much criticised in his day, and subsequently;[1] and, as with Amis, Dickens's personal life, especially the break-up of his marriage, became the subject of public attention and controversy.[2] Few would deny Amis talent; there can be little doubt that he has a way with words; but the higher accolades of a residual humanist vocabulary which can be bestowed on novelists – the creation of 'living characters', humanity, maturity, seriousness, unity – have not always been vouchsafed him. Moreover, changes in social and ethical attitudes have laid him open to a new set of charges to which Dickens, at least in his own time, was largely immune:[3] Amis is a middle-class white European male, and it can be argued that his fiction lacks awareness of the limits that condition may impose on his literary imagination. In particular, it can be said – and has been said, strongly and repeatedly – that his representations of women are sexist: this seems to have been the reason that one of his most powerful novels, *London Fields* (1989), was not shortlisted for the Booker Prize, Britain's best-known literary award (see chapter seven of this Guide); and it is no surprise to find the first paragraph of this novel used as the specimen for dissection in a 1995 essay by Sara Mills entitled 'Working with Sexism: what Can Feminist Text Analysis Do?'.[4]

Any literary evaluation of Amis is further complicated by his enmeshment in the internet of modern – or postmodern – publicity. To put it simply, Amis is a star. Authors have been stars before – Dickens again, or Byron, in the nineteenth century; Scott Fitzgerald or, posthumously, Sylvia Plath in the twentieth. But present-day media, with their unprecedented capacity for multiple reproduction and superfast dissemination, have given literary celebrities a new brilliance and reach. Amis has been photographed and interviewed many times – as Anthony Quinn remarked in 1995, '[t]he Amis interview has become, over the years, a little genre of its own'.[5] He has made television appearances, and there is a website devoted to him (see Bibliography – p. 202 – for details). Intense media scrutiny has been directed upon his personal life, particularly his divorce in 1995 and his remarriage in 1998, his physique, especially his relative shortness of stature (he is five-foot six), the cost and nature of his dental treatment, and the size of publishers' advances for his novels. Like most stars, of course, Amis is not merely a passive victim. From, and even before, the start of his literary career, he has himself used and encouraged the attentions of the media. But the publicity generated around his eighth novel, *The Information* (1995), seemed to spiral out of control; as he told Jonathan Wilson in 1995, '"[f]or a while, it seemed as if I couldn't go to the can without it being in the *Evening Standard* [a London newspaper]"'.[6] The possible long-term effects of this media battering remain to be seen – it is the case that, by November 1999, Amis has published only one short and perhaps minor novel, *Night Train* (1997), and a volume of short stories, *Heavy Water* (1998), since *The Information*. But at the time, he was bullish about its impact: '"this stuff clearly *doesn't* bother me – otherwise I'd be a wreck, curled up behind the sofa in the fetal position."'[7]

Talking to Jonathan Wilson, Amis attributes both his capacity to endure the media blitz and the violent reactions he has aroused to a significant source – his father. For any analysis of the fiction, literary career and reputation of Martin Amis is made even more complex by the fact that he is the son of a novelist who was himself famous and controversial – Kingsley Amis. James Diedrick, in his book *Understanding Martin Amis* (1995), contends that the theory of the 'anxiety of influence' developed by the American critic Harold Bloom is 'central to an understanding of [Amis's] fiction'.[8] Bloom argues that writers – he focuses especially on poets, but the idea can be applied more broadly – are engaged in an Oedipal struggle with the male authors who have gone before them, and that only the 'strong' writer, by a kind of creative misreading and rewriting of his precursors, can forge a voice of his own. It seems likely that the 'anxiety of influence', the Oedipal struggle for one's own style, would be made more complicated – to say the least – when one's literary father is also one's biological father; when father and son differ sharply in their literary preferences ('Kingsley Amis: I hate [Nabokov] like poison. Martin Amis: I think he's marvellous'[9]); and when, as Martin Amis has himself pointed out, '"[m]y father I and both have a corpus of work out there at the same time: that's never happened before . . . no [father–son] pair has stuck with it quite the way we have"'.[10] Moreover, in terms of literary reputation, being 'Kingsley Amis's son' is, as Charles Michener pointed out in 1987, 'a boon to the Amis bashers. The idea that "success" is something inherited and not earned abounds in [England,] this green and not always pleasant land'.[11] But Martin Amis himself has also testified to the advantages of having a novelist father: by his own account, not only did it smooth his initial path to publication – '"[i]t meant that your first novel *would* be published, out of mercenary curiosity if nothing else"' – but it also helped him to bear the pressures of success – and notoriety: '"[a] lot of the things about being a writer don't bother me, like bad reviews, because it's always been in the household"'.[12] In *Money* (1984), the character called Martin Amis, a writer living in London – not wholly to be identified with his creator, but not completely distinct from him, either – presents, perhaps not without irony, the son's assumption of the literary father's mantle as a comfortable, almost homely transition rather than a potentially castrating struggle: '"[i]t's just like taking over the family pub"' (p. 88).

The real Martin Amis had a more erratic childhood and adolescence than his fictional namesake's 'family pub' image suggests. The second son of Kingsley and Hilary Bardwell Amis, Martin Louis Amis was born in Oxford on 25 August 1949; but his parents moved often and he attended over twelve schools in all.[13] In 1961, his father taught at Princeton University, New Jersey, and he spent a year living in the USA. After his mother had divorced Kingsley Amis in 1961, when Martin was twelve, he lived in Spain with her for a year. Later in the 1960s, he acted in Alexander McKendrick's film *A High Wind in Jamaica* (1965) in the West Indies – demonstrating his early interest in the modern medium of cinema. This involved a long absence without leave from the Battersea grammar school at which he was then supposed to be a pupil and the school expelled him.[14] Finally, however, he applied himself to study, attending a series of 'crammers' – private schools offering intensive teaching to get students into university – in London and Brighton – and won a place at Exeter College, Oxford. Studying very hard in his last two terms, he 'got a formal First, coming third in that year'.[15] He briefly took jobs at an art gallery and an advertising agency, and then became an editorial assistant at the *Times Literary Supplement*. Working at the *TLS* by day, he wrote his first novel in the evenings. Published in 1973, *The Rachel Papers* was well received by reviewers and won the Somerset Maugham award for the best first novel by a writer under thirty-five – as his father's first novel, *Lucky Jim*, had done in 1954. In 1974 he was made fiction and poetry editor of the *TLS*. His second novel, *Dead Babies*, came out in 1975 and confirmed him as a writer to watch, even if his work provoked critical reservations. From 1977 to 1979, he became editor of the left-wing journal the *New Statesman*, and his third novel, *Success*, appeared in 1978. It once more aroused mixed responses but showed further evidence of an undeniable talent. By the time *Other People: A Mystery Story* was published in 1981, he was a full-time author, combining fiction with journalism for the Sunday newspaper *The Observer*, for which he worked as a 'Special Writer'. In 1984, the year in which the substantial novel *Money* came out, he married an American philosophy teacher, Antonia Philips; they had two sons, Louis and Jacob, now fifteen and thirteen respectively. A collection of short stories relating to the threat of nuclear war, *Einstein's Monsters*, appeared in 1987; *London Fields* was published in 1989 and quickly ran into the Booker Prize controversy mentioned above; and *Time's Arrow*, on the theme of the Holocaust, came out in 1991. Between 1994 and 1995, he was often in the headlines: he was said to be seeking a half-million pound advance for his next novel; he changed his literary agent, Pat Kavanagh, for the reputedly shark-like American Andrew Wylie; as a result of this, his friendship with fellow writer Julian Barnes, Pat Kavanagh's husband, came to an end; his marriage to Antonia Philips broke up as a result of his relationship with a beautiful American heiress and writer, Isabel Fonseca; he sought costly dental treatment for badly decaying teeth and gum disease; it was revealed that he had an illegitimate daughter, Delilah Seale, born to Lamorna Heath in 1975 and now an Oxford undergraduate; a police report confirmed that his cousin, Lucy Partington, had been one of the victims of the serial killer Frederick West; and, in October 1995, his father, Kingsley Amis, died. The publicity surrounding all these events inevitably affected the reception of his eighth novel, *The Information*, published in 1995 and dedicated to his sons and to Lucy Partington. His life did then settle down to some extent; in 1997, he had a daughter, Fernanda, with Isabel Fonseca; he also published the short novel *Night Train* in that year, and, in the following year, the collection *Heavy Water and Other Stories*. It was also in 1998 that he and Isabel married at a modest ceremony, though not without attracting some media attention: the level of press coverage is indicated by the heading of an article on the marriage in the *Times*: 'Amis, author with £20,000 teeth, has £106 wedding'.[16]

This Icon Readers' Guide is concerned with Amis's work rather than his life, although inevitably an author's life impinges upon his or her work in all kinds of ways. The following chapters take the novels and short story collections in order of publication, looking at each one in turn and tracing its reception from the first reviews to the most recent critical essays, with extracts from the most illuminating examples. As Amis has frequently commented on his own fiction in his interviews, these are also quoted wherever appropriate – though it should be remembered that an interview, while it may radiate the aura of authorial authority, is itself a rhetorical construction, and is likely to have been edited and reshaped by the interviewer, by editors, and, sometimes, by the subject himself.

The Guide offers the most wide-ranging examination of Amis's fiction published so far. Chapters one to three look at Amis's first three novels, *The Rachel Papers*, *Dead Babies* and *Success*, providing extracts from Amis's important 1985 interview with John Haffenden, from James Diedrick's well-informed study *Understanding Martin Amis* (1995), from Richard Brown's sharp analysis of Amis's representations of America and Americans, from David Hawkes's insightful essay on Amis's fiction, from

Neil Powell's thoughtful survey of Amis's first three novels, and from perceptive reviews by Paul Ableman, Peter Ackroyd, Elaine Feinstein, John Mellors, Blake Morrison and Peter Prince. In chapter four, Mary Lamb's perplexing descent into hell in *Other People* is thoroughly traced by Blake Morrison, helpfully illuminated by Amis himself, and intriguingly explored in depth by Brian Finney. The fifth chapter includes Eric Korn's lively and percipient review of *Money*, Richard Brown's remarks on Amis in the USA, Bernard Bergonzi's observations on the fusion of American and English fiction in Amis's fifth novel, Amis's own extensive observations on *Money* to John Haffenden, Karl Miller's fascinating interpretation of it in terms of the orphan and the double, Richard Todd's exploration of its use of the intrusive author in relation to postmodern fiction, and Laura L. Doan's powerful critique of what she sees as its sexist and class biases. Chapter six focuses on Amis's first short story collection *Einstein's Monsters* (1987), with David Profumo's combined review and interview with Amis; Adam Mars-Jones's account in *Venus Envy* (1990), which develops into a powerful general assault on Amis's style; and Rachel Falconer's detailed close reading, which demonstrates how the stories reward serious, sustained critical attention. The seventh chapter begins with the controversy over the exclusion of *London Fields* (1989) from the shortlist of the Booker Prize, Britain's best-known literary award, supposedly on grounds of its sexism; the chapter then goes on to offer extracts from a range of subtle and complex analyses of the novel – Penny Smith reads it in relation to its millennial concerns, Brian Finney explores its dramatisation of the links between murder and the act of narrative, Frederick Holmes sees the characters as authors who try to gain control of their stories but find themselves scripted by the wider culture, and Peter Stokes brings together the novel's concern with authorship and apocalypse. Chapter eight includes Amis's own acknowledgement of his anxieties in writing about the Holocaust in *Time's Arrow*, Roger Scruton's surprising endorsement of the novel, Donald E. Morse's judicious and sensitive analysis of its themes and techniques, Neil Easterbrook's examination of how it implicates the reader and of Amis's use of Robert Jay Lifton's *The Nazi Doctors* (1986), and Richard Menke's fascinating exploration of *Time's Arrow* in terms of thermodynamic metaphors. The ninth chapter considers the publicity surrounding *The Information* and provides extracts from thoughtful reviews by Adam Mars-Jones and Julian Loose and the key portions of the valuable essay by John Nash, which brings together a sustained exploration of the themes of the novel in relation to the publicity surrounding it and the more general debate about the literary canon. Chapter ten concentrates first of all on Amis's most recent novel, *Night Train* (1997), sampling the denunciations by John Updike and Anita Brookner, the strictures of Russell Celyn Jones and the sympathetic reaction of Natasha Walter, and the critically sophisticated reading by Adam Phillips. The chapter concludes by comparing and contrasting the responses of Russell Celyn Jones and Natasha Walter to Amis's most recent collection, *Heavy Water and Other Stories* (1998) – responses in which they reverse the positions they took up in relation to *Night Train* and demonstrate the continued power of Amis's fiction to provoke and divide.

To engage with the fiction of Martin Amis is an exciting experience. The essential criticism gathered in these pages captures that excitement but also goes beyond it to demonstrate that Amis's texts richly reward sustained close reading and analysis. This Guide provides an indispensable context for the greater appreciation and understanding of a writer whose work is defining our time and staking a claim on posterity.

CHAPTER ONE

Postmodern Prurience: *The Rachel Papers* (1973)

IF IT was inevitable that a first novel by a son of Kingsley Amis would attract press attention, it was much less inevitable that the attention would be favourable. But reviews of *The Rachel Papers* were largely enthusiastic, though not unreservedly so. A characteristic response is that of Peter Prince in the *New Statesman*, who acknowledges Amis's 'confidence', 'talent' and 'promise' but judges him insufficiently detached from his unsavoury protagonist:

■ Martin Amis . . . shows great promise in his first novel, and this is all the more hopeful since in *The Rachel Papers* he is labouring under the disadvantage of having to build his story of romantic mishaps and youthful self-discovery around a peculiarly obnoxious hero . . . . . .
[But] I can't help thinking that Mr Amis may have been slightly premature in tackling this particular subject. I hope that doesn't sound patronizing; indeed, Mr Amis in his early twenties shows confidence and talent enough to take on anything – except perhaps Charles Highway at 19 years of age. I just feel that a couple of years further away from that age-group might have usefully distanced the author from his subject-matter; at the moment he sometimes gives the impression of still being rather intimately bound up in its concerns, and I think it makes him at once both too indulgent and too harsh in his judgments. Too indulgent, because every now and then one senses from the author a furtive, rather wistful desire to believe that there *is* after all something of value in Charles Highway's messy chatter, in all those dingy little *aperçus* [insights] and corny paradoxes and fifth-hand aphorisms. Too harsh, because Mr Amis, perhaps through fear of being thought sentimental, refuses to give us any indication that there may be – as in life there almost always is – something much finer in the human being lurking behind the smokescreen of Charles's defensive old chat.[1] □

Prince's view that there is an insufficient distance between author and protagonist in *The Rachel Papers* is echoed by James Diedrick in his book *Understanding Martin Amis* (1995), as the extract later in this chapter demonstrates (p. 19). But it was not a view shared by Peter Ackroyd, reviewing Amis's first novel in *The Spectator*. Ackroyd had no more liking than Prince for Charles Highway; but he judged that, with Charles, Amis had both successfully created, and effectively satirised, a 'substantial' character who was representative of 'the younger generation'. In other words, Ackroyd, in contrast to Prince, felt that a properly critical distance between author and central character had been maintained:

■ Well, you old fogies, you were right after all. Martin Amis has exposed the younger generation for the evil and wretched creatures you always supposed them to be, and his only consolation for them is that, once over the hill of adolescence, they may perhaps improve . . . . . . It is obvious that Martin Amis and I come from widely different social circles, since I have never met people like Charles and Rachel. But it turns out that I don't need to, for Amis has brought them entirely to life. They are so inarticulate and so inadequate that they are quite credible, and Amis has brought off the feat of satirizing his contemporaries while making them both funny and, in a bizarre way, moving. This is the case even with Charles, who is not a character one takes to one's heart. He casts an extremely cold eye on sex and on life, in that order, and yet remains at the mercy of his moods.

Highway has the young man's gift for dissecting appearances: accents and social mannerisms are relentlessly exposed, while his own become self-conscious in the extreme. The narrative is often very funny indeed, but I suspect that Martin Amis is getting the last laugh. Charles Highway is so much the archetypal youth, of a certain time and a certain class, that he is necessarily a comic creation. Sex is nowadays the *vox populi* [the voice of the people] and *vox dei* [the voice of God] if certain clergymen have anything to do with it, but for Highway it is a road paved with bad intentions. Although his descriptions are lurid and mechanical to the point of nausea, he has all the fascination and prurience of a naughty little boy who has been caught doing something nasty. There is, in fact, a little boy struggling to get out of Highway's gawky frame – no more so than in the remarkable passages of adolescent *angst* [anxiety] and nostalgia. Martin Amis has fashioned a substantial character out of the rag-ends of our frantic contemporaries, and he has done so without any facile commitment to their means and ends.[2] □

Both Ackroyd and Prince characterised *The Rachel Papers* as a novel about adolescence and Martin Amis himself, looking back on his first book from the 1980s in a conversation with John Haffenden, categorised it as belonging to the 'genre' of 'the adolescent novel'. The discussion provides Amis, prompted by Haffenden's questioning, with an opportunity to make two significant observations on his first novel – that Charles is a 'nascent literary critic' and that the novel, though comic, subverts the expectations associated with traditional comedy:

■ [*John Haffenden:*] *The only novel you've written where irony wasn't required, it seems, was* The Rachel Papers, *where Charles Highway is in a way a self-ironist. He has a literary self-consciousness which in other novels you might reserve for the authorial voice . . .*

[*Martin Amis:*] Yes, the only twist I was conscious of giving to the adolescent novel – the genre to which *The Rachel Papers* belongs – is that Charles Highway is a budding literary critic, whereas the narrators of such novels are usually budding writers. During one particularly painful and messy episode with Rachel, for example, he says '[b]ut these are matters for the psychologist, not for the literary critic' (p. 179). [The text of the novel in fact reads: '[w]hether The Second Incident was a result of The First Incident is a matter for the psychologists, not for the literary critic'.] He is a nascent literary critic, with all the worst faults of the literary critic – that comfortable distance from life. The only come-uppance he gets is from the university tutor who interviews him towards the end (pp. 209–11). Reading the book again after five years I saw with pleased surprise that the tutor was an author-figure, because all my other books have author-figures. He scolds Charles for his misuse of literature. Charles is a crude case of someone who tries to turn literature to his own advantage – using Blake, for example, to seduce girls. Critics do this too, in a sense, the bad ones.

. . . Would you go along with the idea that whereas the novel traditionally adjudicates right and wrong and punishes bad characters, literature actually offers false models for life, which is in reality more messy and less exact?

That's certainly true. In a comic novel the rejected heroine would usually be given some good lines – lingering to set the record straight – but in *The Rachel Papers* Charles Highway says on the last page, '[s]he left without telling me a thing or two about myself, without asking if I knew what my trouble was, without providing any sort of come-uppance at all' (pp. 218–19). You can see the whole process of meting out apt punishments or improbable conversions becoming rather strained even in the nineteenth century, and indeed in Shakespeare . . .'[3] □

Haffenden's observation about the 'self-consciousness' of Charles Highway is echoed by James Diedrick in his exploration of the novel as a 'comedy of self-consciousness'. Diedrick's account of *The Rachel Papers* is the most considered discussion of the novel to date, and the extract that follows covers a number of important aspects: the way in which Charles's thoughts and actions do not originate wholly with himself but are shaped by a broader cultural logic; the novel's intertextuality – its network of allusions to other texts; and its methods – of which intertextuality is one – of distancing Charles from his creator:

■ *The Rachel Papers* . . . is an audacious first novel. Written by a practi[s]ing literary critic about a would-be literary critic, it makes high comedy out of its own self-reflexiveness . . . . . . In the hands of a less gifted writer, this self-reflexiveness might have become tiresome self-indulgence. But *The Rachel Papers* possesses a ferocious verbal energy that animates every page, and its author has managed to transform his own artistic self-consciousness into a dramatic monologue on the subject spoken by a fully realized character whose obsessiveness becomes the stuff of serious comedy . . . . . . There is something chilling about this comedy, however, since the dehumanization it captures has its source in a social and economic system. Charles's most intimate thoughts and actions are never wholly his own, shaped as they are by a cultural logic that penetrates even the unconscious . . .

The title of the novel is similarly double-voiced. It comes from Charles himself, yet it evokes more famous literary predecessors: *The Bickerstaff Papers* (1708) [Jonathan Swift (1667–1745)] and *The Aspern Papers* (1888) [Henry James (1843–1916)]. The 'Rachel Papers' are the mass of notes, diaries, and memoranda that Charles spends the last five hours of his nineteenth year shuffling and reshuffling . . . The novel's twelve chapters are structured by the clock, beginning with '[s]even o'clock: Oxford' (p. 7) and ending with '[m]idnight: coming of age' (p. 205). While each chapter is rooted in a precisely realized present, much of the novel's action takes place in a complex series of flashbacks ranging back in time from a few days to several years. By revisiting the past (or rather his literary rendering of it) Charles attempts to construct his currently older, supposedly wiser self. This narrative structure creates much of the comedy of self-consciousness that is *The Rachel Papers* . . . [But] Charles's endless literary self-fashioning is more than a symptom of his self-consciousness; it is part of what Amis has called his own 'genuine idea about modern life – that it's so mediated that authentic experience is much harder to find'.[4]

As befits a novel about self-consciousness, the plot of *The Rachel Papers* concerns Charles's own obsessive plotting: to achieve his twin, intertwined desires of entrance to Oxford and Rachel Noyes. He achieves both, the first on the first attempt and the second (as Rachel's last name implies) after an initial rejection. But his efforts in both cases are so compulsively, self-consciously calculating that they nearly extinguish the genuine passion that may have originally motivated them. From the first, Rachel functions at least in part as a fantasy-projection of Charles's own upwardly mobile aspirations (her first name is a virtual anagram of his own). Unlike his current girlfriend, who works contentedly at a pet food store, Rachel is studying for university, and has a tony [stylish, fashionable] Hampstead address. Her apparent refinement holds the same allure for Charles as an Oxford degree, and her involvement with another man, an American, increases her desirability. By the time he wins her affections, however, he has already judged her wanting: 'Rachel's character was about as high-powered as her syntax' (p. 72). Reductively imagined by Charles, she *is* her prose. Midway through his account of their initial lovemaking, Charles's present-tense voice breaks in to record that his experience was nothing like that which D. H. Lawrence's novels celebrate; it was 'an aggregate of pleasureless detail, nothing more; an insane, gruelling, blow-by-blow obstacle course' (p. 149). Similarly, when Charles writes his Oxford entrance essays, Chaucer, Shakespeare, Blake, and Hardy become occasions for rhetorical performances designed to demonstrate his precocity and 'characteristic knowingness' (p. 181). He is finally brought up short late in the novel by the Oxford don who evaluates these essays. His rebuke speaks to Charles's treatment of people as well as literature: '"[l]iterature has a kind of life of its own, you know. You can't just use it . . . ruthlessly, for your own ends"' (p. 211).

This comeuppance is one of the ways Amis places distance between himself and Charles. The others are more subtle, and presume wide acquaintance with many of the writers referred to in the novel. Of the more than one hundred authors and literary texts alluded to in *The Rachel Papers*, two are of crucial importance to the novel's themes: John Keats's *The Eve of St Agnes* (1820) and [Jonathan Swift's] *Cassinus and Peter* (1731). Keats's poem is a lushly sensuous rumination on the relationship between romantic desire and self-deception. As soon as Madeleine and Porphyro consummate their passion, wind and sleet assail the window-panes of Madeleine's chamber, portending future troubles. Immediately after Rachel admits to Charles that she has lied to him about her father, and Charles has curtailed an admission of his own waning feelings toward her, Charles reports that 'the wind outside, which had been strong all evening, started to make cornily portentous noises, cooed from behind the cellar door, fidgeted with the window-frames' (pp. 203–4).

In the previous chapter Charles was confronted by two graphic reminders of Rachel's bodily nature, and this fundamentally alters a relationship which he reports 'had been . . . straightforward and idealized . . . utterly without *candour*' (p. 178). This chapter is subtitled '(the Dean of St Patrick's)' (p. 162), a reference to Jonathan Swift, and the unnamed poem that shapes this chapter is the once-infamous 'Cassinus and Peter', a satirical portrait of a Cambridge undergraduate driven to hysteria by his discovery that his beloved 'Celia, Celia, Celia shits!'.[5] Unlike Cassinus, Charles is aware of the role self-deception plays in his desire, but the sexual double standard still holds sway over him. Despite his longing for authenticity, his Keatsian desire to embrace pure sensation, few of Charles's experiences are direct ones. In one of his many moments of self-criticism, he indicts himself for this: 'I will not be placed at the mercy of my spontaneous self' (p. 176).

Charles's preternatural self-consciousness as he composes his one and only narrative is analogous to Martin Amis's own as he wrote his first novel in the shadow of his famous novelist father.[6] How to put oneself on the map, place enough distance between oneself and one's most significant precursor? . . . . . . [The relationship between Charles and his father in the novel] is not unlike the relationship between *The Rachel Papers* and *Lucky Jim*. Both are first novels by gifted comic writers, and bear many family resemblances, from mastery of dialect and dialogue to delight in comic incongruities. But *The Rachel Papers* is clearly, defiantly different than *Lucky Jim* . . . . . . Charles Highway has clearly read *Lucky Jim*, because midway through the novel he explicitly rejects Jim Dixon's maxim [that 'nice things are nicer than nasty ones'[7]] and replaces it with his own down-and-dirty comic aesthetic: '[s]urely, nice things are dull, and nasty things are funny. The nastier a thing is, the funnier it gets' (p. 88). Expressed so crudely, this may sound like little more than an adolescent male's malicious sense of humor – and Martin Amis's way of tweaking his father. But it is in fact consistent with Charles's earlier aesthetic announcement: 'I had begun to explore the literary grotesque, in particular the writings of Charles Dickens and Franz Kafka, to find a world full of the bizarre surfaces and sneaky tensions with which I was always trying to invest my own life' (pp. 63–64). The fictions of Dickens and Kafka often combine cruelty and laughter. So do the satires of Jonathan Swift. What is emerging here is Martin Amis's own literary manifesto – one part exorcism of his father's precedent, one part declaration that his own province is the comedy of the grotesque.

Charles's assertion that 'nasty things are funny' comes at the beginning of a chapter titled 'Nine: the bathroom', where he speculates about his 'anal sense of humour' ('very common among my age group'). As he speculates further about its source, he suggests that it stems from a '[s]ound distrust of personal vanity plus literary relish of physical grotesqueries' (p. 88). This brings Swift to mind, whose own representations of bodily excesses are inseparable from his Christian humanism. Vanity was one of Swift's favorite satiric targets, and he deflates it by rubbing his readers' noses in the corruptibility of their fleshly selves. Amis's own aesthetic of the carnal in *The Rachel Papers*, however, is less moralistic, and more transgressive, than Swift's . . . . . .

All of the potentially serious emotional scenes in *The Rachel Papers* are . . . curtailed, or inadequately realized (a weakness that will continue to plague Amis's fiction). When Rachel initially declines Charles's advances, for instance, his reaction is surprising ('I felt completely hollow, as if I were a child' (p.86)) because glibness and calculation have so dominated his account of his relationship to her. Charles wants to represent his affair (to the reader and Rachel) as his first emotionally serious relationship, but it is never convincingly rendered as such. Similarly, near the end of the novel Charles has a final confrontation with his father, which becomes a reconciliation. But Charles's emotional freight is so quickly unloaded, and his expression of solidarity with his father so pat, that it seems like another verbal pose.

Given the parodic nature of *The Rachel Papers*, this is not surprising. While the novel can be read as a (male) adolescent coming-of-age story, it can just as easily be taken as a *parody* of the genre, not to mention a parody of the kind of comic romance Kingsley Amis produced in *Lucky Jim*. Parody is subversive, representing a rejection of social or aesthetic authority, but it doesn't elaborate alternatives. Unlike Jim Dixon, who clearly becomes the moral center of *Lucky Jim*, Charles Highway remains something of an enigma at the end of *The Rachel Papers*. He is not simply a satiric target; *The Rachel Papers* may be a satiric comedy, but it is not a full-fledged satire. Author and reader may laugh at Charles's excesses, but they are also implicated in them. *The Rachel Papers* is Amis's first achievement in that most demanding of narrative modes, the dramatic monologue – which requires that the novelist make his own voice heard through and sometimes in spite of the first-person narrator. It is a form Amis raises to the level of high postmodern art in several of his later novels, when his narrators bear fewer resemblances to him than Charles does. In *The Rachel Papers*, it is not always clear where Amis stands in relation to his narrator.[8] □

Diedrick seems to imply here that the confusion he sometimes perceives between Amis and Highway is a weakness. David Hawkes, however, in his essay on Amis for Scribner's *British Writers: Supplement IV* (1997) acknowledges the possibility of such confusion but attributes it more to insensitive reading than authorial slackness. Like Diedrick, Hawkes draws contrasts and comparisons between the first novels of father and son, affirming that '*The Rachel Papers* is a response to and an updating of *Lucky Jim*'[9] and that Charles Highway is 'Jim Dixon transposed from the 1950s to the 1970s';[10] but this makes Charles a different kind of literary character altogether:

19

■ Another way of putting this would be to say that while Jim Dixon is a realistic character, Charles Highway is a postmodern character who lives through literary texts – both the ones he reads in order to find out how to act in real life and those he writes as records and analyses of his real life . . . In fact, Highway has no 'real' life at all; he experiences the world on an entirely textual basis . . . . . .

When *The Rachel Papers* was published, Amis was a clever young man, just down from Oxford, with literary aspirations. His novel paints a portrait of a clever young man with literary aspirations about to go up to Oxford. As in *Lucky Jim*, such plot as there is involves the seduction of a young woman, but *The Rachel Papers* is primarily an analysis of Charles Highway's adolescent character, written in the tradition of Goethe's *The Sorrows of Young Werther* (1744; final version, 1787) or Salinger's *The Catcher in the Rye* (1951). With such a book there is an inevitable temptation to identify the writer with his creation; Kingsley Amis was so annoyed that people identified him with Jim Dixon that he became Evelyn Waugh instead. The egregious Charles Highway is dangerously similar to what the average reader knows about Martin Amis, and many readers have formed permanent antipathies toward Amis on that basis. A sensitive audience, however, will notice the way in which Highway is subtly but deliberately differentiated from his creator. For example, he puts a good deal of emphasis on his own artificiality, constantly reminding us that he is playing a series of roles, acting out scenes from the books he reads. At times this knowledge seems to develop into an awareness that he is a character in a narrative written by someone else . . . . . .

. . . Highway progresses from being a self-conscious manipulator of his own persona to intimating that even his 'true' personality is a literary construction. He ultimately tires of Rachel when it is revealed that she, too, has built up a fictional image for herself, inventing stories about a glamorous Parisian father who fought in the Spanish Civil War . . . . . . When she is no longer a character in one of his stories, or when she invents a character for herself, she loses his attention. Highway can only perceive the world through his writing and his reading: he first greets Rachel with a quote from Alfred Tennyson [In fact, Charles improvises a creative misquotation from Tennyson's poem *Tithonus* (1860), rendering Tennyson's original third line, 'Man comes and tills the field and lies beneath'[11] as 'Man comes and drinks the wine and lies beneath' – though characteristically he thinks '[Rachel] wouldn't get the reference and would simply think I was being hearty' (p. 34)]; to facilitate seduction he leaves Jane Austen's *Persuasion* (1818) on the bed and discusses William Blake; to delay orgasm, he mentally recites the poetry of T. S. Eliot. Other characters are similarly defined by their relation to literature. For instance, when George Eliot's *Daniel Deronda*

(1876) is mentioned, Highway's boorish, proletarian brother-in-law remarks, "'I've seen that. BBC 2'" (p. 143). Rachel is writing a paper on it in school, and Highway falsely denies having read it. The only significant rebuke Charles receives comes from the tutor who interviews him at Oxford: "'[l]iterature has a kind of life of its own, you know. You can't just use it . . . ruthlessly, for your own ends'" (p. 211). But he can – and does – right up until the end. When Rachel reproaches him for the '"*horrible*"' letter he has written to tell her their affair is over, he replies, "'[t]he content or the style?'" (p. 218). He does not reform, remaining resolute in his determination to manipulate his personality as circumstances dictate: 'I will not be placed at the mercy of my spontaneous self' (p. 176). There is more curiosity than contrition in his musing on the novel's last page: 'I wonder what sort of person I can be' (p. 219).[12] □

There is one aspect of Charles's manipulation of his personality which is not mentioned by Hawkes, or by Ackroyd or Prince, and is only alluded to very briefly by Diedrick: this is his attitude to the USA. But *The Rachel Papers* does invoke the USA to some extent and marks the beginning of an engagement in fiction with America that will develop significantly in subsequent novels, as Richard Brown points out in 'Postmodern Americas' (1994):

■ Charles Highway, who fast-talks, writes and womanizes his way through cramming college into Rachel and Oxford in *The Rachel Papers*, is a Londoner. The smooth, wealthy De Forest Hoeniger, principal rival for Rachel's affection is an American: a stereotypical one (Charles's imagination is full of satirical grotesques) before whom he is at first embarrassed and over whom he eventually triumphs, only to sicken with disgust at the achievements of his predatory sexual acquisition. When Charles's shadowy natural father appears with Vanessa 'just flown in from New York' (p. 105), he can give full vent to a construction of American identity that justifies his hatred:

'Because they're violent. Because they only like extremes. Even the rural people, the old reactionaries in the farms, go out blowing niggers' heads off, roast a Jew or two, disembowel a Puerto Rican. Even the hippies are all eating and mass-murdering each other.' (p. 107)

Much of Highway's sex-life and mind-life are a reflection of Anglo-American semiotics. Being clever about the English literary tradition of Milton and Blake is a potential means of advancement for Charles but 'the most violent and tuneless of all [his] American LPs, *Heroin* by the Velvet Underground' (p. 55) is his best strategic tool for casual seduction. The copulation and disgusted sex-fantasy that emerges in the souring of his relationship with Rachel in the tenth chapter is justified in the context that he has 'been reading a lot of American fiction' (p. 184, evidently a reference to the scene from [Norman Mailer's novel] *An American Dream* (1965) that Amis describes in *The Moronic Inferno* (p. 63)).

It might be said of Charles Highway that he becomes or nearly becomes the symbolic America that he hates. Indeed the narrative of his personal development may be another version of the flawed Eden-cum-Utopia which he describes in one of his own more inspired passages of student literary criticism (p. 112). Ironically what may save Charles is the academic canon of English Literature, the safe classics his adolescent brilliance can engage, evade or subvert but which can still (as is shown in the put-down/acceptance he receives from the Oxford don who examines him for University entrance at the close) show him to himself for what he is.[13] ☐

It is interesting that, in all the extracts quoted so far, including those from Amis himself, the words of the Oxford don are held to comprise an authoritative judgement on Charles, rather than as themselves open to question. This perhaps says something about the prestige of Oxford dons, (even when they look like 'hippies' (p. 208)) and about the tendency of present-day critics to identify with teachers of literature. But might not the view that 'literature has a kind of life of its own' be seen as a cliché of the conventional literary criticism of the time, which reflects adversely on the don's supposed commitment to new American writing?

Doubtless, however, the sentiment helped to reinforce Amis's reputation as a promising young novelist who could both vividly portray adolescence but showed reassuring signs of incipient maturity. With *The Rachel Papers*, he was safely launched; indeed it seems to have become a model of the kind of work a budding young novelist should produce, for the first novel of American author Jacob Epstein, *Wild Oats* (1980), allegedly plagiarised phrases from *The Rachel Papers*.[14] But now the second novel, usually regarded as a dangerous obstacle in a writer's progress, lay ahead for Amis – most people with any acquaintance with modern literature have heard of *Lucky Jim*, but how many could easily recall the title of Kingsley Amis's second novel?[15] Martin Amis had proved that he could produce a first novel to set alongside his father's, but what would he do next? The second chapter of this Guide answers that question.

CHAPTER TWO

Country-House Carnage: *Dead Babies* (1975)

A MIS SOON followed up his first novel with a second, in 1975, whose very title seemed designed to shock – *Dead Babies* (it was temporarily retitled *Dark Secrets* for a paperback edition).[1] Shock effects continued throughout the novel, as reviewers observed. But John Mellors, in a perceptive notice in *The Listener*, also detected a conventional theme, and a central sentimentality absent from *The Rachel Papers*:

■ Everyone in Martin Amis's sad, savage and (at times) extremely funny satire *'tends to be either drunk or stoned or hungover or sick'* (p. 31). Living mainly on a diet of drugs, gin, strong champagne cocktails, 'para-natural Whiski' (p. 107) and hardly any food, the degenerates in *Dead Babies* are constantly retching, vomiting and ejecting burps . . . like [']mouth farts' (p. 114). But it is mental sickness from which they suffer most acutely: 'cancelled sex' (pp. 31, 148, 192, 199, 201), 'lagging time' (pp. 31, 133, 134), 'false memory' (pp. 31, 57, 148, 169, 177, 178, 179, 201) and 'street sadness' (pp. 31, 57, 111, 169, 179, 201). Their lives are cancelled very nastily in the Mansonian mayhem at the end ['Mansonian' here alludes to Charles Manson, the leader of a group of hippies who savagely murdered the pregnant actress Sharon Tate and her three guests in California in August 1969].

The title-phrase is used by Amis's characters to pour scorn on outmoded concepts like jealousy, faithfulness and love, and by Amis himself to describe his cast, the six 'Appleseeders' living in Appleseed Rectory in Hertfordshire and their four guests, a golden-hearted whore and a 'triad' or 'troy' of Americans. The time is the future, into which the dead babies have grown up through a period when 'sexual lassitude and disgust seemed to be everywhere among the young, and two-night stands were becoming a rarity' (p. 82); but the business of the satirist, as Amis points out in a quotation from Menippus [which

serves as the epigraph of the novel], 'is not prophecy, just as his subject
is not tomorrow . . . it is today' (p. 10). [Menippus, who lived in the first
half of the third century BC, originated the Menippean satire, a mixture
of prose and verse, which influenced later satirists such as Petronius,
author of the *Satyricon*, and Lucian.[2]] Yet Amis's theme is a conventional
one – that relationships without affection are boring, meaningless and
sterile . . .

Martin Amis is obsessed by bodily functions and dwells with
loving distaste on the digestive processes and on 'gaping vaginas,
rhubarb penises and gouged behinds' (p. 181). He is witty: '"a cooked
breakfast – it would be like going to bed in pyjamas or reading an
English novel"' (p. 21). His dialogue is brilliant, particularly the conversations between the *blasés* Appleseeders and Marvell, the earnest
American; when the cynical Quentin teases him by making remarks in
favour of getting married '"to keep sex emotional"', Marvell is horrified,
and protests that '"[t]he iconography of desire's too pervasive now"'
(p. 137). The description of the obese Whitehead family packing their
grotesque limbs into a small car (pp. 144–6) is quite Rabelaisian
[Rabelaisian means 'of or like François Rabelais (1494?–1553?) in his
writings; marked by exuberant imagination and language and coarse
humour and satire'.]. But beneath the skilfully presented shock-effects
of *Dead Babies*, there is a sentimentally sweet and squelchy centre – a
flavour I did not detect in Amis's first novel, *The Rachel Papers*.[3] □

Sentimentality was not a flavour that the novelist and poet Elaine
Feinstein tasted in *Dead Babies*, but she went further than Mellors in
affirming its difference from *The Rachel Papers*. It seemed clear to her that
Martin Amis did not mean to try to clear the hurdle of the second novel
by attempting to imitate his first triumphant leap:

■ Second novels are difficult; following success is difficult; one thing
Martin Amis ensures: *Dead Babies* offers no repetition of the joyous
hilarity of *The Rachel Papers*. It is more like a declaration of war on the
assumptions that made the first book possible. And it is not for the
squeamish. To give what seems to me a most telling example of the
games Amis now plays with language, the title [a]rises out of a piece
of invented and ambiguous slang: don't give me . . . all this ['"]dead
babies"' (pp. 56, 95, 137, 169). His purpose in pushing the stylishly
foul-mouthed to this point is similar to his intention in throwing his
privileged and corrupt adolescents into a future where the really cool
can enjoy the last reaches of the technology of sex and violence, while
the rest of humanity hangs about raggedly under the stanchions of
some overhead bypass. This poor distorted generation, full of hatred
for their parents, and terrified of any form of compassion or gallantry,

is described with a total ferocity which is nevertheless frequently comic. Giles's opening dream of losing his teeth, one by one, into the mouthpiece of the telephone, echoes through the book to the point where he cannot bring himself to articulate the word 'dentist' [In fact, it seems to be the word 'teeth' that gives Giles particular trouble – see p. 211]. A sexual encounter intended to evoke *Story of O* eroticism collapses with Andy's penis caught in his zip (p. 85). Nevertheless, the book is a long way from a romp. Rather as I hope for society that this is no true prophecy, I hope for Martin Amis that the nightmare of this vision will rapidly become part of his past. In the meanwhile, it is a remarkable fantasy.[4] □

Feinstein's definition of *Dead Babies* as a 'fantasy' was echoed by Peter Ackroyd in his *Spectator* review: he also found 'farce, and melodrama' in the novel; but he resisted the invitation of its epigraph to classify *Dead Babies* as a satire, as John Mellors had done. Ackroyd was, however, akin to Mellors in bringing a charge of sentimentality against the novel though he redefined sentimentality as an excessive devotion to one reality at the expense of all others which was evident, for him, in the novel's 'obscenity'.

■ At first sight *Dead Babies* might be, as a fetching quote from Menippus . . . suggests, a 'satire'. It is set in an indefinite future, and it chronicles the amphetamine highs and venereal lows of a group of the liberated young, so liberated in fact that they have lost even themselves in the process. But sex and drugs have already been abandoned as stimulants by serious hedonists, and at this late date [1975] any satire on them would be misdirected. Also, Martin Amis's characters are so singular and so quirky that they would be crushed out of recognition by the engines of conventional satire. *Dead Babies* is if anything a fantasy since Amis has turned some familiar neuroses and some conventional dreams into the healing patterns of violence and comedy. The rest is farce, and melodrama.

Having got these little matters of definition sorted out, it is as well to say at the beginning that *Dead Babies* can be an extremely funny book, all the more comic for squeezing the lemons of 'taste' and 'seriousness' for all they're worth. It is an inverted, and often perverted, image of mannered country-house comedy. Appleseed Rectory, where the gang all meet, is *'a place of shifting outlines and imploded vacuums; it is a place of lagging time and false memory, a place of street sadness, night fatigue and cancelled sex'* (p. 31). The murky background of Martin Amis's victims is sketched in, onanistic [masturbatory] nightmares are introduced with trumpet and fanfare, rainbow drugs are dispensed, and everyone sits back for the fun to begin. It doesn't, of course.

Mr Amis doesn't create a particularly complex story, nor does he take his plots very far or very fast, and the brunt of his comedy lies in the clever manipulation of language and the general sharpness of his descriptions. All human aspirations, all of Man's little decencies, the dignity of our procreative functions, the life of our souls, the wealth of inter-personal relations, the facilities of human expression, all of them come under Amis's hammer. By no stretch of the mind is this a life-enhancing vision, but his writing has all the horrified perceptiveness of someone wrinkling up his nose – or worse – at something nasty . . . In fact, *Dead Babies* is a comedy at the expense of everybody in its pages. And although a sharp vision can sometimes give Amis's prose a perfect pitch, it becomes not so much sharp as narrow and eventually threatens to shrink the book down altogether. The general messiness and the futuristic shock become too messy and too shocking, and the sentimentality which hovers around all obscenity (which is, after all, an excessive devotion to one reality at the expense of all others) suffocates some of the preceding wit and humour.[5] □

One aspect of *Dead Babies* not raised by Ackroyd and Feinstein, but briefly alluded to in John Mellors's description of Buzhardt Marvell as 'the earnest American', is the representation of characters from the USA in *Dead Babies*. In his contribution to *Forked Tongues*, Richard Brown finds that the portraits of Americans, in Amis's second novel, as in his first (see p. 21), are 'stereotypes':[6]

■ One group of the party of sick hedonists whose wild debauch at the Appleseed Rectory leads them to well-deserved destruction is classified, in the cast list that prefaces the novel, as '*The Americans*' (p. 11). During the stylized introductions to the suave, cynical and/or grotesque sex-and-drug crazed Brits, what we first hear of the trio of Americans is that they are involved in a sexual grouping described as a '"troy"' (p. 21). They enter as an absurd version of Rabelaisian erotic dystopia from the country of the unrestrained self. Roxeanne (at least from Keith's point of view) is: 'one of those terrifying, genetics-experiment, gate-fold American girls – well over six foot in her platforms, a bonfire of lambent red hair, breasts like zeppelins, large firm high backside, endless legs' (p. 54). And the leading figure in the American group Marvell Buzhardt (counterpart to the British host Quentin Villiers) offers up the philosophy that justifies their deeds: '"*Fuck* all this dead babies abo[ut] love, understanding, compassion – use drugs to kind of . . . cushion the consciousness, guide it, protect it, stimulate it"' (p. 56).

American literature comes in for its usual roasting in the book. To 'Mailer' (p. 40) is part of the group's porno-taxonomy [that is, its classification of sexual acts], and there is some clever comedy where the English and American languages clash in dialogue. Andy Adorno's memorable definition of the British team as '"ecstatic materialists"' who '"grab whatever the fuck's going"' (p. 155) suggests that they are as bad, if not worse, themselves. It may or may not be significant that it is when the English and American characters are fully merged in their transatlantic meeting of competitive self-destruction that their own death wish drives them to destruction, just as their worst nightmare, the mysterious Johnny, had turned out to be none other than an 'other self' of Quentin Villiers.[7] □

Neil Powell, discussing *Dead Babies* in his survey of Amis's first three novels, finds the characterisation of the Americans even more grotesque than that of the English characters, but points out that the Americans are finally less destructive than the apparent English gentleman. In the extract from his essay which follows, Powell also usefully suggests some of the literary allusions in the novel:

■ [*Dead Babies*] is full of literary and other allusions: a novel of Iris Murdoch's is mentioned ([*The Black Prince* (1972)] pp. 45, 45–46), reminding us that this enclosed country-house plot is a development or a perversion of a typically Murdochian world; Quentin's magazine *Yes* has 'won outspoken praise from William Burroughs, Gore Vidal, Angus Wilson' (p. 53) – writers evidently among Amis's influences and his targets. On a different level, the idea of flower-power gone to seed is plainly suggested by 'Appleseed' (Apple was of course the Beatles' company) while it is no coincidence that the diabolical drug-mixer, Marvell Buzhardt, shares a name with [the seventeenth-century poet Andrew Marvell,] author of 'The Garden'.

The Appleseeders are a grotesque bunch. The sanest of them is probably Diana Parry, who 'spends a lot of the time wondering what the hell she's doing in Appleseed Rectory' (p. 78) and who, before the final catastrophe[,] asks: '"Don't you think we must have made a mistake a long time ago to end up like this. That something went wrong and that's why we're all so dead now . . . Baby?"' (p. 169). Her boyfriend, Andy Adorno, is a pastiche of trendy machismo: keen on drinking, fighting and swearing, but sexually disappointing and the only character to respond in a conventionally 'sentimental' way to the bizarre death of The Mandarin, Celia's cat, which goes berserk after Marvell has drugged its food:

Andy returned for the last time to The Mandarin's body. 'I loved that cat,' he said unsteadily. 'I did.'
'It just checked out, man,' said Marvell.

'Yeah,' said Andy, breathing in. 'But Jesus I hate this no-good motherfuckin chickenshit weekend.' (p.177)

That provides a marginal degree of redemption for Andy. Celia is the least vividly realized of the Appleseeders, largely because her main function is to be married to the 'superman' Quentin Villiers ('[t]he versatility of the fellow!' (p.53)) who is the presiding or at any rate the manipulating genius behind Appleseed Rectory and who

> can talk all day to a butcher about the longevity of imported meats, to an air-hostess about safety regulations in the de Gaulle hangars, to an insurance salesman about post-dated transferable policies, to a poet about non-typographical means of distinguishing six-syllable three-lined stanzas and nine-syllabled two-line ones, to an economist about pre-war counter-inflationary theory, to a zoologist about the compensatory eye-movements of the iguana. Just so, he can address a barrow-boy in rhyming slang, a tourist in yokel French, a Sunderlander in Geordie, a Newmarket tout in genteel Cambridge-shire, a gypsy in Romany. (p.53)

He is, then, a kind of Everyman. But we are warned:

> Watch Quentin closely. Everyone else does. Stunned by his good looks, proportionately taken aback by his friendliness and accessi-bility, flattered by his interest, struck by the intimacy of his manner and lulled by the hypnotic sonority of his voice – it is impossible to meet Quentin without falling a little bit in love. (p.53)

The two remaining residents are Giles Coldstream – perhaps the one real comic creation in the novel, endearingly neurotic and gin-sodden, obsessed with dentistry – and Keith Whitehead. Little Keith is the Court Dwarf, revoltingly obese, distinguished from the others by a background which might be called 'ordinarily' dreadful rather than modishly, affluently dreadful. He suffers and (therefore?) survives.

Even more grotesque are the three Americans – Marvell Buzhardt, Skip Marshall and Roxeanne Smith – who seem to be the forces of destruction, who frighten even Diana and Andy, and who more than frighten Keith. But they are merely catalysts: the real danger, and the source of the novel's thriller-aspect, lies elsewhere.

The hurtling, obsessive obscenity of *Dead Babies* . . . is in the end, as it is intended to be, numbing: that, after all, is part of the satirist's moral. Yet, like all Amis's novels, the book has a soft side and strikes unexpected notes of wry gentleness: when the assembled company is 'a-wheeze with boredom' after watching 'unspeakable acts' (p.181) (catalogued nonetheless) performed on film and Marvell promises something '"new"' and '"different"' (p. 182), the treat turns out to be a scene enacted with vintage Hollywood decorum. The point, of course, is that it is infinitely more erotic than the hard-core pornography. The watchers, attuned to a more brutalized world, are confused and astonished. But by now it is too late for redemption – as we have been told, in a passage of sudden dazzling eloquence, a few pages before:

> Yes, it was seven o'clock and a pall of thunder hung over the Rectory rose-gardens. The formerly active air was now so weighed down that it seeped like heavy water over the roof. Darkness flowed in the distance, and the dusk raked like a black searchlight across the hills towards them.
> But pity the dead babies. Now, before it starts. They couldn't know what was behind them, nor what was to come. The past? They had none. Like children after a long day's journey, their lives arranged themselves in a patchwork of vanished mornings, lost afternoons and probable yesterdays. (p. 180)

Those two beautifully balanced paragraphs show Amis's writing at its best: in their context – they occur abruptly in the harshest section of the book – they are stunningly effective. However, that awkward 'Yes . . .' hints at a narrative weakness: the problem of tone is no more resolved here than it was in *The Rachel Papers*, and Amis's attempts at ironic or satirical detachment employing updated Swiftian or Fieldingesque devices, are uneasy.[8] □

It is interesting to compare Powell's positive judgement of the passage on p. 180 of *Dead Babies* with that of James Diedrick in the extract that follows. Both critics use the term 'soft'; but for Diedrick it carries a pejorative connotation and is the consequence of a failure of judgement (p. 33). While Diedrick shares Powell's view that the novel is not a total success as a satire, he explores Amis's satirical aims and techniques more deeply, linking them with Menippean satire, with the ideas of the twentieth-century Russian critic Mikhail Bakhtin, and with Denis Diderot's *Rameau's Nephew* (1762):

■ *Dead Babies* is Amis's first and last experiment in formal satire, and it is easy to see why. It exhibits the same verbal inventiveness that characterizes *The Rachel Papers*, but little of its comic high spirits. In place of the fully realized Charles Highway Amis presents ten minimally rendered characters, most of them suffering from *'street sadness'* and *'cancelled sex'* (p. 31), their outward liberation masking inward blight. And they are all forced to serve a satire that is less successful than the satirical comedy of *The Rachel Papers*. Nastiness proliferates . . . but the novel is only fitfully funny. Despite these limitations, *Dead Babies* is full of interest – for readers of Amis as well as students of satire and the novel. It manifests Amis's ambitious experiments with genre, point of view, and voice as he moves beyond the autobiographical locus of his first novel and toward the wider social concerns of his later work.

. . . The narrative [of *Dead Babies*] spans three days, Friday through Sunday. Six English residents of Appleseed Rectory play host to a weekend revel featuring increasing amounts of alcohol, drugs, and thwarted sex. They are joined by a trio of Americans, a young woman from London, and the mysterious 'Johnny', who turns out to be a double of one of the other characters. The authorial persona, who appears occasionally to remind the reader of his control over the other eleven, constitutes a shadowy twelfth character. The 'dead babies' of the title refers to a variety of humanist beliefs that most members of the group have declared defunct. This phrase is evoked whenever any of these beliefs threaten the narcissistic ethos articulated most aggressively by Marvell Buzhardt. Buzhardt is American, a 'postgraduate in psychology, anthropology and environment at Columbia University' (p. 55), and the author of *The Mind Lab*, which promotes the hedonistic use of psychoactive chemicals. As the weekend proceeds he distributes a variety of these drugs to the Appleseeders, fostering in each an illusory sense of power and control. The increasingly outrageous, ultimately deadly effects of his prescriptions constitute Amis's judgement on the ethos that produced them.

As *Dead Babies* opens, the reader learns (p. 14) that Quentin Villiers, the lord of Appleseed estate, has been reading *Rameau's Nephew* by Denis Diderot, one of the great Menippean satires of the eighteenth century. Amis is here providing one of many intertextual clues to his own narrative program. Mikhail Bakhtin provides an extended definition of this form of satire in his book *Problems of Dostoevski's Poetics*, which was reviewed in the *Times Literary Supplement* in 1974, during Amis's tenure as fiction and poetry editor.[9] The most important characteristic of the form, Bakhtin writes, 'lies in the fact that the most daring and unfettered fantasies . . . and adventures are internally motivated, justified and illuminated here by a purely ideological and philosophical end – to create *extraordinary situations* in which to provoke and test a philosophical idea'. The testing of this idea or truth is given priority over 'the testing of a specific individual or social-typical human character'.[10] It is clear from the beginning of *Dead Babies* that the characters will be subordinated to the ends of satire. After briefly introducing the main English characters, the narrator announces '[t]hese are the six that answer to our purposes' (p. 30). Later, answering the anguished soliloquy of the endlessly victimized Keith Whitehead ('"who's doing it all to me, eh?"'), the narrator is even more explicit: 'you simply *had* to be that way . . . merely in order to serve the designs of this particular fiction' (p. 162).

Menippean satire is a hybrid form. 'The organic combination of philosophical dialog, lofty symbolism, fantastic adventure and under-world naturalism is a remarkable characteristic of the menippea', Bakhtin writes.[11] Each of these elements is given play in *Dead Babies*. Amis stages several dialogues ('Those conversations' (pp. 135, 155, 165), he calls them) between Marvell and various Appleseed residents that echo those of the two speakers in *Rameau's Nephew*. In Diderot's dialogue, one of the speakers is an unrepentant hedonist and hypocrite who insists his position is the necessary outcome of the materialist philosophy Enlightenment reason is founded on. He is opposed by a speaker who clings to the belief that civic virtue is com-patible with materialistic determinism. In *Dead Babies*, Marvell is the voice of hedonism, and he articulates certain au courant ideas of his generation. It is left to Quentin to oppose Marvell's posthumanist values, at least rhetorically. He defends love, monogamy, even feudal-ism, often sounding like an eighteenth-century English squire. He is an anachronism, in other words. Marvell, on the other hand, echoes another representative of the eighteenth century, one who has gained a certain currency in the twentieth: the Marquis de Sade. Sade's celebra-tion of perversity was not a rejection of Enlightenment values so much as a dark variant of Enlightenment mastery over nature. In a similar sense, Marvell exemplifies one logical outcome of contemporary Enlightenment thinking. He uses Andy Adorno's embrace of a guerrilla theater group called the Conceptualists, who believe that '"Other sex is to do with choice rather than urge"', to argue that '"perversion is justified – no, *demanded* – by an environment that is now totally man-made, totally without a biology"' (p. 170). Marvell is a late-twentieth-century embodiment of the same presumptuous and reductive rationalism that satire has traditionally opposed.

Although his assumptions tend to dominate these philosophical dialogues, Marvell's 'values' are implicitly critiqued by a pattern of 'lofty' symbolism. *Dead Babies* is divided into three sections; the list of 'main characters' is arranged so as to emphasize two groups of six and three; the action takes place over a three-day weekend; the sexual preference of the Americans is the ménage à trois; the neurosis (or psychosis) of each character is traced to the Oedipal triangle. The weekend orgy of sex, drugs, and depravity that constitutes the action of *Dead Babies* is a kind of infernal parody of the Last Supper, with pre-siding host Quentin Villiers ultimately revealed [as] the Antichrist (his last name evokes the word 'villain' and anagramatically contains the word 'evil'). There is even a parody of the crucifixion when the long-suffering dwarf Keith Whitehead is roped to the blossoming apple tree in the rectory garden, where 'two grimed hypodermics hung from his bloated arms' (p.205). '"We're ecstatic materialists"' (p.155), crows Andy in a moment of drunken epiphany, but ecstasy is conspicuous only by its absence. In this extreme satire on counter-cultural liberation theology the sacraments of drugs and sex substitute for emotional or spiritual ones, but they never bestow even fleeting grace. For all the compulsive talk of and graphically rendered attempts at sexual congress in the novel, only one couple consummates their desire, and this event leaves the woman in tears.

Body fluids of all kinds flow copiously in *Dead Babies*, but they are not purgative. They express the varieties of personal and social disease produced by everything from parental neglect to the aestheticization of violence. In Menippean satire, as Bakhtin writes, 'the idea . . . has no fear of the underworld or of the filth of life',[12] and Amis, providing proof, rubs the reader's face in it. The worst tendencies of the present are exaggerated and projected into a postseventies future that has become a theater of cruelty, with the body as its stage. The simulated beating of an aged comedian that the Appleseeders witness at a venue called 'the Psychologic Revue' (pp.100–6), is brutal and shocking, but it is mirrored to varying degrees in the pain and humiliation the characters visit on one another. Keith, described in the character list as 'court dwarf' (p.11), is fed experimental drugs by Quentin and Andy, who simultaneously delight in and learn from the spectacle of his reactions. Later, in back-to-back scenes of shocking detail, he is sexually assaulted by the three Americans. Physical anxieties and humiliations are commonplace in *Dead Babies*, from Giles Coldstream's dental nightmares to Andy's bouts of impotence, which strike hardest when he meets a woman he can't dominate. The narrator offers brief but graphic sexual histories for each character, and these, along with their physical eccentricities, tend to define them. In a novel, this formula would seem hopelessly reductive. In a satire on narcissism, it serves to suggest what life has been reduced to.

The satire in *Dead Babies* is not quite so fixed as this reading has so far suggested, however. It is more than a conservative howl of obscene rage at moral decline (although like all satire it is motivated in part by conservative impulses). It is closer in spirit to the philosophical open-endedness of *Rameau's Nephew* than the stable moral ironies of Swift's *A Modest Proposal* (1729) (by titling his satire *Dead Babies*, Amis is aligning it with Swift's shocking *Proposal*, whose speaker calls for the killing and eating of Irish babies). Swift always maintains a clinical distance from the characters and narrators who are the targets of his satire; Amis is to varying degrees complicit with his. This is registered in *Dead Babies* in varying ways, most noticeably in Amis's uncertain control of tone at crucial moments. While he strives for and usually maintains a coolly detached point of view, at times his judgement fails him and his writing goes soft. Near the end of the novel, for instance, just before doom descends, the narrator abandons satire for bathos:

> But pity the dead babies. Now, before it starts. They couldn't know what was behind them, nor what was to come. The past? They had none. Like children after a long day's journey, their lives arranged themselves in a patchwork of vanished mornings, lost afternoons and probable yesterdays. (p. 180)

Verbal triplets are a hallmark of Amis's style; here they strive for a portentous tone that clashes with the novel's black comedy.

A more complex manifestation of this open-endedness can be found in the character of Quentin Villiers. Although he mouths the traditional pieties of love, commitment, and paternal responsibility, he actually represents a trap laid for the reader, a false alternative to the excesses of the others. His heart is the darkest of all. He is finally more like de Sade than Marvell himself: a monster of perversion and rapacity. Readers seeking safe harbor with Quentin find themselves alone and unprotected in the final storm. In an important sense Quentin, who combines civility and sadism, deference and control, who has one foot firmly planted in the eighteenth century, symbolizes the historical conditions that gave rise to the Marvells of the contemporary scene . . . At the end of *Dead Babies*, having killed his wife, Diana, and Marvell, Quentin sits in the Appleseed Rectory kitchen, waiting for Keith to arrive. He has arranged evidence that will implicate the Conceptualists in all the killings and free him from suspicion. '[H]*is green eyes flashed into the dawn like wild, dying suns*' (p. 224).[13] □

In contrast to Diedrick, David Hawkes sees the final revelations about Quentin not as opening out *Dead Babies* but as confining it more tightly within a pessimistic perspective upon late twentieth-century humanity that anticipates Amis's subsequent fiction, in which 'the demise of the soul will figure alongside the death of love and the degradation of art as the characteristic developments of the postmodern era'.[14] With hindsight, it can be seen that the hope expressed by Elaine Feinstein earlier in this chapter (p. 25), that the 'nightmare . . . vision' of *Dead Babies* would soon become part of Martin Amis's past, was largely a vain one. None the less, his next novel, *Success*, would see a slight lifting of the darkness, a move from country-house carnage to the urban struggle for survival in 1970s London.

CHAPTER THREE

Snakes and Ladders: *Success* (1978)

WITH THE publication of Martin Amis's third novel, *Success*, in 1978, his literary reputation began to change. There were the stirrings of an awareness that here was a writer who was starting to create an *oeuvre*, a distinctive body of work of his own; he was no longer merely the talented son of a famous literary father, even if references back to Kingsley remained irresistible for reviewers. *Success* offered an opportunity, not only to discuss a new novel by Martin Amis, but also to set that novel in the context of a growing corpus of fiction. This is evident in the review of *Success* in the *Times Literary Supplement* by Blake Morrison, author of an important study of the literary 'Movement' of the 1950s with which Kingsley Amis had been closely associated.[1] In the extract that follows, Morrison compares *Success* to Amis's two previous novels, *The Rachel Papers* and *Dead Babies*, and judges that, while *Success* 'lacks some of the imaginative power of *Dead Babies*', it is, none the less, 'Martin Amis's most assured work so far':

■ [Martin Amis] has brought to the fashionable 'set-pieces' of the 1960s and 1970s (adolescent sex in *The Rachel Papers*, drugs and communal living in *Dead Babies*, and now bisexuality and incest in *Success*) an old-fashioned Swiftian disgust for the human anatomy. He skirts the genres of romance and soft porn, but derives much pleasure from debunking them, from speaking of what in those genres must always go unspoken (ugliness, dirt, age, excreta, self-disgust). In the latest novel we have a 'dented backside', 'tropical armpits' (p. 19), breasts which are '[g]reat plates of blancmange the size of knapsacks, topped by curlicued sausage stubs' (p. 90), a man with all his teeth pulled out whose 'fag-ends sometimes go red and heavy in the slack corner of his mouth' (p. 35).

Gregory Riding is squeamish about such things. He is appalled by the 'grim femininia' of the girl he's sleeping with, 'the ghostly smells that issue from her pouches and vents . . . the underworld effluvia she leaves glistening on your sheets' (p. 17). Fortunately Gregory need not often tolerate unpleasantness: he is, he assures us, rich and aristocratic, drives a 'powerful . . . car' (p. 19), has a prestigious London art gallery job, is much pursued by glamorous members of both sexes. His evenings out at the fashionable Torka's throb with excitement. Terry, his foster-brother and flat-mate, is not so lucky. Adopted at the age of nine by Gregory's father – 'Riding Sr was an insatiably compassionate man (i.e. off his chump in a posh kind of way . . .)' (p. 26) – he has never overcome his squalid lower-middle-class origins, and lives in a 'world of cheap eateries and drab bedsitterdom' (p. 153). He worries about losing his job, his legs are so short that Gregory is 'amazed they reach the ground' (p. 113), and his dream of a rare sexual conquest dissolves when the callous Gregory takes his girl.

Or, rather, seems to take her: we have no omniscient authorial voice here, only the testimonies of Terry and Gregory themselves. And once we are warned by Terry that Gregory is 'a liar . . . the author of lies' (p. 88) we begin to suspect that 'the horror of being ordinary' (p. 48) has driven him to desperate invention. Terry, too, as he takes revenge on Gregory by sleeping with his neurotic sister, Ursula, discovers that success is mainly a matter of 'style' (clothes, attitude, language). Gradually he begins to behave and talk ('a rather marvellously tarty woman' (p. 177 [Compare p. 89, where Gregory says 'this rather marvellously tarty girl'])) rather as Gregory had done: they might almost be one person so interchangeable are the roles of failure and success.

Almost, but not quite: the novel never sinks to a platitudinous 'success is merely an attitude of mind' because it contains elements of social allegory which suggest that the success may be 'real'. Terry, whose surname is Service and who works in Masters House (pp. 33, 217), is emphatically the 'coming' (p. 194) man (the pun neatly equates social and sexual achievement), and his ascent is imbued with a political significance: he and his kind 'are the masters now'. The structure of the novel forces the reader to feel ambivalent about this. Each of the twelve chapters presents first Terry's voice, then Gregory's, and the voices compete for our sympathy. Terry says at the outset that he wishes to make us hate Gregory, and for much of the novel he succeeds; but at the end, with Ursula dead, Gregory broke and broken, and Terry increasingly vicious, our sympathy may have shifted.

Success lacks some of the imaginative power of *Dead Babies*, and reservations may be felt about the at times sentimental handling of the 'dead sister' theme – reservations which even Terry's self-conscious 'I'm so sentimental these days that I squelch when I walk' (p. 106) cannot dispel. But the narrative economy and manipulation of sympathy makes this Martin Amis's most assured work so far. The presentation of city life in its sadness is forceful in itself, but what is especially impressive is that all the detail counts. The tube trains, the restaurant meals and the 'fucked-up hippie' (pp. 64, 99, 126, 143, 177, 209) by whom Terry measures his own social status: all these play a part in the overall design.[2] □

Morrison's praise for *Success* was not endorsed by the novelist Paul Ableman, who reviewed *Success* in the *Spectator* and criticised it as largely tedious, overfree with four-letter words, often sloppily written, lacking in significant purpose, and imitative – but none the less exhibiting talent:

■ Martin Amis's third novel concerns two young men who share a London flat. Gregory is handsome, witty, elegant and derives from landed gentry. His foster-brother, Terry, is a product of the slums. While still a child, Terry saw his younger sister murdered by their brutish father who was then carried off to retribution. Left alone, since his mother had previously suffered the same unkind fate at the hands of her spouse, Terry was adopted by Gregory's kind-hearted parents. Now the two boys have grown up. The novel spans a year in their lives and is divided into twelve sections, corresponding to the passing months.

The book is narrated alternately by Gregory and Terry. Presumably the intention, analogous to that of [Lawrence] Durrell (1912–1990) in the [*Alexandria Quartet* (1957–60)], is to provide different perspectives on the same sequence of events. But for such a device to engage and hold the reader's interest, the events themselves must be interesting. Unhappily much of the action in *Success* is pedestrian and the necessity to plod through it twice becomes tedious.

Terry has a girl friend called Jan. Gregory calls her June [or Joan]. This is a fair sample of the level of variation of perspective. There is, however, a ponderous differentiation of diction. Gregory talks like a super-dandy out of [Ronald] Firbank and Terry like a super-yob. Neither of them is very convincing as a person but this drawback is somewhat mitigated by the reader's growing perception that the book is a parable about the decline of the old order in England and the new raj [reign] of the yobs . . .

Miranda, Gregory's sister and Terry's foster-sister, joins the m[é]nage. Her role, apart from the provision, in the massage-parlour sense of the word, of relief is to go quietly '*tonto*'. This is a word much favoured by Mr Amis and used by him as synonymous with 'bonkers', although my Italian-English dictionary says it means stupid or silly. There is not, in fact, much erotic relief in *Success*. In dismal compensation, there is an abundance of what unenlightened folk would call bad language . . . . . . This schoolboy flaunting of 'rude words' is distressing, and not merely as a symptom of imaginative poverty or poor taste. The right to use such words in literature has been laboriously won over the centuries. *Success* is the kind of novel that gives libertarianism a bad name . . . There is a lot of sloppy writing. Gregory says of Terry: '[h]is . . . teeth . . . taper darkly off into the metallic hecatomb of his jaws' (p. 184). A hecatomb is, of course, an animal sacrifice and not a kind of mausoleum. [In Greek and Roman Antiquity, a 'hecatomb' meant a 'great public sacrifice', properly of 100 oxen; it has come to mean, figuratively, a 'sacrifice of many victims'.] The get-out available to authors who use fictitious narrators is to attribute mistakes to *their* ignorance. Happily, there is one, out of many, terminological faults in *Success* which has a built-in safety device against this defence. Gregory, the arch-aesthete, contemplating Terry's bed, refers to it as: 'Terence's large and unfastidious double bed' (p. 24). The use of such an unfelicitous term as 'unfastidious' robs Gregory of the very quality (fastidiousness, in fact) which the observation is meant to demonstrate. But such matters, albeit material, are quibbles.

Much more damning is the fact that it is hard to discern any purpose behind *Success* other than the desire to write a novel. The split narrative belts on, desperately hoping for something good to turn up. Here there is a plod through Becketland and next a meander through Kafka country. One could, in fact, relate fragments of the novel to a whole spectrum of modern masters. But stylistic versatility doesn't necessarily generate a work of art.

And yet *Success* bristles with evidence of talent. 'When I said that pathetic thing to Gregory and stumbled down the stairs, whose face burnt the hotter with embarrassment and remorse? Mine, mine. Why? I'll tell you why. Because I have no pride, and they merely have no shame' (p. 140). The build-up is adequate, if not elegant, but the final epigram is subtle and haunting. '[W]hy is it always clichés that make you cry?' (p. 202). The question might seem an invitation to any critic to guffaw but in fact, and in context, it is genuinely touching. 'A blue light was shooting round my room like a spectral boomerang' (p. 203). One of many stabbing images. And there is much more detail one could praise.

But alas Mr Amis distrusts his own creative imagination. There is a sub-text to this book, a surreal, lyrical novel about the eerie quality of urban life as ancient norms crumble and machines evolve like drosophilae [fruit-flies used extensively in genetic research]. But Mr Amis only harvests it in moments when his guard is down. Then he remembers that he is the most with-it penman around and quickly shifts his narrative back to the plane of trendy cynicism. It is hard to escape the feeling that subconsciously Mr Amis regards *Success* as a stance rather than a novel.³ □

Where Ableman saw *Success* as a montage of modernist fragments, James Diedrick felt that it was a work in which Amis had left behind the 'stylistic patchwork' of his first two novels, along with their 'occasional wavering of tone' and 'sometimes intrusive self-reflexivity', and replaced them with 'a rigorously controlled narrative' whose structure demonstrates that the 'narrative "doubling" characteristic of both *The Rachel Papers* and *Dead Babies*' had been taken further and become 'an organizing principle'.[4] In the extract that follows, Diedrick also suggests significant intertextual references in the novel and analyses the ways in which the narratives of Greg and Terry first engage, then estrange, the reader. He then moves on to provide an analysis of the 'social and familial causes of [the] respective pathologies' of Terry and Greg and to link it with the first stirring of Thatcherism:

■ Taken together, [the dramatic monologues of Greg and Terry] form an 'X' whose intersection marks the death of Greg's sister Ursula, to which both men have contributed. It also represents the crossing point in the fortunes of each: while one brother falls in the world, the other ascends. As this geometry suggests, and even granting the precisely rendered differences between the two [compare this with Ableman's remarks on p. 36, about the 'ponderous differentiation of diction'] they emerge as doubles of one another, much as Quentin and Andy do in *Dead Babies*. Only now such doubling is an explicit theme . . .

Success also manifests some significant intertextual 'doublings'. The first of these is hinted at in the book's dedication: 'To Philip' (p. 5). Philip is the name of Amis's older brother, who was named after the poet Philip Larkin – a regular visitor to the Amis household during Martin Amis's childhood.[5] Martin Amis has written of Larkin's work with great admiration,[6] and Larkin's 1946 novel *Jill* anticipates *Success* in its focus on a young working-class man in awe and envy of his decadent, aristocratic Oxford roommate. In addition, Amis's treatment of the damage Terry suffers at the hands of his father, and Terry's own oft-repeated lament that he is 'fucked up' constitute a narrative excursion into the nihilistic territory Larkin explored in his 1971 poem 'This Be the Verse', with its bleak opening stanza: '[t]hey fuck you up, your mum and dad / They may not mean to, but they do / They fill you with the faults they had / And add some extra, just for you'.[7] In his own narration, Terry implicitly doubles himself with Oliver Twist, emphasizing the Dickensian qualities of his orphaned childhood, from the grim and violent squalor of his early years to his fairy-tale ascension into privilege when he is adopted by Gregory's wealthy family. Ultimately, however, Terry comes to resemble the Artful Dodger more than Oliver.

Vladimir Nabokov also haunts the margins of *Success*. Its title is also the title of a novel by the fictional author featured in the first book Nabokov wrote in English: *The Real Life of Sebastian Knight* (1941). Nabokov's novel is narrated by Sebastian Knight's half-brother, who searches in vain for the definitive truth about a person he feels he is virtually *becoming* by the end of the quest – a doubling echoed in a different register at the end of *Success*. In his first essay on Nabokov, published two years after *Success*, Amis claims that Nabokov's characteristic literary mode is the 'sublime', focused not on some ideal world, but 'directed at our fallen world of squalor, absurdity and talentlessness. Sublimity replaces the ideas of motivation and plot with those of obsession and destiny. It suspends moral judgements in favour of remorselessness, a helter-skelter intensity'.[8] This description certainly applies to Amis's own procedures in *Success* (and most of his other novels), as does his comment about *Lolita* in a later essay: '[i]t constructs a mind in the way that a prose Browning might have gone about it, through rigorous dramatic monologue'.[9] As with all dramatic monologues, *Success* expects a great deal of the reader, who is left to construct the truth from the unspoken gaps in and between each narrative.

Success encompasses a year in the lives of Greg and Terry, who share a flat in Bayswater . . . The novel begins in January and ends in December, emphasizing a cyclical pattern consistent with the place-trading fortunes of the two: in the end, as in the beginning, one is abject, the other ascendant . . . . . . Despite their mutual malice, Greg's and Terry's voices initially engage the reader with their immediacy, their dialectical authenticity, and their confessional intimacy. The foster brother's narratives are dialogic: each speaker is intensely aware of the other speaker and of the reader. Their remarks are sprinkled with direct addresses to an assumed listener. 'I'm drinking a lot these days', Terry says in the first chapter, adding '[w]ouldn't you be?' (p. 12). When his turn comes, [Greg] says of his decadent friends, '[t]hey're marvellous fun – you'll like them' (p. 41). Each also intermittently quizzes or counsels the reader about his counterpart. 'Has he said anything to you about it?' (p. 45), [Greg] asks after reporting what [Terry] has told him about his liaison with [Greg's] ex-girlfriend Miranda, and [Terry asks if Greg has 'said anything' to the reader about Terry's relationship with Ursula (p. 173)[10]].

Greg and Terry's repeated interrogatives function like hooks, pulling the reader into their perceptual worlds, their quandaries and queries. Terry's early questions are particularly endearing in this regard . . . . . . For a time then, and to differing degrees, the reader feels close to the two narrators, and implicated in their stories, almost as a relative would. Indeed, each speaks to the reader with the intimacy and special pleading that a sibling might, seeking an ally. Amis wants

THE FICTION OF MARTIN AMIS

the reader to experience the way these two men think, and what they represent, from the inside, and the hothouse atmosphere induced by their narratives achieves this. So do the suggestions that they are symbolic doubles . . .

[There are] many explicit warnings in the novel, voiced by Amis through his characters, that his two narrators are unreliable, that the reader needs to be on guard. It is an especially apt warning in regard to Greg: the most shocking scene in the novel, his brutal seduction of Terry's would-be girlfriend Jan, turns out to be a product of Greg's delusional imagination. It is also one of the ways Amis engineers a progressive withdrawal of sympathy and identification from Terry and Greg, encouraging the reader to evaluate the underlying social and familial causes of their respective pathologies.

There is in fact something uncomfortably close about the intimate relationship initially established among foster brothers and reader in *Success*, and the reader's recognition of this coincides with consecutive revelations of the literal incest that exists at the corrosive center of the novel. Terry was nine when his sister was killed by his father. Greg was nine when he initiated an incestuous relationship with his sister Ursula. Abused and victimized women thus define the family histories of both characters. Through special pleading, Greg tries to convince the reader that his intimacy with Ursula is exempt from moral censure. With sneering superiority, he calls the prohibition against incest 'a strip of warped lead from the gutter presses, a twitch in the responses of philistines and suburbanites, a "sin" only in the eyes of the hated and the mean' (p. 66). He claims that he and Ursula came together innocently in childhood, clinging to one another in the absence of parental warmth.

From Greg's earliest confessions, however, it is clear that incest is both the product and the embodiment of the pathological narcissism that forms the ground of his being. Greg's description of Ursula's response when he first caressed her alludes to Narcissus's own immobilizing stare into self-reflecting waters. It reveals more about his own desires than his sister's: 'Ursula looked up at me encouragingly, her face lit by a lake of dreams' (p. 68). In one sense all of the doubling in the novel, and all of the abuse and betrayal, double back to this primal moment. It initiates a kind of narcissistic withdrawal from the larger world and from other people that blights Greg's later life. As an adult, he is unwilling to face the fact that his continuing intimacies with his sister have emotionally maimed her and driven her to suicide. When he does turn his mind to her, his thoughts are self-damning, and reveal his essential infantilism. 'Why does she cry so much *now*? What else can she be crying for but the lost world of our childhood, when it didn't seem to matter what we did?' (p. 117).

Terry harbors a different kind of pathology. Significantly, it is well adapted to the world of late-seventies London, a world where 'socio-sexual self-betterment' (as both Greg (p. 43) and Terry (p. 36) term it) is the ruling ethos. Thus it is not surprising that once Terry gains the social upper hand, he should take up where Greg has left off. He coaxes Ursula into his bed, pressures her to repeat sexual acts she performed on Greg, and hastens her self-destruction. Out of gratitude, he offers a kind of mechanical reciprocation, unaware that Ursula takes no pleasure in his advances. When she does finally come to him for sexual comfort, after Greg has permanently rejected her in a fit of jealous pique over Terry, their union is brief, fitful, and desperate. Terry's self-absolving description of their last conversation before Ursula's suicide precisely captures his own emergent sociopathology: 'I merely pointed out, gently but firmly, that there was no sense in which I could assume responsibility for her, that you cannot "take people on" any longer while still trying to function successfully in your own life, that she was on her own now, the same as me, the same as Greg, the same as everybody else' (p. 207).

The moral monstrosity spawned by this obsession with success is the central vehicle of Amis's social satire in *Success*. The novel was published the year before Margaret Thatcher rose to power as head of England's Conservative Party; Terry and Gregory's acrimonious coexistence prophetically captures the increasingly intertwined, antagonistic relationship between the monied classes and their envious, entrepreneurial rivals. As Graham Fuller has written, *Success* is 'a parody of England's class war, with Gregory and Terry symbolizing the spiritual decay of the landed gentry and the greedy self-betterment of the "yobs", each appraising the other's position with eloquent disgust or shameless envy'.[11] In one sense both Terry and Greg personify versions of the philistinism and greed that many of Thatcher's critics predicted would be her ideological legacy.[12] □

With the benefit of historical hindsight, Diedrick is able to perceive a prophetic quality in *Success*, and to argue, with some plausibility, that Amis's third novel is more insightful and enduring than its first reviewers realised. But it remains the case that if Amis's literary career had stopped with *Success*, he might still be regarded as a minor figure. Neil Powell's essay on Amis, an extract from which was included in the previous chapter, appeared when *Success* was Amis's most recent novel. The overall aims of this essay were to provide a considered assessment of Martin Amis's first three novels, to characterise the kind of success he had so far achieved and to identify general problems which his work seemed to raise. Powell acknowledged that Amis had 'certainly been the most praised and the most publicised new writer of full-length fiction in

England in the past decade', but suggested that the sort of success his novels had enjoyed so far was that of 'books which are distinctively of their time and which . . . succeed through accuracy of detail and of tone';[13] it remained to be seen whether they would be promoted to the category of books which are enduring successes. At the end of his essay, Powell picks out what he sees as three major problems with Amis's work to date:

■ The first, rather slippery one involves the distinction between pornography and literature: it seems to me that in all three novels – but most noticeably in *Dead Babies* – there are passages where the ironist's or satirist's distancing fails entirely. This is an aspect of the uncertainty of tone which so often weakens Amis's writing. Pornography fulfils a simple and perhaps necessary purpose; whereas literature is altogether more complicated. We need to distinguish between them not for censorious reasons but because the two things demand different kinds of intention and response. A work of literature may be endangered where the simpler level of intention and response gets in the way of the more subtle and complex one: such a confusion happens too often in Amis's novels and provokes those familiar comments ('Extravagantly sexual . . . highly enjoyable') which are quoted on the paperback editions of his books and in which reviewers, understandably enough, attempt to have it both ways. Among a novelist's desperate remedies, the gratuitous, knowing obscenity – like the one-line joke – is a stand-by to be used sparingly.

The second problem is related to the first. Because Amis's characters live in an echoing present ('The past? They had none.' (*Dead Babies*, p. 180)), their allusions and their vocabulary belong to a world of crazily foreshortened historical perspectives. A central passage in *The Rachel Papers* (pp. 97, 98, 102) presupposes a detailed knowledge of *Sergeant Pepper's Lonely Hearts Club Band*; Andy, in *Dead Babies*, habitually adds a redundant 'is all' to the ends of his sentences; Terry, in *Success*, obsessively uses the word '*tonto*', in italics, an extreme example of localized slang which seems to mean 'mad'. These are random instances of an overstrained contemporaneity: the cumulative effect of such things is drastically to restrict the potential range of the novels.

But what about the potential range of *the novel*? What effect is Amis's success, or *Success*, likely to have upon the language of fiction? In Arnold Bennett's *The Old Wives' Tale* (1908), the final section is called 'What Life Is'. That too is a second-division novel, though a remarkably good one, and in its intention of providing a detailed record of two contrasting sisters' lives it has something in common with *Success*. Amis is in many ways the more polished and skilful of the two writers, but it is Bennett's 'life' which moves and convinces. Why? Not, I think, because life has changed (though obviously it has) but because, whereas in Bennett language is enriching, in Amis it is deadening, reductive. One has, in *The Old Wives' Tale*, a deep sense of both change and continuity in historical time, sustained by Bennett's allusions to real events of some importance and to alterations in the texture of life. In Amis, the resonance has gone and the language of fiction has become as formulaic and as ephemeral as last year's pop music. Stifled by its insistence on the present, by its pop and media allusiveness, and by its introverted slang, Amis's language becomes *only* of its time and lacks even the ambition of timelessness.

Except, that is, for those moments – the occasional patches of brilliance in *Dead Babies*, the end of *Success* – when Amis seems to reach out towards a larger fictional world: then one can see what a fine writer he could be if he were to allow himself a greater historical range, a deeper commitment to the enduring realities of time and place. I hope that his future novels will show a decisive break with (to borrow a line from Thom Gunn) 'the limitations where he found success'[14] and will find him using his talent more positively, less defensively. But success is a funny thing, and it may take time to grow out of it.[15] □

It could be said that Amis began to try to grow out of success in his fourth novel, *Other People*. As the next chapter will show, the results were not judged to be wholly successful, but they certainly proved to be perplexing and fascinating.

CHAPTER FOUR

Descent into Hell: *Other People: A Mystery Story* (1981)

IN *THE Novel Today* (1990), Allan Massie, a reviewer and critic who is himself a novelist, proposed that '[i]t was not till his fourth novel, *Other People*, that Amis began to escape from the limiting condition of being bang up to the minute, of having the ear of his exact contemporaries, and only theirs'.[1] But initially, *Other People* proved perplexing to reviewers, presenting problems of definition and comprehension. In the *Listener*, for example, Victoria Glendinning began her review by an apparently confident categorisation of the novel – 'Martin Amis has written a modern morality' – only to call herself into question in the next sentence – '[a]t least I think he has',[2] and to start her final paragraph by reclassifying *Other People* as 'a fable'.[3] She also acknowledged that she found the novel 'quite hard to understand'.[4] That challenge to understanding was also addressed by Blake Morrison, who, as with *Success*, once again provided, in the *Times Literary Supplement*, the most substantial review of an Amis novel, registering the perplexity that *Other People* produced, the change of style it exemplified and, along with some other reviewers – for instance, Alan Hollinghurst[5] and John Sutherland[6] – affixing a label, perhaps too easily, to its technique: Martian – the technique associated above all with the poet Craig Raine and his poem 'A Martian Sends a Postcard Home' (1979),[7] in which familiar objects and activities, like books, telephones and going to the toilet, are described in unfamiliar ways, as if seen with the estranging eyes of an alien visitor to earth:

■ We knew where we were with Martin Amis's fiction, or thought we did. Black humour, metropolitan satire, Swiftian obsession with the bodily functions – with three novels and a handful of short stories the boundaries of his fictional world looked to have been decisively drawn. But where are we now? A young woman wakes in an institution of some kind. She walks down its corridors with 'heavy curved extensions [shoes]' (p. 14) attached to her feet. She watches packs of 'trolleys [motor vehicles]' (p. 16) charging noisily along the street. She classifies people, bizarrely and it seems arbitrarily, into six different kinds. She gazes upwards at 'extravagantly lovely white creatures – fat sleepy things [clouds]' (p. 17) and 'slow-moving crucifixes [aeroplanes]' (p. 18). She feels to be on the verge of some 'inscrutable, ecstatic human action' (p. 17). She appears to have lost her bearings; and so have we.

Other People is subtitled [*A Mystery Story*] and like most mystery stories withholds its chief secret until the end. But one of its mysteries – Martin Amis's change of style, and the resources he draws on in order to bring it about – is to be solved by looking not at the last page but at the back cover. [This is, of course, the back cover of the first hardback edition in 1981 – some public library copies retain this cover and photograph, which confirms Morrison's description of it.] This shows the author sitting, cigarette in hand, reading what we can just about make out to be the *New Statesman*, a magazine of which he was once the literary editor (and it's the arts pages he's perusing), but which he left in order to write full-time. The photograph is perhaps a way of reminding cognoscenti [those in the know] that one of Amis's achievements on that paper was to give some prominence to a poetry which specializes in presenting the familiar world through the eyes of a fascinated alien – a poetry associated with Craig Raine, Christopher Reid and others which has since been given the name 'Martian'. *Other People* is a Martian novel – not the first perhaps (William Golding's *The Inheritors* (1955) and a host of science fiction novels have prior claims) and not the whole way through but to an extent that suggests he has adopted some of the techniques of recent poetry for his own ends (the fact that his name is an anagram of 'Martianism' may not be entirely beside the point).

Amis is a self-confessed raider of others' texts, and makes no attempt to conceal the borrowings (especially those from his contemporaries) of *Other People*. Indeed the shift in mode is one which the second chapter explicitly draws attention to. 'Between ourselves, this isn't my style at all really. The choice wasn't truly mine, although I naturally exercise a degree of control. It had to be like this . . . she *asked* for it' (p. 21). 'She' is the heroine, Mary Lamb, who – as the voice also tells us at this point – appears to be going through an experience not unlike amnesia. She is also, it seems, suffering from nominal aphasia, a complaint which afflicts George Zeyer in Kingsley Amis's *Ending Up* (1974) and which is defined there as 'that condition in which the sufferer finds it difficult to remember nouns, common terms, the names of familiar objects'.[8] For Mary, innocent as her name suggests, the world is a riddle, and we are forced to do a certain amount of decoding on her behalf . . .

The 'dirty sheath of smudged grey paper that came and went every day' (p. 57), with men on its back pages costing lots of money, is a tabloid newspaper; knitting needles in a restaurant are chopsticks (p. 120); a 'glistening dumb-bell' (p. 112) proves to be the receiver of a phone.

That last image might come from Christopher Reid's poem 'Baldanders';[9] other passages read like prose drafts for the 'Yellow Pages' section of Craig Raine's *The Onion, Memory* (1978)[10] . . . . . . The proliferation of correspondences, of everything looking like something else, reinforces the novel's main theme, which is Mary's search for her double, the person she perfectly resembles, the lost self of a former life. The search begins in the lower levels of society, where Mary is befriended by an alcoholic half-tramp, half-prostitute, Sharon, who takes her money, cleans her up and pairs her off with Trev, whose speciality is sex with violence . . . Mary batters his face with a brick, runs for it, and hides out with Sharon's alcoholic parents, Mr and Mrs Botham[,] who allow her to go about educating herself in earnest. She explores her body . . . reads Shakespeare and Jane Austen, gets to know London. The idyll ends when Trev comes for his revenge: he is repelled, but in the process Mr Botham's back is broken and Mary has to move on.

Breakage is a dominant motif in the novel and wherever Mary goes she leaves a trail of destruction behind her: broken backs, broken jaws, broken noses, broken necks, broken spirits, broken hearts. Her next home is a hostel for girls who . . . have 'gone out too deep in life' (p. 70) . . . Mary stays there long enough to find a job as washer-up in a café and then moves into a squat . . . with two men from work. Russ and Alan are a re-working of Gregory and Terry in *Success*. Russ is slim, loose, sidling and in some of the novel's funniest scenes fantasizes about his peremptory treatment of famous film actresses . . . Alan is pale, frightened and prone to wrench fistfuls of hair from his scalp, thus adding to an already serious baldness problem. Here are the classic dualities of Martin Amis's fiction: buoyant self-assurance as against self-loathing[;] preening, arching, craning and gliding as against whining, whing[e]ing, fawning and breaking down. But, as in *Success*, the gap between the two gradually narrows: Russ is hung up about being illiterate; it is Alan who manages to sleep with Mary; and the rivalry of the two men proves to be a form of mutual dependence, a desperate double act.

Mary's search for her own double is meanwhile proceeding. Through the mysterious policeman, Prince, who is called in on each of her various mishaps, she learns about Amy Hide, a girl whose disappearance has led to a man being held on a murder charge. Is Mary herself Amy Hide? . . . It is on Prince . . . that Mary depends for her ultimate revelation, and with whom she is paired in yet another strange doppelgänger [double] . . . . . .

Though it has its twists and surprises to the end, the plot of *Other People* is somewhat perfunctory ... there is none of the tightness and narrative subtlety of *Success*. Interest is concentrated, instead, on the playing off of two narrative voices: one knowing, the other unknowing. The latter is Mary's or something like it, bemused by 'the astronomical present' (p.29). The identity of the second voice remains a puzzle until the final pages, and is indeed the novel's chief thriller element. Snappy and snappish, this voice hectors the reader, corrects misapprehensions, parades its familiarity with the ways of the world. At times it seems to be an authorial voice exulting, in self-conscious post-modernist fashion, in its omniscience and control. At other times we suspect that it must belong to the person at the heart of the novel's crime mystery. These impressions are perfectly compatible, of course: both people may be said to control Mary's outcome; both have the power to kill her off.

There is in the end no single answer to this novel's mystery ... [11] □

Despite the thoroughness of his review, Morrison seems finally to remain perplexed by *Other People*. Tackled by John Haffenden about the confusion the novel caused, Martin Amis himself acknowledged it meant that he had, in a sense, failed, and proceeded to provide some very helpful explication:

■ [*John Haffenden:*] *I think readers can often feel defeated by the riddle of* Other People. *Among other critics, I think, Paul Ableman said that the end of the novel left us with what he called 'the shoddy enigma of an author's refusal to clarify his meaning rather than the authentic one of a mystery too profound for clear expression'.* [12] *Could you take this opportunity to provide a little explication?*

[*Martin Amis:*] There is a consistent but not a realistic explanation of the book. In fact, only Ian McEwan 'got' the book, as it were, and I must admit to failure here – because I thought readers would understand by the end. The simple idea of the book – as I point out several times in the text – is, why should we expect death to be any less complicated than life? Nothing about life suggests that death will just be a silence. Life is very witty and cruel and pointed, and let us suppose that death is like that too. The novel is the girl's death, and her death is a sort of witty parody of her life. In life she was Amy Hide, a character who was privileged in all kinds of ways and made a journey downward through society – as some very strange people do: downward mobility is largely a new phenomenon, and it's a metaphor for self-destruction which some people seriously do enact – and therefore her life-in-death is one in which she is terrifically well-meaning and causes disaster. In her real life as Amy Hide she was not well-meaning, and brought disaster on herself. The Prince character, the narrator, has total power over her, as a narrator would, and also as a demon-lover would. At the very end of the novel she starts her life again, the idea being that life and death will alternate until she gets it right: she will go through life again, she will meet the man at the edge of the road, she will fall into the same mistakes . . . but actually I wanted to suggest on top of everything else that she would in fact get it right this time. There is another complicated layer which has to do with the fact that in the Amy Hide life the Prince character was as automaton-like as she was, and didn't realize what was going on; in the death he *does* realize what was going on, and at the end he doesn't any more – he again becomes an actor in this life. The idea is that you are on a wheel until the point where you can get off purely by behaving well – by meaning well *and* doing well.

So the narrator and Prince are the same voice – I think I picked up one clue in the fact that the narrative voice and Prince describe squats in the same terms: '[p]eople are serious about living together' (pp. 106, 125) – and I'm glad you confirm the identification.

Yes, and as narrator and as murderous demon-lover he has equal power to knock her off: they are exactly analogous.

In one sense, I suppose, it's an epistemological novel – being concerned with how we know anything – which matches your consuming interest in punning and the place of language in interpreting the world.

Yes. As you know, it was said to be a Martian novel, although I began it a year before Craig Raine's Martian poem appeared.[13] The *donnée* [basic assumption] for me was the chance to describe the world as if I knew nothing about it, and perhaps it did fall prey to a rather elaborate set of metaphysical notions. It is not an ideas-novel in the sense that I believe in reincarnation or anything of that sort; it's just a way of looking at life.[14] □

Although Amis takes issue with the view that *Other People* is a 'Martian' novel, James Diedrick, in *Understanding Martin Amis*, firmly reiterates this view. Diedrick points out that Amis himself, just over a year before *Other People* came out, had published a poem in the *New Statesman*, called 'Point of View', which might itself be seen as 'Martian' in its disturbing representation of the perceptions of social deviants – 'To the mature paedophile / A child's incurious glance is a leer / Of intimate salacity'.[15] The whole poem appears as prose in *Other People* (pp. 186–7), and provides, Diedrick suggests, a microcosm of 'the denaturalizing of conventional understanding that characterizes the novel as a whole'.[16]

Diedrick also draws attention to an older practice of defamiliarization which may inform Amis's fourth novel – that represented by William Wordsworth's contributions to *Lyrical Ballads* (1798)[17] which, as Samuel Taylor Coleridge put it, aimed to 'give the charm of novelty to things of everyday . . . [to awaken] the mind's attention from the lethargy of custom . . . [and to remove] the film of familiarity' which inhibits our full appreciation of 'the loveliness and wonders of the world'[18] – but with Martin Amis, defamiliarisation can also reveal the ugliness and horrors of the world – not least its violence.

It is this aspect of *Other People* which Brian Finney explores in his 1995 essay 'Narrative and Narrated Homicides in Martin Amis's *Other People* and *London Fields*'. As his title suggests, Finney's focus is on the relation in Amis's fiction between narrative and the representation of violence and murder; *Other People* is the first of Amis's novels to combine violence with the presence of the narrator in the story, a combination exemplified by the identification, confirmed by Amis in his Haffenden interview, of the narrator with Prince, who is also Mary's murderer:

■ Why do death, murder, and victimization appear so frequently in Amis's fiction? The answer lies not just in the murderous nature of contemporary civilization. It also has to do with the nature of the narrative act. In his later novels, beginning with *Other People*, this prevalence of violence against one or more of the characters is accompanied by the introduction into the narrative of the narrator in person . . . This typically postmodern device draws attention to the highly ambiguous role played by any narrator in fiction. Whoever narrates a story both creates and annihilates characters . . . . . .

Other People opens with a confessional Prologue by the narrator. 'I didn't want to have to do it to her. I would have infinitely preferred some other solution. Still, there we are. It makes sense, really, given the rules of life on earth; and she *asked* for it' (p. 9). The narrator simultaneously expresses his sense of guilt and immediately proceeds to spread the responsibility for what he has done and is about to do to the novel's protagonist, Mary Lamb, as she calls herself at first. He blames both 'the rules of life on earth' (or the fallen nature of humankind) and Mary whose fall from grace leads to her demand for retributive justice. *Other People* is subtitled *A Mystery Story*, and its first mystery is the identity of its narrator. This narrator never allows us to forget his controlling presence for long. Every chapter, except the first and the final four making up Part Three, has a section typographically distinguished from the rest of the narrative in which the narrator directly addresses the reader in the second person. Even the first chapter has the Prologue, just as Part Three has an Epilogue, in which the same device is employed.

Invariably these sections encourage readers both to reflect on whatever topic has governed the preceding action and to recognize their own complicity in it. In effect his readers repeatedly are being removed from the fiction by a philosophizing narrator only to be returned to the action by the narrator who forces them to recognize the similarity between whatever action the narrator has been describing and their own experiences. In Chapter 7, for instance, Mary enters a Church-Army Hostel for Young Women where everyone has taken a smash to be there. 'Have you ever taken a smash in your time?' asks the narrator. Not content with dragging us in, he proceeds to offer advice that simultaneously subtly adds to our knowledge about him. 'If you see a smash coming and can't keep out of the way – don't break. Because if you do, nothing will ever put you back together again. I've taken a big one and I know. Nothing. Ever' (p.70). In describing his own fall, this Humpty-Dumpty narrator is also returning us to the action of which he is a mysterious part. Is his fall involved in Mary's fall prior to her loss of memory? We are forced back into the narration to find out. These metafictional interruptions do not have the effect that Martin Amis's father, Kingsley, always charges him with creating – they do not alienate the reader from the story.[19] They are a basic ingredient of narration, one that has been employed in rather different ways by comic novelists since the time of Cervantes and Fielding.

At the same time the narrator never lets us forget that we share with him the responsibility for subjecting Mary to the hell that the book's title alludes to. In *Huis Clos* (*In Camera*) (1945) Sartre depicts hell as other people.[20] Amis's *Other People* is a depiction of a modern hell in which Mary, suffering from memory loss, is forced to rediscover her debased earlier self (or other person) overseen by the all-seeing narrator who enters the action in the form of a police detective called John Prince. It takes the reader most of the book to appreciate the fact that Prince and the narrator are the same person. This is because Prince, like Mary, has a past – as her murderer. He is simultaneously Prince Charming and the Prince of Darkness. He is a Manichean demon-lover. In her previous existence as Amy Hide, her sister tells her, '"[y]ou said you loved him so much you wouldn't mind if he killed you"' (p.186). And it appears that he did kill her. Amis provides a clue to the significance of this dual role: 'the narrator is the murderer and the writer and the murderer are equivalent in that each has the power to knock her off'.[21] As readers, we are invited to enjoy a story about a woman who gets murdered by participating ourselves in her literary murder. We are both spectators of the action and aiders and abettors of the murdering author/narrator.

At the beginning of the novel, Mary finds herself in a kind of limbo where she is forced to rediscover her past life from a position of innocence. This Martian aspect of the book is more original than many of the reviewers allowed . . . Mary's amnesia allows Amis to bring to life the present unencumbered by the preconceptions of the past. 'When the past is forgotten, the present is unforgettable' (p. 56). Without a memory Mary is dazzled and dazed by her perceptions of the moment. She begins her life in death as a natural victim for whom sex, for instance, is a strange practice she cannot get the hang of. Trev, the first man to have sex with her, is a natural sadist. But all she can make out is that '[h]is two tongues wanted her two mouths' (p. 46). Repeatedly Amis is able to achieve effects as unusual as this, to defamiliarize our automatized response – in this case to the modern novel's statutory sex scene. At the same time, Amy's experience is being vividly evoked by a narrator who is responsible for subjecting Mary to the pain she undergoes from Trev's brutal sexual exploitation of her body. The narrator could interfere at any point, but does not. What is more, we would not want him to. We participate in his sadistic treatment of her. And he will not let us forget it. 'I've done things to her, I know, I admit it. But look what she's done to me' (p. 106). Having made her the type of character she is (one who is to be found in contemporary life), the narrator then exonerates himself and us by claiming that she has invited his (and our) victimization of her.

The entire book can be seen as living through or living back her life at or after the moment of her death at the hands of her lover . . . In life, as Amy Hide, she started off leading a privileged existence and gradually descended the social scale as she self-destructed. In the novel she begins her fictional existence among tramps and slowly rises through the book's circles of living hell to sadistically dominate a decadent aristocratic household headed by Jamie. Amy Hide was malevolent and consciously brought disaster on herself and others. Mary Lamb is well-meaning and unconsciously brings about the same effect. The innocent Mary of the nursery rhyme who had a little lamb is patiently brought by the narrator to rediscover within her self the Amy Hide hiding there. Mary, the Dr. Jekyll figure of this novel, sees Amy, her Mr. Hyde, lurking in her reflection in the mirror. 'She is afraid that her life has in some crucial sense already run its course, that the life she moves through now is nothing more than another life's reflection, its mirror, its shadow' (p. 97). She has passed through the looking glass of death to confront her life in reverse. It takes her almost the whole of the book to rediscover 'the power to make feel bad' (p. 116) that caused Prince to murder her in life and that she finally turns on Jamie with such devastating effect that she breaks through the mirror to her old self: '[s]he had torn through the glass and come back from the other side. She had found her again. She was herself at last' (p. 200). She *is* other people. Mary is also Amy. Prince is not the only character to reveal Manichean duality. Mary/Amy also has to be restored to a sense of her power for good and evil. She is representative of her era – complex, neither heroine nor villainness, yet capable of moral choice.

Amis's concept of life-in-death has proved difficult for most readers to grasp, and many reviewers of the book have complained that the mystery was unsolvable. Amis insists that he does not believe in reincarnation (though the book makes use of the concept). . . . In other words he has employed a purely fictional device to make strange . . . the ordinary and everyday. Words, language come to be associated by Mary with structure, meaning, the meaning of the past. 'Each word she recognized gave her the sense of being restored, minutely solidified, as if damaged tissue were being welded back on to her like honey-cells. Even now she knew that language would stand for or even contain some order, an order that could not possibly subsist in anything she had come across so far' (p. 40). But language is the lethal instrument of the murderous narrator. It returns Mary to knowledge of her past existence as the destructive Amy. At the same time, language, Mary discovers, can be deceptive. Put to narrative use it can fabricate events. Reading popular romances, she realizes 'that stories were lies, imagined for money, time sold' (p. 74). Amis, of course, is simultaneously reminding his readers of their part of the narrative bargain – they have paid him to murder Mary for their amusement and to make her torments sufficiently empathetic to induce those readers to feel drawn into her predicament, to feel that their money was well spent. Is Amis deliberately employing language as a metaphor with which to associate order (especially narrative order) with fabrication? . . .

So Amis employs a fiction on which to predicate this novel. But he does provide the attentive reader with clues about the nature of this narrative premise. For example, when Prince takes Mary to the hell-like night club where she gets murdered a second time, he says to her: '[i]s there life after death? Who knows. Actually I wouldn't put it past life, would you? That would be just *like* life, to have a trick in its tail . . . ' (p. 125). The section following this in which the narrator addresses the reader takes the question up:

> *Is* there life after death? Well, *is* there?
> If there is, it will probably be hell. (If there is, it will probably be murder.)
> If there is, it will probably be very like life . . . (p. 127)

All versions of life after death have been modeled on life, the only experience we are permitted. If we have made the present-day world a form of hell-on-earth, Amis posits, then why should we expect the afterlife to be any different. And yet there is still the possibility of exercising moral choice, both in this world and in death. Prince acknowledges this possibility when he pleads with Mary: 'get it right next time, be good next time. Oh Mary – heal me, dear' (p. 82).

[Amis] chooses to follow Mary's rediscovery of her past fallen self, the self that has the power to make Alan, her lover, feel bad enough to hang himself when she breaks with him, just as Amy made short work of her lover, Michael Shane, in her past life. The long Part Two follows Mary's journey of upward social mobility and downward ethical behaviour as she becomes 'like other people' – 'getting fear and letting the present dim' (p. 96). Part Three, a mere eighteen pages long, opens with Amy (as she now acknowledges herself) living with Prince in a state of blissful domesticity. 'She wasn't sure whether this was love' (p. 210). Yet she feels that she has lived long enough. 'He can come for me now' (p. 217). He does just that. He takes her back to the now deserted hell-like night club. '"You're already dead – can't you see?"' he asks. '"Death is terribly easy to believe"' (p. 222). That message is spoken both by Prince to Amy and by the narrator to the reader. We have all made a similar mess of life in general. Prince murders her once more. The last chapter ends with Amy aged sixteen finding herself back home just prior to meeting her demon-lover who made her turn bad in her first life. This circular definition of hell is reminiscent of Sartre's *Huis Clos*, which ends, 'Eh bien, continuons'[22] ('Oh well, let us go on'). Amis seems to be asking us, are we destined to continue making the same errors as those who have gone before us? But also, are writers (and readers) condemned to go on murdering their characters to create new worlds that are always old?

Amis claims that the novel implies that this time round Amy will get it right, although it is unclear where in the text this is definitively suggested. Of more interest is his remark that the Prince figure who is about to encounter her at the end of the Epilogue has reverted to someone 'as automaton-like as she was, and didn't realize what was going on'[23] (p. 48). The narrator says, 'I'm not in control any more, not this time' (p. 224). He appears to be suggesting that by the end of the narrative the near omniscient narrator is as much in the power of the character he has been victimizing as she was in his power earlier. Her power has finally worked on the conscience of her murderous creator/narrator. He is a prisoner of his own fiction and is returned to the hellish cycle from which only a reformed Amy can set him free. Both the narrator and the reader (who has been encouraged throughout to identify with him) end up caught in the web of the fictional construct they have been conspiring together to weave around the hapless Mary. But Mary is also Amy, and only Amy can release the narrator from his guilt at having ended her life. This is a refusal of narrative closure with a vengeance.[24] □

The 'hellish cycle' identified by Finney is one of those elements which make *Other People* more unsettling, and more powerful, than Amis's first three novels. The start of this chapter cited Allan Massie's judgement that those first three novels might have shocked Amis's elders but in no way disturbed his own generation. *Other People* was different; while it was 'unsatisfactory', 'principally because of its indeterminate centre', it was 'disturbing as none of his previous books had been, because [Amis] was now admitting to ignorance of certain aspects of personality, which he had formerly presented with a glib assurance'. Amis's fourth novel demonstrated his 'ability to develop';[25] as the next chapter of this Guide will show, that ability would be spectacularly confirmed by his fifth novel, whose very title seemed to sum up the mood of the 1980s: *Money*.

CHAPTER FIVE

Self's the Man: *Money: A Suicide Note* (1984)

THE PUBLICATION of *Money* marked a new phase in Martin Amis's career. A sustained and substantial work, it aroused interest in three main respects. The first and most immediately arresting was its vibrant narrative voice; the second was its portrayal, through that voice, of a narrator-protagonist, John Self, who could be seen to embody the acquisitiveness of the 1980s in the era of Thatcher and Reagan, the desire, above all, for money; the third was its use of what Richard Todd, in an essay quoted later in this chapter (pp. 70–3), calls 'the intrusive author',[1] the author who appears as a voice, perhaps even as a character, in his own text, as one 'Martin Amis' does in *Money*. In a lively and perceptive review in the *Times Literary Supplement*, Eric Korn responded enthusiastically to the narrative voice, highlighted the novel's exploration of corruption by money, and discussed the 'intrusive author': he also pointed out how the quality of the narrator's discourse exceeds, at times, the confines of John Self – a feature that Richard Todd will explore further (p. 71) – and criticises the plot of the novel. Finally, Korn relates it to Amis's earlier work and suggests that he should now shed some of his recurrent themes:

■ One of the chief glories of Martin Amis's elaborate, enticing, subtle, irritating, overpowering new fiction is the astonishing narrative voice he has devised, the jagged, spent, street-wise, gutter-wise, guttural mid-Atlantic twang, the buttonholing, earbending, lughole-jarring monologue with all 'the energy, the electricity . . . all the hustle and razz' (p. 96) of midtown, fastfood, fastbuck, fastfuck Manhattan, of the dangerous districts uptown where everything is frazzled, charred, blistered (like the narrator), the sleaze and grate of *louche* [disreputable, shifty] London-on-the-make, a compelling, obsessive, obscene voice that carries the reader through this longish, dense, full, at times overlong . . . novel, a voice that carries you unresisting to unexpected endings . . .

Who is this prole, this Goth, this foul-mouthed clockwork orange, this upstart, this servant-when-he-reigneth, and what is he doing in New York, pawing and porning and porking about, on a business assignment that apparently offers unlimited money in exchange for little talent, and endless time for booze and hangovers and drugs and junk food and junk sex? He is called John Self (a nudging sort of name, but you will be nudged much harder later), chain-smoking ('[u]nless I specifically inform you otherwise, I'm always smoking another cigarette' (p. 8)), wrecked ('200 pounds of yob genes, booze, snout, and fast food . . . charred and choked on heavy fuel' (pp. 31–2)), and he is there to make a movie with the apparently limitless funds of younger, smarter, fitter Fielding Goodney. Behind him he has left poor faithless Selina Street, streetsmart, bedsmart, with her brothel underwear and pornographic games; in New York is his good angel Martina Twain (another nudge); she's uncorrupted, unbarbarous and – I thought – unzestfully (or at least a little too reverentially) described, but alcoholic excess makes him miss their breakfast date by twelve hours . . .

All told an unsuccessful trip, this first one (the first of four yoyo excursions across the Atlantic which comprise the novel), with nothing achieved, mysterious unsettling phonecalls from a vengeful victim . . . a near terminal humiliation at tennis from Fielding, seven Fastfurters at a sitting, sundaes of bad dope . . . Great Lakes of drink, Pentathlons of onanism [masturbation], *suffering* . . . . . . He staggers back to London where a fawning reporter asks: '"what's it feel like? You're one of the top commercial directors in the country, you're only thirty-five, you're about to make your first feature"' (p. 51). Well, yes, we had been wondering what exactly his skills were; later it transpires, unsurprisingly, that his fame is based on an unflinching use of flesh to sell, unsurprisingly, 'smoking, drinking, junk food and nude magazines' (p. 78). The film they are making is called *Money* (or *Good Money* or *Bad Money* as time goes on) and Self's the man ['Self's the Man' is the title of a poem by Philip Larkin[2]] who is wholly corrupted by money, who wholly corrupts money and with money, who is lifted and eventually dropped . . . by money, bad money driving out good in a moral Gresham's Law [bad money drives out good]. This is the significance of the novel's (and Self's) recurring concern with the pornographic: not corruption by sex, but the corruption of sex by money . . . . . .

Something else happens on that first Manhattan fling. Invited to a dinner party by Martina where there will be some writers, a Nigerian novelist, Fenton Akimbo, and critic Stanwyck Mills (Martin Amis can use joke names without catastrophes of embarrassment),[3] he rejects the offer vehemently. 'A writer lives round my way in London. He looks at me oddly in the street. He gives me the fucking creeps' (p. 39). The aside lies there ticking quietly, gives another warning rumble a score of pages on (p. 60), and ten pages beyond that it goes off.

Oh yeah, and a *writer* lives round my way too. A guy in a pub pointed him out to me, and I've seen him hanging out in Family Fun, the space-game parlour . . . This writer's name, they tell me, is *Martin Amis*. Never heard of him. Do *you* know his stuff at all? (p. 71)

At this point, the reader, harangued by tricky Self . . . and Self's tricky author, must resist the urge to reply 'Yes, I do, as a matter of fact, and please get your elbow out of my spleen'. Of course Self hasn't heard of Amis, for Self is a proclaimed illiterate ('it all came down to a choice between pain and not reading. I chose not reading' (p. 42)). Chivvied by Martina, he thinks *Animal Farm* childish, Desdemona an adulteress, *The Catcher in the Rye* a miracle of polished prose. Self reads, peruses rather, only the rawest of vulval glamour mags; his shelves and Selina's contain about a dozen books: *Treasure Island, Silas Marner, The Pardoner's Tale, The Diamond as Big as the Ritz, Success!* (Amis's last novel but one was *Success* without the exclamation [mark] . . .). But Self is an unreliable narrator, whose prose has already spilled over the cramping confines of his dialect. Would an illiterate describe the experience of '[being] bopped by a mad guy' as 'qualitatively different, full of an atrocious, a limitless rectitude' (p. 38), a Jamesian or Borgesian cadence? His conscience too overflows, though quirkily, the narrow confines of his egotism. 'I must marry Selina. If I don't I'll just die. If I don't no one else will, and I'll have ruined another life. If I don't, I think she might sue me for every penny I have' (p. 173). Even pornotopia palls. 'I suspect I'm not cut out for brothels', he ruminates, in one, where, by the by, he has given the name of Martin: 'I can't help getting engaged on the human scale, minimal though this is, fight it though I do' (p. 102).

Money runs into difficulties. The wayward dirigible of its plot is repeatedly snared, and ripped, on the prickly skyscraping egos of its future stars, the geronto-macho Lorne Guyland, the sterile Madonna Caduta Massi, Butch Beausoleil, the female flesh interest, and Spunk Davis, about whose name Self anticipates a little difficulty for the British market. The infighting and negotiations among the cast are the most uncomplexly entertaining parts of the book . . . . . .

In successive novels, as his characters grow more repugnant, Amis has manipulated the distance between himself and them. He is not, and even in 1973 wasn't, the Charles Highway of *The Rachel Papers*, the one who is advised to '"for Christ's sake stop reading all this struc-turalist stuff"' (p. 211); but there is a zestful closeness between them.

In *Dead Babies/Dark Secrets* there is a malign *diabolus ex machina* who suddenly becomes aware of 'all the blank wrong yesterdays' (p.219) [*diabolus ex machina* means 'devil out of/from the machine' – Korn is adapting the more common phrase *deus ex machina*, the god out of/from the machine, a 'power or event that comes in the nick of time to solve difficulty', a 'providential interposition, esp[ecially] in [a] novel or play'. Originally the phrase *deus ex machina* referred to the 'god from the machinery' . . . by which in [the Greek] theatre the gods were shown in the air]. In *Success* the narration (and the nastiness) is cunningly divided between the two near-twin foster brothers. (The protagonist of *Other People*, a far less satisfying construction than *Money* for my money, is not nasty: but then she is hardly alive.)

    Money is exhilarating, skilful, savvy. It manipulates the plot . . . as painlessly, as inexorably as it manipulates the reader. And this is a root of discontent: the structural wit, the metaphysics, is less interesting – to me, perhaps to him – than the diction and character. Hence the nastiness is sympathetic, the vice enticing . . . Amis manipulates Amis: when he denounces Sin it's only Self-abuse. And now that the Swiftian, the planet-wide disgust ([i]f you don't like it here, Mr Martian Amis, why don't you go back where you came from?) of the earlier novels is alleviated, shouldn't some of the recurrent themes be shed? It's retiring age for the worry about falling teeth and falling hair, [and] the phrase . . . 'What's the point of her if she doesn't do that?' – i.e., fuck (*Money*, p.244)[,] cook (*Other People*, p.158), allow you to do whatever the hell you like (*Success*, p.82)?[4] ▢

Korn's by that time corny pun 'Martian Amis' alludes, of course, to the 'Martian' technique of seeing the familiar as strange which, as the last chapter demonstrated, was noted by reviewers and critics in Amis's previous novel *Other People*. If the Martian perspective is less evident in *Money* (though, as Richard Todd suggests, it is not wholly absent (p.73)), this is perhaps not only because its novelty has worn off, but also because Amis has not had to travel to a hypothetical Mars and back to find a point of view that is vividly different but strangely familiar: he has merely had to fly to and from the USA. As Korn's review alliteratively underlines at the outset, *Money* is set in 'fastfood, fastbuck, fastfuck Manhattan' as well as the '*louche* London-on-the-make' that had earlier figured, in its premonitory phase, in *Success*. The first two chapters of this Guide cited Richard Brown's discussion of the representation of Americans in *The Rachel Papers* and *Dead Babies*: but those were Americans abroad, in England; it is *Money* that actually goes to America and shows Americans at home. Brown begins his account of *Money* by linking it with Amis's collection of essays on America, *The Moronic Inferno* (1986):

■ A key term that recurs throughout *The Moronic Inferno*, producing and defining the Dickensian grotesques of America whom Amis seeks out, is 'money'. *Money*, Amis's fifth novel published inevitably in the year of dystopias 1984, might be read in and through these essays. He wrote of the popular American TV evangelists in 1980: '[m]oney is the two-way traffic of the religious TV industry: money is taken from the viewers in the form of sacramental contributions; money is 'returned' to them in the form of celestial jackpots . . . Money is its own vindication; money is its own just cause' (p. 113). The circularity of such money/ religion figures largely in the novel, whose anti-hero John Self survives as '"commercial [director]"' (p. 51) in the financial hinterland of the movie industry, linking actors[,] writers and directors to the all-important '"money genius"' (p. 52) Fielding Goodney in order to make a film called *Good Money* that turns out to be little more than a financial trick played on Self in which he is duped into bankrupting himself.

The novel begins with a pointedly American scene: a New York in which Self seeks Goodney to set up the first deal through a minefield of junk food and pornography. Even the cab driver has views which make him an extension of Charles Highway's nightmare exaggeration of American violence and racism [see p. 21 of this Guide]. The reader is thrown into America immediately not only by settings but also by the personality and the language of the first-person narrator John Self whose very body is the city; his toothache its 'upper west side' (pp. 26, 75, 76, 112, 357). Amis creates for him a brilliantly fast-paced new idiom packed with brand names (his car is a Fiasco; he takes a sleeping pill called Serafim), and terms like 'rug-rethink' (pp. 83, 273), 'handjob' (passim), 'sack talent' (p. 57) and the word 'pornography' used as a positive term (which are types of usage that the British reader will probably register as 'Americanisms'). As Self says on the comic names of characters in the book: '"lots of Americans are called things like that. They've all got names like Orifice and Handjob. They don't notice. They think it's cool"' (p. 247). So it is something of a shock to the English reader (no doubt a relief to the American) to find that stereotypically Mailerish and American John Self has, in fact, an English background and even refers to himself as an Englishman (p. 20), though he also admits to being 'half American and half asleep' (p. 9). 'I pitched my voice somewhere in the mid-Atlantic' (p. 206), says Self in his own defence, implying that Amis . . . may find aspects of his writing emerging from that space between.

The narrative alternates between an American film industry, with its vain and self-seeking 'stars' Lorne Guyland and Butch Beausoleil, seen through vestigially English eyes, and a west London publand (the pub that Self frequents in London, since he was 'born upstairs' (pp. 59, 145) and where he meets the English writer 'Martin Amis' is called the Shakespeare) defamiliarized as through the eyes of an American. But Anglo-American cultural mixedness prevents the polarities from stabilizing. Self's 'American, but English-raised' girl-friend Martina Twain[,] 'a real boss chick . . . with a terrific education on her' (p.39), who teaches him to read George Orwell and *Othello*, helps both to identify England as a place of culture in the novel's Anglo-American dichotomies and also to subvert such identifications. Selina [S]treet, his London girlfriend, whose 'brothelly knowhow and top-dollar underwear' (p.14) call up American currency, similarly serves to destabilise stereotypes.

Self's eventual undoing at the hands of American Fielding Goodney may be prefigured in the story of his Uncle Norman who had believed America to be 'the land of opportunity' (p.207) but ended up coming home none the richer and living in a 'home' (a 'home' is significantly defined as a place 'where money isn't worth anything' (p.208) [In fact, the idea that America is 'the land of opportunity' is attributed to Self himself, rather than directly to Uncle Norman – 'I have always understood that America is the land of opportunity' (p.207) – but he quickly brings it under the sign of irony by telling the story of his uncle's business failures in the USA]). Self too ends up back 'home' and almost inadvertently begging in the London Underground with his dubious new girlfriend, Georgina. But this opposition too is undercut, perhaps, by Fielding's Enlightenment English writer's name [that is, Henry Fielding (1707–54), author of *Tom Jones* (1749)], and by the fact that it is Martina's English husband, Ossie Twain, who works 'in pure money . . . nothing to do with anything except money, the stuff itself' (pp.119–20), who is both Selina's secret lover and the true instigator of Self's supposedly clandestine relationship with his wife, as well as sharing his name with America's comic genius Mark Twain [(1835–1910), author of *The Adventures of Huckleberry Finn* (1884)].[5] □

Brown's sense that in *Money* the oppositions between England and the USA are both highlighted at times, and at other times blurred by a merging and an exchange of qualities, is echoed by Bernard Bergonzi in his observations on the way Amis's fifth novel brings together elements of English and American fiction which had been sharply distinguished when Bergonzi had originally compared and contrasted them in his study *The Situation of the Novel* (1969; 2nd edn, 1972). In an interview in 1990, asked how he saw the relationship between the English and American novel today, Bergonzi replied:

■ At that time [in the 1960s and early 1970s], one did have this sense, which was rather encouraged by certain critics and indeed novelists, that English fiction was domestic and dull and commonplace and small-scale, whereas the Americans were going for the biggie and everything was up for grabs there. That was a kind of myth, if you like, a literary critical myth . . . But now there's much less of a clear distinction. For instance, Martin Amis's *Money* seems to me a most brilliant novel which has a great deal of American writing in it – Mailer, Burroughs and so on – but which is also a painfully sharply observed work of English social comedy: he's got them both going at the same time.[6] □

The English aspect of *Money* is underlined by Amis in his interview with John Haffenden, when he talks about his reasons for setting it in 1981 and refers, not to events in the USA at that time, but to the Royal Wedding of Prince Charles and Lady Diana, and the riots in Brixton, Liverpool and other English cities. The conversation goes on to cover a range of important aspects of the novel which was, at the time of the interview, Amis's most recent one: the plot, the apparent arbitrariness of the ending, the significance of John Self, the author appearing as a character, the moral dimension of the work, and its sexual, possibly pornographic scenes:

■ [*John Haffenden:*] Money *is set in 1981: was it begun then?*

[*Martin Amis:*] I started it in 1980. It could have been set any time, but the conjunction of the Royal Wedding and the riots in 1981 seemed a natural timetable for the book. I also thought it amusing to write an historical novel about something which actually happened only the other day . . . . . .

I wonder how much the business of plotting a novel matters to you, particularly when you often seem so possessed by the central characters of your books? Money *might well have worked simply as a scathing chronicle of John Self's degeneration through drink and sex and power, whereas you introduce the twist of having him undone by the manipulator, the phoney Fielding Goodney. It might strike one as a trick ending when the bulk of the novel has given us perhaps too few suggestions that Goodney is the antagonist.*

It has been said already that the plot is almost a distraction in this book, but I think it's important that Fielding Goodney is like an artist. I don't understand it fully yet, but I'm sure it all has to do with that idea. Everyone in the book is a kind of artist – sack-artists, piss-artists, con-artists, bullshit-artists – and perhaps this leads on to something I will understand and write about later. There is a type of person who is a handsome liar, a golden mythomaniac, who lies for no reason, without motivation. It's a great affront to the novel, because A.C. Bradley and that whole school of humanistic criticism tell us that people behave for reasons, whereas – if you read *The Sun* every day, and keep your wits about you in the street – you see that motivation has actually been exaggerated in, and by, the novel: you have something much woollier than motivation.

The Martin Amis character in Money *suggests that motivation must now be seen as something more inward and neurotic.*

Yes, motivation has become depleted, a shagged-out force in modern life.

In Money, *however, the reader has seen too little of the character or thoughts of Fielding Goodney even to feel concerned about whether or not he has motivation. We may be amused or disturbed by the trick or gimmick of the plot, but he is presented more or less as a suave ideal in John Self's eyes.*

Yes, 'ideal' is right: he is meant to seem like an absolute given, like Quentin in *Dead Babies*. He embodies confidence, which is at last in my novels identified as a psychopathic state. The last chapter says that confidence is a wildly inappropriate response to present-day life. Fielding Goodney is meant to embody and show the weakness of such a state of mind . . . I remember telling my father three years ago that the plot of *Money* would all be based on a totally unexplained confidence trick which I meant to be as bald and brutal as possible – absolutely unexplained – and I think that's quite a good analogy for money . . . . . .

With respect to your . . . novels, it can, I think, raise an uncomfortable paradox in the reader's mind that you can write with a Nabokovian writerly relish and at the same time keep up the indignation usually expected of the satirist.

I'm never sure that what I've been writing is satire. *Money* is a sort of dramatic monologue, but Self never actually *says* anything intelligent in the whole book. At one point he asks Martina Twain why she likes him: '"Why?" Because I'm so twentieth century? "Why?"' (p.334). It's important that he doesn't actually *say* '[b]ecause I'm so twentieth century', since all his quoted remarks are fumbling.

He sees himself as a representative figure?

He suspects that he is, yes. Another example is when he reads in the newspaper about that girl who is allergic to the twentieth century – all

modern fabrics make her roar with rejection – and he thinks, 'I am
addicted to the twentieth century' (p. 91). I do mean him to be a consumer, and he is consumed by consumerism, as all mere consumers
are. I also mean him to be stupefied by having watched too much television – his life is without sustenance of any kind – and that is why he is
so fooled by everyone; he never knows what is going on. He has this lazy
non-effort response which is wished on you by television – and by reading a shitty newspaper. Those are his two sources of information about
the planet. On four or five occasions his mind stretches to thinking
about Poland, and he always sees it as a sort of soap opera: he wonders
about Danuta Walesa, for example, and hopes she's had her kid OK.

In Money *you* [include] *a me-persona, 'Martin Amis', so that nobody might
identify you with your hero, John Self, indulging a wet, drunk fantasy.*

I was wondering whether I did put 'me' in there because I was so
terrified of people thinking that I was John Self. But actually I've been
hanging around the wings of my novels, so awkwardly sometimes,
like the guest at the banquet, that I thought I might jolly well be in
there at last. Also, every character in this book dupes the narrator, and
yet I am the one who has actually done it all to him: I've always been
very conscious of that, and it is perhaps an index of how alive and
unstable my characters are to me . . . . . .

*Do you recognize in yourself a puritanical streak? After all, you do believe in
innocence – simple innocence and criminal innocence – and in corruption.*

I have strong moral views, and they are very much directed at things
like money and acquisition. I think money is the central deformity in
life, as Saul Bellow says, it's one of the evils that has cheerfully sur-
vived identification as an evil. Money doesn't mind if we say it's evil,
it goes from strength to strength. It's a fiction, an addiction, and a tacit
conspiracy that we have all agreed to go along with. My hatred for it
does look as though I'm underwriting a certain asceticism, but it isn't
really that way: I don't offer alternatives to what I deplore.
    I am clear about the moral transgressions and even the occasional
strengths and steadfastnesses of my characters, but I don't ever feel the
need to point them out. I may be just a victim of what I take to be the
nature of moral thinking in our time, which is actually lazy. At one
point in *Money* John Self thinks, '[w]hat is this state, seeing the difference between good and bad and choosing bad . . . okaying bad?' (p. 26),
and he decides – though I don't know if I spelt this out in the final
draft – that it's a state of corruption. A certain sort of perverse laxity
about oneself, moral unease without moral energy. I think people do

and always will have moral awareness, but the executive branch is weak at the moment; and perhaps I reflect or connive at that in not sorting out reward and punishment . . . . . .

Do you feel any need to justify what some readers may consider to be pornographic scenes in your novels? In your profile of Gloria Steinem you recorded her view that pornography is part of the conspiracy of '"anti-woman warfare"', and you went on to suggest that it might be better to see it as 'mere weakness and chaotic venality' (Moronic Inferno, *p. 139). This question may relate to certain heavy passages in* Money: *do you feel yourself to be something of a male apologist in respect of pornography?*

I think the feminists have got a very strong argument against pornography, but I don't think it's a civil-rights issue. Many women take pornography as an organized attack but it isn't that: it's just a nasty way of making money for all the people who are in it . . . . . . There are certainly one or two pornographic scenes in *Money*, and they're there for the effect they have on the narrator: he has no resistance to pornography, or to any other bad thing. It's very easy for me to decide that I don't write pornography, because I'm sure that one of the definitions of pornography would have to be that the creator of pornography is excited by it, and I'm not excited by anything except by how I'm going to arrange the words. All definitions, by the way, would have to include the element of money.

You somehow managed to make John Self in Money *both obnoxious and endearing, but could it not be said that in creating the excitement of his vulgar and meretricious career you are inviting readers to indulge their bottom-line impulses and erotic drives?*

If his erotic drives were stronger, then presumably pornography wouldn't have such easy access to him. Pornography isn't really erotic, it's carnal; it's a frippery for the jaded, and jadedness is again an enemy of eroticism. John Self likes everything that's bad – that's the trouble with him – he has no resistance, because he has no sustenance, no structure. Pornography is one of his many symptoms, if you like. The crucial pornographic scene is when he is seduced, as it were, by his then stepmother, Vron. That's his nadir in the book: everything has collapsed, so why not do the worst thing? Then he is beaten up, and told that his father isn't his real father; so it had to be the worst possible sex. The artistic objection is the only objection. But it seems to me that it's John's worst moment, and the idea of pleasure isn't in that scene at all: isn't he in fact getting the lesson of pornography? It never occurs to me that the reader could find such a scene titillating, because that's just not what I'm thinking about . . . . . .

You include two strings of literary allusions in Money: *to* Othello *(about 1604) and to Orwell's* Animal Farm *(1945) and (perhaps slightly less)* Nineteen Eighty-Four *(1949). How important were these allusions in your planning of the novel, and do they in fact amount to a mythic structure in your mind? Or are they just curlicues* [decorative curls or twists]*?*

I asked Saul Bellow if [*The Adventures of*] *Augie March* (1953) had a mythic structure, and he said that it just had a patina. You don't want to be fondling the elbows of thesis-candidates. There is a strong Shakespearian theme in *Money*, and it's impossible not to think of Shakespeare as a sort of writer-god. John Self's interpretation of *Othello* is that Desdemona is being unfaithful, because fifty pages earlier he's seen a pornographic film which uses the same plot – plus graphic infidelities. Shakespeare is the model or taunting embodiment of what he's excluded from, and Fielding Goodney's relation to John Self is really that of Iago. Though Self, of course, isn't Othello – he's Roderigo, the lecherous spendthrift and gull. When Goodney fights with him, he appears to say "'[o]h damn dear go . . . Oh and you man dog'" (p. 350); later on the Martin Amis character tells Self that the words might have been 'O damn'd Iago, O inhuman dog' (*Othello*, Act 5, Scene 1, Line 64[7]) (this is the best line in the play and says everything about Iago), at which point John Self thinks Martin Amis is talking about his own car! ('He drives a little black Iago, a 666' (p. 272).) Martin Amis says, "'Fascinating. Pure transference'" (p. 377), because at that moment Fielding Goodney had thought he himself had been betrayed, whereas in fact he had been the betrayer.

I'm not a great Orwellian, but I wanted *Animal Farm* because of the animal imagery in my book, and I thought it would be wonderfully funny if someone could read *Animal Farm* just thinking it was an animal story and not an allegory.

Did you have any sense of Fielding Goodney, being a type of O'Brien [the interrogator in Orwell's *Nineteen Eighty-Four*], *persecuting this victim of modern society, John Self?*

The wised-up operator, the one who knows all the uncomfortable truths: there was a glimmer of that, but it doesn't have particularly wide emphasis. The point of it is that John Self's education is under way, but he still sees himself as on the O'Brien side whereas in fact he isn't: he's a victim. He likes the sound of classless Oceania, and he sees himself as an idealistic young corporal in the Thought Police, but the reader suspects that he's more of an occupant of Room 101.

Is John Self a nihilist, and would it not have been logical for him to have died at the end of the book?

He does end up dead in a way – outside the novel, outside money and *Money*, in endless and ordinary life. To describe him as a nihilist is stretching it. What he lives through may be a sort of nihilism, but he has no informing ideology of the way he lives.[8] □

One of the features of *Money* which Amis and Haffenden discuss and which reviewers such as Eric Korn and critics like Richard Brown noted – the presence of a writer called Martin Amis in the novel – is further explored by Karl Miller in his fascinating book *Doubles: Studies in Literary History* (1985; 1987). Miller identifies Amis as 'the latest of Anglo-America's dualistic artists' who creates, in *Success, Other People*, and, above all, *Money*, three examples of an 'orphan delirium' in which orphan and double meet:

■ *Money* is an obscene orphan delirium, that of the guttersnipe film-maker John Self, who shuttles in continuous escape between London and New York, and is ripped off by a tempter, a money-man. The movie they are making is a family romance in which Self's own orphan-oedipal predicament is mirrored. One of the most brilliant strokes in the annals of the genre is delivered when the narrator, Self, takes up with a serious-minded, not to say disapproving writer by the name of Martin Amis, who rewrites his movie, and narrowly beats him at chess. (The symbiotes play chess together in *Success* . . .) After his victory, 'Martin Amis' offers poor Self what comes across as an authorial apology for making him up and putting him through this turmoil.

The reader is plunged into a momentous, aerial, ethereal, lunar, pre-menstrual, manic, antic, frantic 'panting present' (p. 208), of ups and downs, fights and flights and gutters. Here is an antinomian duality which is also an emetic, diuretic, onanistic duality. Here is a narcissist who is never done playing with himself, and not only at chess . . . Onan is an orphan, and there are two of him [In the Old Testament Book of Genesis, Onan, ordered by his father to make his brother's wife pregnant in order to produce a child for his brother, 'spill[s] his seed on the ground, lest he should give seed to his brother' (Genesis, 38:9). 'Onanism' is a term that means interrupted intercourse, or (as in this case) masturbation]. Masturbation, no less than suicide, is a dualistic proof, and both proofs are furnished in the course of Self's self-exposure.

The duality of the novel can be further characterized in terms of its way with women. [In his poem 'A Bookshop Idyll',] Kingsley Amis – Martin Amis's father – has suggested in his time, unequivocally enough, that

> Women are really much nicer than men:
> No wonder we like them,[9]

but has been thought to have withdrawn the suggestion in his recent fictions. And now his son has joined this debate about the strangeness of women – attractive women in particular. The heroine of *Other People* feels that women go a little mad once a month (p. 188). 'Women are more civilized,' reflects the hero of *Money* (p. 331), a ferocious consumer of pornography who treats them as sex objects. Father and son have seemed to punish an excessive or delirious machismo, and yet they have been charged with misogyny. Arguments break out as to whether or not these writers really like them.

'The world wavers,' the novel reports (p. 202). 'People are doubling' (p. 63). The doubling in the novel itself is both intricate and strategic, ranging as it does from alter egos to double-takes and double-pates (there's a scalper's keen interest in hairstyles, 'rugs'). Duality drops a tear when the Selves, if that is what they are, the narrator and Martin Amis, watch the Royal Wedding of Prince Charles and Lady Di on television, and accuse each other of being moved. In New York, the disgusting Anglo-American Mid-Atlantic Self makes friends with sensitive sky-blue-blooded Martina Twain . . . , who points him towards a better life, subjects him to opera and evening dress, waters her plants, and serves as a sort of bridge between Self and the sobersides Martin Amis, over there in London reading and writing for all he is worth: Martina lends support, in other words, to the impression that the two males are sharers of a life. Reading is an activity in relation to which Self is something of a remedial case, and Martina has him trying his hand. After a while he finds he no longer *likes* what he wants: a version of Ovid's dualistic *deteriora sequor* – of that famous self-disapproval – which can be read as a sign of grace, and of change. ['Deteriora sequor' is from the Latin phrase 'Video meliora, proboque; / Deteriora sequor' – 'I see the better way and I approve it; [but] I follow the worse' – or, as John Self puts it, '[w]hat is this state, seeing the difference between good and bad and choosing bad . . . ?' (p. 26).]

So Onan lets up and learns to read fancy books, and to write one. Onan and double meet. As usual in the literature of such conjunctions, the excluded is seen to escape, and in this work the escapes would appear to be from troubles and fiascos in which a first exclusion is repeated or remembered: we gather that John Self has a family which is anxious to exclude him (his mother is dead and his father proves false) and from which he is anxious to escape. At all events, he is a self-proclaimed 'escape artist' (p. 393) who can execute a 'full escape posture' (p. 228). He strives upwards, with the help of aeroplanes. 'Away! I thought, as we climbed through the air with the greatest of ease' (p. 92). 'Away' is Keats's word [in his poem 'Ode to a Nightingale' (1820) – 'Away! Away! for I will fly to thee'], and this may even be Keats's exclamation mark. Allusion and parody are a dimension of the book's duality. Self 'moves like a ghost' (p. 222) as if to pour one of his countless drinks – the stride alluded to here ('strides' means trousers in the street talk of the novel) is that of the ravishing Tarquin in *Macbeth*; and he then supposes himself in hell. Film is called a '"delirium"' (p. 226) and people are 'paranoid' (pp. 239, 240): this, too, is allusive. The novel . . . observes that even the most confident are afraid: and 'confidence' is another time-honoured term. Brash John Self attempts suicide. This confidence-man comes to regard confidence as a *'psychopathic state'* (p. 393). Nervousness is best. The novel carries and declares a range of co-ordinate fictions, including Melville's novel [*The Confidence-Man: His Masquerade* (1857)], and precipitates the arguments and debates of traditional duality into the panting present tense. It updates such concerns as 'possession' and puts a view of this, and of the superstitions of the past, to which many people would now assent:

> these tribes of spacefaced conquered would brood about God, Hell, the Father of Lies, the fate of the spirit, with the soul imagined as an inner being, a moistly smiling angel in a pink nightie, or a grimacing goblin, all V-signs, bad rug and handjobs. But now the invader is a graph shadow swathed in spools and printouts, and he wears an alien face.
>
> I sometimes think I am controlled by someone. Some space invader is invading my inner space, some fucking joker. But he's not from out there. He's from in here (p. 330).

Parody and allusion, then, are compounded by affinity. The later Bellow is evident in the novel, as are the terrors of Mailer and Mickey Spillane. Like Bellow, Amis likes to write about change, metamorphosis, what he calls 'turnaround'. The problems raised by his novel are problems familiar to the reader of the literature of its affinities, which has witnessed a turnaround from the condition of the novel to the condition of the poem, and a new kind of subordination to the author of the other people he creates. This novel bears a relation to its author which makes it difficult for it to end. And indeed it is not altogether easy to say where it begins: some of the phobias which attack the Self sensorium – that of the disappearing penis, and of the borrowing of smelly second-hand clothes – are borrowed from the orphans in *Success*. Self is that rare bird, the dipsomaniac masturbator, and he is a man who can barely read who has written a fancy book which quotes from Keats and Shakespeare. He is a man who confesses what can appear to be less intelligible to himself than it is to that other man whose name is on the title-page – and to whom, at the time of Self's suicide attempt, there is a bewildering, or obfuscating, direct allusion, an allusion which operates quite independently of the presence in the novel of a 'Martin Amis'. We may conclude that Self is not a person but a part, a burlesqued proclivity, a preposterous Jonsonian humour, a bundle of at times incongruous – as distinct, we may feel, from dualistically inconsistent – bad habits. If he is the expression of some ulterior self-disapproval or disavowal, what are its scale and proportions? Where does it end? It is as if these bad habits are being made endlessly delightful, by an unending author. With such fictions, it is sometimes possible to sense that only the one man is on show, to doubt the authenticity of those characters who trail no shadow of a Siamese connection with the author. But this is not to doubt the authenticity of the show itself, or its appeal to *semblables*, to a paranoid orphan readership.

It is also possible to doubt whether this is a book about money. John Self coins it and blues it, but other things matter more. Nevertheless *Money* is its title, and in the autumn of 1984 a book entitled *Rich* is due to be published by the poet Craig Raine, who will be treated by some, and not for the first time, as Martin Amis's Martian Twain. Such coincidences or designs belong to a semaphore whereby these same *semblables* communicate. It signals the existence of a community of strangers. And on this occasion it signals that 'Martian' and 'alien' and 'orphan' are collusive terms. There exist a literature and an environment in which the individual who feels himself invaded, from without or from within, is perceived as an invader. Here once more are the orphan and the double.[10] □

Miller's interpretation of *Money* in terms of 'the orphan and the double' is developed by Richard Todd in his exploration of the notion of 'the intrusive author' in postmodern fiction. In a paper delivered in 1985 and published in 1990 in a collection called *Exploring Postmodernism*, Todd presents his analysis of Amis's *Money* and Alasdair Gray's novel *Lanark: A Life in Four Books* (1981) as 'a protest at the *exclusiveness* of the premature canonic status [John Fowles's] *The French Lieutenant's Woman* (1969) has gained in discussions of British postmodernism during the past fifteen years or so'.[11] His essay proceeds on the assumption 'that Gray and Amis, far more insistently than Fowles or any of his more tentative imitators such as Malcolm Bradbury (in *The History Man* (1975)), use the device of the intrusive author to exploit self-reference and self-reflexiveness in a number of interesting and noteworthy ways'. In particular, Todd contends that the more intrusive the authorial presence, the less dominant are those references to history and to place, such as occur in *The French Lieutenant's Woman*, which serve both to invoke and subvert the conventions of realism: the primary concern becomes not to subvert realism but to explore 'the self-referent and the self-reflexive'[12] and to foreground their style – particularly in *Money*, the 'stylistic foregrounding' of which shows 'more evident virtuosity' than *Lanark*, although the latter has 'noteworthy stylistic attributes'.[13] Todd first discusses *Lanark*, and then moves on to *Money*, arguing that in this novel, as in Gray's, the 'use of the device of the intrusive author is integrally related to its self-reflexiveness'.[14] He begins his discussion of *Money* by relating the question of its intrusive author to Amis's own fame or notoriety and to his previous novels:

■ The self-reflexiveness of *Money* takes on especially interesting dimensions as we consider the high public profile Martin Amis has maintained in Britain since emerging as a novelist of some stature as early as 1975, while still in his mid-twenties . . . the son of a famous literary father, [he] has not only had no difficulty in achieving notoriety but has seemed actively to court it, and it has proved hard for London's literary establishment to speak rationally of his work and personality. To his enemies (and there seem to be many) he is seen as the leader of one of the most powerful and influential literary cliques of this or any other age . . . But to his admirers Amis is (among many panegyrics [words of praise]) the finest prose stylist of his generation. The title and subject-matter of his third novel, *Success*, might thus be regarded as fascinatingly self-reflexive. *Money* is Amis's fifth novel, and he is still only in his mid-thirties . . .

It has been argued by Karl Miller that Amis's last three novels, *Success, Other People*, and *Money*, all share a common interest or even theme, in that all three are 'fictions . . . turmoils, in which orphan and double meet'.[15] This is certainly true, although one might well develop the point by noticing that Amis has increasingly obsessively started to explore the relationship between what one can only call the different orders of reality to which orphan and double belong . . . . . . *Money* . . . turns the screw [still] further. The orphan in this urban satire is named John Self . . . Self in fact meets two versions of the double: in London he encounters a writer named Martin Amis, whom he eventually coerces into rewriting the script of *Money* after the previous scriptwriter's failure to make it sufficiently attractive to the four leads, all of whom have refused their roles; in New York he is pursued by Martina Twain, who introduces the largely unread Self to works such as *Animal Farm*, [and] *Nineteen Eighty-Four*, and takes him to see Verdi's *Otello* – meanwhile we discover that Martina's husband Ossie has been having an affair with Self's girlfriend Selina Street.

Self is not, in fact, strictly speaking, an orphan, and one of the components of the rather complex denouement of *Money* concerns his discovery of his true paternity. On his own account Self was born 'upstairs' (pp. 59, 145) in a London pub called the Shakespeare. Believing himself to be the son of Barry Self, he eventually discovers that his true father is Fat Vince, 'beer-crate operative and freelance bouncer at the Shakespeare', who has 'been in and out of this place every day for thirty-five years' (p. 145). Martin Amis, also 35 in the year of *Money*'s publication (although of course younger in the year – 1981 – in which the narrative is set), is introduced gradually into the narrative, and, on the first occasion they meet, Self, not notably literate, asks Amis: '"Your dad, he's a writer too, isn't he? Bet that made it easier."' Amis's reply is worth recording: '"Oh, sure. It's just like taking over the family pub"' (p. 88). The *TLS* reviewer of *Money* [Eric Korn] reminded its readers that one fat Englishman had crossed the Atlantic a generation before[16] [The reference here is to Kingsley Amis's novel *One Fat Englishman* (1963)]. It seems to me that we are presented in *Money* with a number of instances of self-reflexiveness being confronted so explicitly (the nomenclature is clearly to be seen as part of the process) that we are forced to examine the extent to which the novel's various voices both are and are not claiming to be aspects of a single consciousness. One of the fascinating features of *Money* is, indeed, the voice of the narrator, a voice that, stylistically speaking, is explicitly virtuoso, yet whose owner is at pains to tell us that he has read little and absorbed less. This feature of the narrative is closely related to the interesting mis-hearings that are dotted around the text: Self, who in any case suffers from a 'fresh disease . . . called tinnitus' (p. 1), is often 'hearing things' as well as frequently blacking out on account of powerful combinations of drink and drugs and *not* (as he discovers to his cost at the novel's end) hearing or recalling or being capable of taking in information that really matters. In a brothel in Manhattan he tells a girl called Moby that his name is Martin and that he is a writer: he is flummoxed by her reply: '"John roar mainstream?"' [genre or mainstream?] (p. 100). Talking to his sinister agent Fielding Goodney, Self makes a note of a possible substitute star, Nub Forkner:

"That's o-r-k, Slick," said Fielding.
    I glanced down at the page. "That's what I've got."
    " . . . You read much, John?"
    "Read what?"
    "Fiction."
    "Do you?"
    "Oh sure. It gives me all kinds of ideas. I like the sound and the fury," he added enigmatically. [*The Sound and the Fury* (1929) is a novel by the American writer William Faulkner (1897–1962) which takes its title from a phrase in Shakespeare's *Macbeth* (composed probably 1606) – '[Life] is a tale/Told by an idiot, full of sound and

fury,/Signifying nothing' (Act 5, Scene 5, lines 25–27).[17] Todd also cites the misheard quotation from *Othello* discussed earlier in this chapter (p. 65) by Amis himself.] (p. 219) . . . . . .

Yet when all this is said, the voice, with its hectic pace and tone – even the violence and the profuse and candid sexuality, the urban satire mediated through a flaunted stylistic virtuosity such that the only semi-colon in something like 200,000 words of text occurs in the last sentence (p. 394), after a figurative allusion to their absence (in terms of the novel's pace) some 80 pages earlier (p. 312: 'I want to slow down now, and check out the scenery, and put in a stop or two. I want some semi-colons') – despite all this, the voice of Self is very much the voice Amis uses elsewhere; and this seems to me to represent an explicitly considered solution to the problem of how, in a text of this kind, one conveys a narrator of Self's philistinism, whose final discovery is that all the money he believes himself to have been earning forms part of an operation he has been tricked into financing himself, a rip-off Martin Amis admits his complicity in. Perhaps emblematic of the difficulty such a text presents is the chess game Self and Amis play towards the end. Self is in fact an excellent player, surely a deliberate and flagrantly unexpected attribute, and he is 'zugzwanged' by Amis after a cliff-hanging game. Despite Self's having used the word earlier in his narrative (p. 119), he now, at the end of their game, has to ask Amis for a definition of it ('"What the fuck does that mean?"'); Martin Amis replies: '"Literally, *forced to move*. It means that whoever has to move has to lose. If it were my turn now, you'd win. But it's yours. And you lose"' (p. 379). Elsewhere, both Martin and Martina severally explain aspects of what we must call the experience of literature to Self. Thus Martina:

> talked about the vulnerability of a figure unknowingly watched . . . The analogous distinction in fiction would be that between the conscious and the reluctant narrator – the sad, the unwitting narrator (p. 132).

And Martin tells Self:

> 'The further down the scale [the hero] is, the more liberties you can take with him. You can do what the hell you like to him, really. This creates an appetite for punishment. The author is not free of sadistic impulses' (p. 247).

It is in the light of this self-reflexive complexity of 'voice' in *Money* that we should also see the pervasively arresting topographical description of both Manhattan and London. Here are two examples selected virtually at random, the first reminding us that Amis has also published a work of nonfiction entitled *The Invasion of the Space Invaders* (1982):

> I spent an improving four hours on Forty-Second Street, dividing my time between a space-game arcade and the basement gogo bar next door. In the arcade the proletarian ghosts of the New York night, these darkness-worshippers, their terrified faces reflected in the screens, stand hunched over their controls. They look like human forms of mutant moles and bats, hooked on the radar, rumble and wow of these stocky new robots who play with you if you give them money. They'll talk too, for a price. *Launch Mission, Circuit Completed, Firestorm, Flashpoint, Timewarp, Crackup, Blackout!* The kids, tramps and loners in here, they are the mineshaft spirits of the new age . . . In the gogo bar men and women are eternally ranged against each other, kept apart by a wall of drink, a moat of poison, along which the mad matrons and bad bouncers stroll (pp. 24–25).

> I walked back to my sock in the thin rain. And the skies. Christ! In shades of kitchen mists, with eyes of light showing only murk and seams of film and grease, the air hung above and behind me like an old sink full of old washing-up. Blasted, totalled, broken-winded, shot-faced London, doing time under sodden skies (p.159).

Readers familiar with recent developments in British literature will notice something of the so-called 'Martian' school of bizarrely figurative expressiveness, a characteristic use of the English language that has been suggestively compared to the 'metaphysical' style of the late sixteenth and early seventeenth centuries. My point in drawing attention to this characteristic of *Money's* topographical descriptions is to insist that in devising a voice for John Self, the extra-fictional Martin Amis has, it seems to me, quite explicitly chosen to use his own, a voice that is clearly recognizable from his own other published fiction. I am convinced that we should see Amis's strategy as a deliberate choice that illustrates a self-conscious confrontation of the problem of solipsistic 'closure' and not – instead – as illustrating any kind of limitation of which no awareness has been shown.[18] □

Todd concludes that *Money* and *Lanark* 'each represent different ways of responding self-reflexively to a perceived threat of solipsistic closure, a threat that . . . may be particularly urgent in contemporary fiction in Britain because of the perceived weight and multiplicity of traditional approaches to realism. Gray and Amis have pushed the postmodernist device of the intrusive author to a point where stylistic and topographical elements have become practically autonomous of any reference to that tradition'.[19] He suggests that what Amis offers 'may be, as [Karl] Miller has claimed, generically innovative in its linking of the device of the intrusive author to an obsession with orphan and double in a tradition whose roots can be traced at least as far as a Gothic text such as James Hogg's *Confessions of a Justified Sinner* (1824)',[20] and affirms that 'Amis's treatment of his self-reflexive theme is combined with a stylistic virtuosity (to which topographical elements are *subordinated*) that suggests a yet more thoroughgoing fragmentation than does Gray's. Such fragmentation confirms, more strongly still than in Amis's previous fiction to date, our sense of a single selfhood complexly refracted through the existence of various, duplicitously conflicting, voices.'[21]

In an essay that compares Amis's *Money* with Caryl Churchill's play *Serious Money* (1987), Laura L. Doan is more critical of Amis than Korn, Miller and Todd. Both Amis's and Churchill's texts, Doan proposes, appear to challenge the new Thatcherite attitude that money, like work, should no longer be a 'dirty word', and both seem 'to question the legitimacy of an ideology founded upon the primacy of greed as a motivating factor'. Moreover, both, 'though at variance with one another, demonstrate how, in the real economy and within the economy of the text, class and gender intersect to maintain or transform existing systems of power'. While Churchill views the economic system as a model for all power structures and can thus incorporate a critique of both class and gender relations, Amis 'scrutinizes the ideology of the economic system [but] elides a sustained critique of the class system. In this "exposé" of capitalist greed, financial success remains an exclusively middle-class, male prerogative'.[22] Although Amis shows 'how the individual – a working-class male – can be easily victimized and lose control', this 'restricted focus hinders a critique of the gender system which is, instead, upheld and reified (i.e., maintained). In Amis's novel, women's relationship to money must be mediated through men in the form of sexual favors. His resulting equation is thus: woman + money = object.' This is Doan's account – and critique – of *Money*:

■ Narrator-protagonist John Self is the victim of an elaborate money conspiracy perpetrated by Fielding Goodney, a financier-cum-confidence man, involving regular surveillance of Self, innumerable anonymous telephone calls, and several actors posing as potential investors. Weakened by his dependence on sex and booze, Self walks straight into the trap set by Goodney, the very fellow Self believes he's soaking for millions of dollars. Self collaborates with Goodney, a self-described *good* capitalist (p.30) and 'old money' American, because Goodney promises to secure financial backing for a movie Self wants to direct, variously entitled 'Good Money' and 'Bad Money'. The epitome of the sexist, racist homophobe, Self is a self-made man who has risen from a working-class background – his family runs a seedy strip joint – through his work as a director of crass commercials. Recklessly spending what he thinks is Goodney's money, Self actually shrinks his own bank account; in the end, his newfound wealth is lost. Destitute, Self returns to his former position as a scrounger from the working-class. His egocentric surname aptly conjures up a char[a]cter whose obsessive self-indulgence leads to his financial ruin and, by extension, invests the narrative with the sense of a cautionary tale for 'every*man*' who might find himself in Self's place.

Partly because Self tells his own story (meaning that he is never in possession of all the information he needs to understand what is happening), and partly because Amis eschews the convention of character motivation in the novel ('motivation has become depleted, a shagged-out force in modern life' [see p.62 of this Guide]) the reader never suspects that Goodney is a scoundrel or even that Self is an unsuspecting victim.[23] Amis provides neither advance warning nor ad[e]quate preparation for the revelation. He justifies his disinterestedness by arguing that the scam is irrelevant. Just as Goodney plays a confidence trick on the protagonist, Amis practices his trickery on the reader by setting up an elaborate ruse with no explanation. Yet, by the time the author reveals this twist of events, the scam works more as an unwanted distraction than as a clever trick, producing greater ambiguity than Amis bargains [for]. The novel, Amis explains, is in essence an intense character study of John Self, but the text is in many ways less concerned with Self – and his quest for financial gain – than with the encoding of the life-controlling power systems in discourse that determine the possibilities and constraints of 'Self-control' . . . . . .

John Self fails to recognize his own state of disempowerment within the social structure, but he understands that there are others on the outside who desire inclusion and who want to broaden the parameters of power. He names them in a kind of litany of the marginalized:

> Everyone is determined to be what they are: it's the coming thing. Women want out from under us men. Faggots and diesels won't be humped by the hets. Blacks have had it with all this white power . . . Now even the paedophile . . . dares show his shadowed face: he wants a little respect around here (p.324).

Here the writer Martin Amis betrays his own bourgeois liberal bias through the words he places in the hero's mouth. Self says 'women' and 'blacks' as opposed to 'cunts' and 'wogs', but calls gays and lesbians 'faggots and diesels', instead of using the terms they have chosen to identify and empower themselves. Is this the linguistic slip of the hero or his author? If it is supposed to be Self's slip, it seems inconsistent: he uses negative labels for women elsewhere, and does not show the slightly heightened consciousness that the switch to women in this context would entail. As Amis's slip, it shows to what extent he is limited by the values he is supposedly criticizing. Conditioned by the liberalizing changes that have granted a degree of validity to the causes of blacks and women, Amis easily uses 'respectable' labels for them, but gays and lesbians, who have been less successful at gaining such credibility, retain their marginal status through the use of pejorative labels. In either case, like his hero, Amis seems to recognize the significant relation between social identity and political power, but he tends to diminish its force by subsuming it under the rubric of mere *self*-identity.

As Self notes, the incursion of the disempowered into the spheres of power is based on reclaiming the legitimacy of their own identities. Self's insight is inspired by the incredible variety of pornography he continually consumes, which, based on the laws of supply and demand, reflects both the diversity of humankind *and* the objectification of women. Here, ironically, pornography – a form of representation hardly notable for its conspicuous concern for the individual – expands Self's awareness of others. Class is noticeably absent from the list because, unlike the boundaries of gender, race or sexual preference, Self believes that class barriers can be breached by the acquisition of great sums of money.

John Self is a *parvenu par excellence*. In his world view, life presents an endless series of unlimited possibilities for those who possess, and are obsessed with, money. As Self explains, 'the thing I want more than anything else . . . is to make lots of money' (p. 92). Self continually offers praise for the beauty and versatility of money, the one thing he says he loves: 'Selina [his girlfriend] says I'm not capable of true love. It isn't true. I truly love money. Truly I do. Oh, money, I love you. You're so democratic: you've got no favorites. You even things out for me and my kind' (p. 238). However, the financial success promised and facilitated by new Conservative ideology embodies an implicit threat to the class system. Consequently, Self's absolute and dangerous faith in money as the great equalizer between the social classes leaves him vulnerable, as he himself dimly recognizes: '[w]*ithout money, you're one day old and one inch tall. And you're nude too'* (p. 383). Self thinks that money will help him transcend his class, that the ruling class will now treat him as one of their own, and because he wants so much to believe that the empowered will play by the rules of the game, he becomes an easy target for a scam.

Amis takes exceptional care to ensure that the narrator-protagonist, so disgusting in his values and lifestyle, cannot be mistaken for the writer by literally putting himself into the text. Martin Amis, the character, is a suave, intelligent, highly educated, comfortably middle-class writer who quite obviously finds Self, and what he represents, unsavory. By carefully exploring the minutiae of Self's daily thoughts and actions, Amis the writer nearly succeeds in calling the newly Americanized British economic system into question. Yet Self's quest for status in an upper middle-class society that excludes members of the working class is doomed to fail from the start. Self can never shake off the stigma of his working-class manner, accent and values, whether he is in England or America – and he blithely travels between New York and London as though from Pimlico to Portobello Road. When in London, Self manages to avoid Soho, but fraternizes either with down-and-out middle-class drop-outs, or returns to the comforts of the topless bar he calls home. In New York, a city that brings out the worst in him, Self heads directly to seedy bars, nightclubs, porn shops and junk food restaurants. Even in the dubious classlessness of American society, Self finds the world he can afford – expensive health clubs and restaurants, or the highbrow entertainment of opera and literature – uncomfortable and alien. He is nothing more than an upstart who tries to stick his nose where it doesn't belong and who is 'rightfully' excluded by the upper middle-class types whose sensibility he offends and whose security, comfort and financial resources he threatens. In the end, Self's entrapment in the working class marks a return to the familiar stereotype of the working-class *parvenu* who, predictably enough, is punished, not for his obsession with money or heady desire for power, but for assuming he could move into this [é]lite club . . . . . .

[In *Serious Money*, t]he primary target of [Caryl] Churchill's sustained critique . . . is not the class system but the equally oppressive gender system. The stock exchange offers the ideal venue to examine how patriarchy distributes power. John Self's world of money-making and movie-making would seem an equally suitable venue for Amis to examine the dynamics of the gender sy[s]tem, but, once again, he is reluctant to acknowledge how the economic system works as a paradigm [model] of other power systems. For Amis, to be authentically working-class means to be sexist, and so he imbues Self with the prejudices associated with the working-class stereotype. As a result, Amis's protagonist resides within, as Beno[î]te Groult puts it, 'a completely falsified world in which sex is artificially separated from life'.[24] Thus the first thing Self asks himself when he meets a woman is 'will I fuck it?' (p.238). By substituting 'it' for 'her', Self, like the pornography he devours, denies woman personhood, placing her in the ultimate state of disempowerment and disembodiment. In fact, Self's dependence on pornography suggests the crucial nexus [link] between the woman as pornographic image and his own objectification of women.

Because Self views life through the prism of money, he divides women roughly into two categories: whores and non-whores. Self affirms Selina's assertion that 'men use money to dominate women' (p. 90), and complacently recognizes women's greater potential for victimization but, rather than register concern, the thought fuels his suspicion that women somehow deserve it: '[i]t must be tiring know-ledge, the realization that half the members of the planet . . . can do what the hell they like with you'. Masculine identity depends utterly on women who are pleased, in Self's parlance, to get 'groped or goosed or propositioned' (p. 14) – never loved. Women are the vessel for all Self's beliefs about sex, money and power, and he inevitably imposes his value system on them in the same way he imposes his body:

> I saw [Selina's] performing flesh in fantastic eddies and convul-sions, the face with its smile of assent and the complicit look in the flattered eyes . . . the arched creature doing what that creature does best – and the thrilling proof, so rich in pornography, that she does all this not for passion, not for comfort, far less for love . . . she does all this for *money*. (p. 37)

Since, as [Suzanne] Kappeler argues, '[t]he objectification of women is a result of the subjectification of man', Self's assumption about Selina's motivation is hardly surprising.[25] By persuading himself that she does it all for money, Self justifies his own transference of love from the individual to money. Blinded by such demeaning attitudes toward women, Self misses clues that might have forestalled his own victimization. For instance, the misogyny implicit in his first thoughts upon meeting the lesbian feminist screenwriter for his movie project prevents his assimilating the information she will offer later:

> [Doris] stood there . . . No matter how butch and pushy they get, girls will never lose this air of sensitive expectancy. Or I hope they won't. She wore roomy dungarees and a much-patched flying jacket – anti-rape clothes, mace clothes. They didn't work. Now here's someone, I thought to myself, here's someone who's really worth raping (p. 58).

Self's inability to heed either Doris's warning of a scam or any other advice women might offer increases his vulnerability. Women, Self asserts, lend a helping hand because they have ulterior motives, usually involving money; their advice, therefore, is worthless and should be ignored . . . .

The different ways in which Amis and Churchill inscribe the interconnectedness of money and sex clarify one of the most fundamental differences between the two texts. Amis elects to stay within the patriarchal gender boundaries by upholding the pattern of dominance and submission; hence, John Self wonders if the 'Quid' will be 'slapped about and gangbanged on the international money market' (p.242; compare p.154). When Self talks about being 'pussy-whipped by money' (p.270), the language, laden with pornographic imagery, incorporates sexual aggression and reveals his ambivalence in [priorities] – money or sex . . . . . .

Amis's *Money* and Churchill's *Serious Money* are essentially about control. John Self's victimization is brought about by that which he can control – his own greed – and by that over which he has no control, the class system. And here we find the seeds of Amis's undoing. The invention of an outrageous anti-hero cannot mask a failure to fulfill the grander aim of unmasking the ideological underpinnings of Thatcherism. Amis gestures towards the daring and radical in order to disguise his conservative appropriation of the classist stereotype of a protagonist who meets his expected demise. The character of John Self simply cannot work as a metonym [that is, a part which stands for a whole] for Thatcherism. The discourse of Amis's novel ostensibly exposes the false tenets of the new Toryism and impugns the greed of Thatcherite England in order to call for the transformation of the existing capitalist system. However, by casting his protagonist as a member of the working class, Amis endangers this purpose and instead devises a telos [end] that valorizes [upholds the value of] the class and gender systems.[26] □

Doan's strong criticism of the sexism and class bias of *Money*, her refusal to be seduced by the narrative voice, contrasts with the enthusiastic response exhibited by other (mostly male) reviewers and critics,[27] such as Eric Korn. The mixed reactions to Amis's fifth novel would be echoed and amplified in the arguments over his next and even more controversial novel, *London Fields*. But this would not appear for five years. Some of the groundwork for it would be laid, however, by the remarkable excursion into the short story form that is discussed in the next chapter of this Guide: *Einstein's Monsters*.

CHAPTER SIX

Writing the Unthinkable: *Einstein's Monsters* (1987)

MARTIN AMIS has written relatively few short stories. As he himself remarks in his 'Author's Note' to *Einstein's Monsters*, in the sixteen years from 1969 to 1985 he had 'managed' only four; but in the two years from 1985 to 1987, his productivity increased: five successive short stories came, and then the flow stopped. It is these five stories that, together with the polemical introductory essay called 'Thinkability', comprise the slender but potent collection whose title, according to Amis, refers not only 'to nuclear weapons, but also to ourselves. We are Einstein's monsters, not fully human, not for now' (p. 6).

In the *Literary Review* of May 1987, David Profumo combined his own commentary on *Einstein's Monsters* with an interview with Amis. The result provides excellent insights into the short story collection from the viewpoint of its author and a responsive reader:

■ [As t]hese five stories emerged . . . [Amis] gradually . . . realised that they shared a common theme: an indignant concern about nuclear weapons. As he explains in . . . 'Thinkability', this was prompted by ['impending fatherhood and a tardy reading of Jonathan Schell's classic, awakening study *The Fate of the Earth* (1982)' (p. 11)]. The resulting stories are powerfully chilling illustrations of the ways in which the fearful threat of nuclear destruction has already poisoned the human spirit.

The first one he wrote [placed third in the collection] remains his favourite. 'The Time Disease' (pp. 69–84) is a sci-fi parody of a mildly futuristic American city where normal values about health and inter-personal communications have become inverted. 'The real inspiration was a revenge on Los Angeles', he explained. 'I'd hated it so much, I'd felt so ill while I'd been there – the smog – I felt really lousy. And the "live-for-ever" culture; the city of narcissists. I thought it would be funny if there was a disease around that encouraged you to live a very unhealthy life. On top of that it's a story about the stupefaction of television. It posits a really outrageous idea that this will eventually fuck up reality, and the rule will be that if people believe things, then it will eventually come to pass.'

Sexual inversion is another theme of the story. 'I find, glancing through the book, there are quite a few AIDS themes, and do you know this charming idea that AIDS may be – and this is a good word – radiogenic [that is, AIDS may be produced by radiation, possibly from atmospheric testing of nuclear weapons]? . . . And if that's the case, AIDS is just the first of several lulus coming our way' . . . . . .

. . . In *Einstein's Monsters* . . . it becomes clear he has gone into the subject [of nuclear weapons] in considerable depth . . . But imaginative writing about the subject seems to be notoriously unstable in itself, and I wondered how much he had been influenced by mainstream science fiction, the genre to which the bulk of the literature [about nuclear weapons] seems to belong.

Martin Amis describes sci-fi as 'a kind of family hobby; also I reviewed it for a good many years in *The Observer* under the pseudonym of Henry Tilney, the hero of [Jane Austen's novel] *Northanger Abbey!'* (1818). He believes there is a prejudice against it as a genre, and that there are some great practitioners in the field. He agrees with his father [see Kingsley Amis, *New Maps of Hell* (1960), a pioneering work in the 'serious' study of science fiction] that the strength of the genre is that it is completely realistic within its own terms of reference, and offers, especially in the dystopian mode, many serious possibilities [a 'dystopia' is a nightmare vision of a future society – as in Aldous Huxley's *Brave New World* (1932) or George Orwell's *Nineteen Eighty-Four*, as opposed to a 'utopia', which is a vision of a supposedly ideal future society, as in Edward Bellamy's *Looking Backward: 2000–1887* (1888) or William Morris's *News from Nowhere* (1890). As the respective publication dates of all these texts suggests, the twentieth century has been more inclined to dystopias]. The novel on which he is currently working – *London Fields* – is itself set twelve years in the future, and has a nuclear background.

Other influences that he happily acknowledges in [his 'Author's Note'] range from J. G. Ballard [(1930–) – both a science fiction and 'mainstream' author – 'to the Salman Rushdie of *Grimus* [(1975)]']. In [regard to] one of the more flamboyant stories, 'The Little Puppy That Could', he records a debt ['to Vladimir Nabokov [(1899–1977)] and Franz Kafka [(1883–1924)]' (p.6)]. The story concerns a post-[nuclear] holocaust community menaced by a monstrous hell-hound to which regular sacrifices have to be offered. Lurid mutants abound in this world-turned-upside-down, but the future is redeemed by an apparently normal puppy who lures the monster to destruction, and is then transformed into a shining youth. Amis describes it as 'a mad literary exercise', and it conjures entertainingly a number of literary stereotypes, from the heroic pet saga to the sunset optimism of brave new worlds.

The most unnerving and tautly written story [in *Einstein's Monsters*] is 'Insight at Flame Lake' (pp. 51–67), the fourth to be written [placed second in the collection]. Dan is a disturbed twelve year old American who is trying to recover from the death of his father, one of the Fathers of nuclear research; he stays with his Uncle Ned and his young wife and baby daughter in their lakeside summer cabin, but his schizophrenia induces terrible delusions. The lake itself takes on explosive symptoms, the skyscapes are deranged, the baby is evil. It's a very unpleasant story, and I asked its author to expand on the background to its composition, and to explain something further about his linking of childhood with the whole business of the nuclear threat.

'Well, he's a kind of nuked schizophrenic, and it takes the form of guilt on his father's behalf. And being able to see wickedness in a baby is more or less the crux of how deformed his mind is. Babies are very much at the forefront of all of this'. . . . it's a question of translating the danger back into accessible human terms. Amis also recalls an early disgust with the idea of nuclear weapons. When he was a child at school he used to leave the room whenever the target maps of the London area were discussed, and he was looked after by a Welsh lady who ascribed her 'heroic migraines' to the atom . . . . . .

[*Einstein's Monsters*] is rounded off with a story entitled 'The Immortals' (pp. 115–27), which looks on a first reading to be a more light-hearted piece. The narrator is indestructible, a permanent observer of the cycle of human history who witnesses its final achievements of autodestruction. Cynical, sophisticated and blasé, he seems to enjoy the god's-eye view of the Wandering Jew, Orlando, or a *Struldbrug*[g] [the legendary Wandering Jew, having refused Christ rest as he carried his cross to Calvary, was 'condemned to wander the world until Christ's second coming';[1] in Virginia Woolf's fantasy novel *Orlando* (1928), Orlando lives from the late sixteenth century into the 1920s; the Struldbruggs are the immortals in Jonathan Swift's *Gulliver's Travels* (1726) whose longevity becomes a curse as they decay]. [B]ut it transpires that this is all a hallucination suffered by a 'second-rate New Zealand schoolmaster who never did anything or went anywhere and is now painfully and noisily dying of solar radiation along with everybody else' [although it should be noted that the narrator describes this perception of himself and his situation as 'a delusion', a 'weird idea' (p. 126) – the reader is probably expected to assume that the 'second-rate . . . schoolmaster' dying of solar radiation is the truth of the matter, but an interesting note of doubt remains]. To the bitter end, the sphere of nuclear experience is seen as a round of successive delusions.

This is gloomy stuff indeed. Martin Amis's version of the world into which his sons have been born is grim, and the apathy level is dangerous. 'All the things we're doing to the planet, like the erosion of the topsoil, all that Green stuff, is very true. But no-one will stop anyone from doing it. And we're hurtling towards an entropy watershed when all the fossil-fuels and the oil run out, and no-one's thinking about change [in this context, entropy means the 'measure of the degradation or disorganisation of the universe' – or, in this case, the planet earth] . . . Because the nuclear weapons, by possibly embodying an end to the human story, seem to have fucked up everyone's idea of where the future is supposed to be'.[2] □

As the short-story writer and novelist Adam Mars-Jones pointed out three years later, however, Amis's charge of apathy in regard to nuclear weapons was not wholly justified. Amis makes no reference in the introduction to *Einstein's Monsters* to what Mars-Jones calls 'the most single-minded demonstration of nuclear protest [in the 1980s], the Peace Camp at Greenham Common, or the larger movement of which it was part'. The reason for this omission, Mars-Jones provocatively suggests, is that the Greenham Peace Camp was a *Women's* Peace Camp, while Amis's 'anti-nuclearism is conspicuously male'.[3]

Mars-Jones made this argument in his pamphlet, *Venus Envy* (1990), published in Chatto and Windus's 'Counterblasts' series, a series that aimed to provide provocative, polemical essays on important contemporary issues. Mars-Jones challenged the way in which masculinity had redefined itself in response to feminism – 'not in the way that feminists might have hoped',[4] but 'in terms of responsibility'. 'A new style has arisen of faintly synthetic introspection, presented as a maturing process unprompted by contemporary debates, which nevertheless reads more convincingly as a rhetorical response to cultural pressure'.[5] Mars-Jones explores this style as it addresses the prospect of destruction by nuclear weapons, and he takes as his examples *Einstein's Monsters* and Ian McEwan's *The Child in Time* (1987). He begins his attack on *Einstein's Monsters* by analysing the introductory essay and arguing that it should be seen as a rhetorical construction which proffers a male anti-nuclearism that marginalises women's voices and disavows the possibility of a link between gender inequality and the threat of nuclear destruction. He then moves on to focus on some of the short stories themselves; the following extract starts with his discussion of these and builds up into a slashing assault on Martin Amis's style in general:

■ The notion that the entrenched destructiveness of our culture has something to do with the jealously defended imbalance between its sexes finds a place in *Einstein's Monsters* only in an inverted form. Bujak, in the story 'Bujak and the Strong Force', seeing gay punks in the street, interprets 'their plight, and their profusion, as an einsteinian matter also' (p. 36). The idea seems to be that such violations of the sexual order stem inevitably from the Bomb's disturbing of cosmic balance. Presumably, then, in a world without the Bomb sexual roles would be properly harmonious. This, of course, is only a passing remark made by a fictional character, but there is an absence of characters who take any sort of opposing tack.

In the story 'The Little Puppy that Could', Amis imagines a post-holocaustal future where the sexual status quo has been deformed and distorted along with everything else. Men have become interchangeable – Tim and Tam and Tom – subject to the rule of monstrous matriarchs who, horribly, demand to be pleasured. Now that fertility is a scarce commodity, the world is held to ransom by a womb and not a penis. The women are given names (Keithette, Clivonne, Kevinia) whose ludicrousness may be meant to derive from the supposed laughter-quotient of the male names on which they are based, but there is a definite edge of hysteria to the humour. What seems to bring out the rancour which the comedy disguises, at least from its author, is the very idea of women with male privileges.

At the end of the story the heroine, the intensely feminine Andromeda, has found herself a real man (a transformed puppy, innocent animal purified by fire): '[h]is arms were strong and warlike as he turned and led her into the cool night. They stood together on the hilltop and gazed down at their new world' (p. 113). The logic here is arsy-versy, but consistent with the rest of the book's theorising. The Bomb has made men effeminate and women repellently assertive. Now a proper polarization of the sexes will make possible some sort of renewal.

A feminist suggestion might rather be that it was a world in thrall to a distorted male identity that made the Bomb in the first place. It seems unlikely that Martin Amis is unaware of this line of thinking. What seems to be at work, here and elsewhere in *Einstein's Monsters*, is *disavowal*, that useful psychological word that means denying something without mentioning it.

The great irony of *Einstein's Monsters* is that a book dedicated to the unapproachable ideal of disarmament should be written by someone so opposed by temperament to disarmament outside the nuclear arena. Martin Amis'[s] progress has not been so much a career as an escalation, the persona increasingly truculent, the style ever more bristling. His very method is overkill. There seems little doubt that in the silos of his notebooks there are stored enough explosive phrases to account for his readers many times over. Though Amis in 'Thinkability' may find the idea baffling, any reader of a page of his mature prose has a pretty good idea of what might be meant by *retaliating first*.

These analogies aren't flippant. Amis himself, despite his remarks about the need for 'decorum' in nuclear discussion, feels free to use the vocabulary of holocaust figuratively. In 'Bujak and the Strong Force' alone, a man who is sensitive to potential violence is said to have a 'fallout detector' (p. 37), Bujak's fist is said to be 'neutronium', to kill a whole family is to 'nuke' them (p. 39) – perhaps to compensate for the nuclear preoccupations in the story seeming rather arbitrarily imposed on its plot. The story of a man whose family is murdered but who takes no revenge could be expressed in terms of the Old Testament giving way to the New, rather than deterrence unilaterally abandoned, but once you've used a nuclear vocabulary it's hard to go back to a conventional one. As the proliferation of nuclear images indicates, whether they are an integral part of the story or not, Amis concentrates on the way the big world infiltrates and corrodes private lives, rather than the other aspect of the traffic, the elusive way that individual behaviour subtends [underlies and upholds] the status quo.

The aggressiveness of Martin Amis'[s] style is of course artificial; it shapes its own highly contrived version of strength and weakness. The monstrous women in 'The Little Puppy that Could' are announced as all-powerful, but are relegated to the role of comic bit-players. The narrator of 'Bujak and the Strong Force', by contrast, is weak, but insistently, buttonholingly, Woody Allenishly weak, and – naturally enough, being the narrator – has control of the point of view, the true seat of power in a story. The hyperbolic phrases Amis gives him promote every flinch into a stylistic swagger, every whimper into a growl.

But if aggressiveness in a style does not correspond to aggressiveness in the world, it does correspond to the power of will. No other aspect of writing responds to pure willpower: sit down at a desk for four hours and you can't guarantee to come up with four satisfactory plot twists or nine convincing insights into character. But you can be pretty sure of coming up with twenty startling images or striking turns of phrase. Even when Martin Amis is treading water he breaks the surface so much it looks like a shark attack.

A style like Martin Amis'[s] represents both a fear and a desire. It represents a radical doubt about the business of writing, an authorial identity crisis that can be postponed by having each sentence declare the presence of the author. Amis'[s] narrators don't venture abroad without a suit, a shield, without a testudo [in Ancient Roman times, a screen formed by a body of troops in close array, with overlapping shields;

more generally, a moveable screen to protect besieging troops] of style to protect them. Here, for instance, are three of his narrators, the weak writer from 'Bujak', a disturbed pre-adolescent ('Insight at Flame Lake') and a citizen of the year 2020 ('The Time Disease'), all deploying one of Amis'[s] favourite tropes [turns of phrase], the cadenced triptych of synonyms:

[1] If the world disarmed tomorrow, he believed, the species would still need at least a century of recuperation, after its entanglement, its flirtation, after its thing with the strong force (pp. 41–2).

[2] Meanwhile I stare into the brilliance and burnish, into the mauve of the MIRVed lake (p. 59).

[3] [U]p there in the blasted, the totalled, up there in the fucked sky (p. 79).

Fear of inauthenticity here leads to inauthenticity of a different sort, not an unsigned painting but a painting composed entirely of signatures. The reader who is reminded by each succeeding sentence of the looming designs of the author is denied much of the traditional pleasure of literature, the pleasure of surrendering to an imagined world rather than being bullied into finding it impressive. The supposed opposition between highly-wrought and unambitious ways of writing on which Amis'[s] style depends doesn't hold up in any case. There is writing which advertises its surprises and writing that simply springs them . . .

It is this absence of a neutral register from Martin Amis'[s] work, oddly enough, that his father Kingsley complains of, the lack of workaday sentences not hell-bent on shock or charm. Here and there in *Einstein's Monsters* Amis hides his hand and aspires to such transparency, notably in the story 'Insight at Flame Lake', which alternates two diaries, of a disturbed pre-adolescent and his uncomprehending uncle. But all it takes is one electric adjective too many and the jig is up, the familiar antagonistic persona reaches criticality.

The other aspect of a style like Martin Amis'[s] is the desire to make a mark at all costs – not the strongest basis from which to mount an attack on the moral blindnesses of the nuclear age. It is noticeable for instance that in 'Thinkability' he has a shot at rendering nuclear war in his particular tone of voice, in a sentence that ends with the distinctive juxtaposition 'the warped atoms, the grovelling dead' (p. 9). Forget the ambition of finding the language of unanimity: this is a holocaust with a monogram, almost a copyright logo.

The military analogies are irresistible, though the ugly sound you hear is only the dull clang of polemic against polemic. Martin Amis'[s] anti-nuclear stance is in the nature of a pre-emptive strike, detonating an issue that might otherwise be used against him. A woman's hand on the button, after all, would do far more damage to his world-view. By striking first, he can cut the supply lines between the nuclear issue and other issues he doesn't want to engage with: feminism and environmentalism, half of humanity and the whole of its home.[6] □

In contrast to Mars-Jones, Rachel Falconer, in her 1998 essay 'Bakhtin's Chronotope and the Contemporary Short Story', offered a more positive account of *Einstein's Monsters*. As Falconer points out near the start of her essay, the twentieth-century Russian critic Mikhail Bakhtin argued that all genres, and distinctions between genres, could be defined by their '*chronotope* (literally, "time space" . . . the intrinsic connectedness of temporal and spatial relationships that are artistically expressed in literature)'.[7] Little work has been done, however, on the chronotope of the short story. Falconer selects *Einstein's Monsters* as one example of a text that has an 'arresting' way of representing time. Amis's collection, Falconer suggests, 'thematizes the lack of agency entailed by a doomed sense of time on the scientific and technological level, where our cosmological timescales dwarf the human life span, and our ability to destroy the planet reduces all time to present crisis[8] . . . the short story form enables Amis to focus on a single theme, the threat of nuclear holocaust, while presenting a range of different responses to it so that no one perspective dominates and the exercise of agency rests finally with the reader'.[9] Falconer develops this argument in a rich and interesting way:

■ The individual stories [in *Einstein's Monsters*] effect various compromises between thinkability and unthinkability, insofar as . . . they do imagine life after [nuclear war]. But they are meant to be thought through and then, if possible, *unthought* . . . the temporal spaces they explore must ultimately remain unactualized for – *unthinkable* to – the reader. Each of the five stories in this collection imagines a different 'unthinkable' post-nuclear future as a potential present. The choice of genre is essential to the preservation of each imagined future's 'unthinkability'. Together, they effect a Borgesian bifurcation of possibilities, with each projected scenario helping to cancel out the others in the sequence. [The reference here is to Borges's short story 'The Garden of Forking Paths' ('El jardín de los senderos que se bifurcan' (1941)), with its famous remark: '[i]n all fictional works, each time a man is confronted with several alternatives, he chooses one and eliminates the others; in the fiction of Ts'ui Pen, he chooses – simultaneously – all of them. *He creates*, in this way, diverse futures, diverse times which themselves also proliferate and fork'.[10]] Three of the five entail futuristic, post-nuclear disaster settings ('The Time Disease', 'The Little

Puppy that Could', and 'The Immortals'), while two have 'realistic' settings in a suspended present, with the holocaust psychologically imminent but the actual explosion yet to come ('Bujak and the Strong Force, *or* God's Dice' and 'Insight at Flame Lake'). Thus the lack of any sequential linkage between one story and the next contributes to the weakened sense of temporal progress as we move out of an extended present ('Bujak' and 'Insight') and from an immediate future ('The Time Disease') to a relatively distant one ('Little Puppy', 'Immortals'). Regardless of the point where it falls along the temporal continuum, each story takes place within a cross section of time that is both 'already present' and 'unthinkably' possible in the future. Two stories end relatively optimistically ('Bujak' and 'Little Puppy'), while the other three invite the reader to reject their imagined futures. The sequence as a whole is not geared toward a more thinkable and potentially more acceptable post-nuclear future, but neither is the implied reader expected to become 'wiser' or 'better prepared' as s/he turns from one story to the next. The sequential disconnectedness between each story and the next allows us to reject each possible future as it unfolds, yet the cumulative effect is of a present that branches into numerous possible futures. In this sense, the short story appears better able than the novel to accommodate a proliferation of potential futures while maintaining a basic narrative logic.

The possibility of an Einsteinian reversal of time occurring at the point of the 'firebreak' is explored in 'Bujak and the Strong Force, *or* God's Dice'. Here the notion of 'holocaust' is applied to an individual's experience of time. Tragedy (if that is the word) occurs out of the blue; it has no motive, no teleology, and no apparent sequentiality until events are later retraced in the court scene. Bujak returns home to find wife, mother, and daughter raped and murdered, then discovers their killers asleep in the house. Instead of taking revenge, he drags them off to the police station and thereby fails to fulfill the reader's (and the narrator's) expectation; for some reason, Bujak chooses disarmament. When the narrator asks Bujak about this years later, he simply says, '"[y]ou must make a start"' (p. 49). For Bujak, this (non)act constitutes a *temporal* reversal, marking a break between one 'life' and the next, in which various aspects of himself are reversed (becoming physically weak where once he was strong, e.g., and verbal where once he was forceful). Curiously, the reversal of time in Bujak's case is made possible by unthinkability. Why does Bujak not kill the two sleeping men? (As the narrator reminds him, '"[n]o court on earth would have sent you down"' (p. 48).) Bujak does not kill them because they have become unthinkable to him – untouchable: '"[r]eally the hardest thing was to touch them at all. You know the wet tails of rats? Snakes? Because I saw that they weren't human beings at all. They had no idea what human life was. No idea! Terrible mutations, a disgrace to their human moulding'" (p.49). The narrative becomes highly paradoxical here, with the 'unthinkable' attaining a regenerative power by virtue of remaining beyond touch. In order to bring the reader to that paradoxical point, the narrator must himself think through the 'unthinkable'. If that unthinkable act is the detonation of a nuclear bomb by one of the superpowers, it is addressed indirectly by means of this 'untouchability'. Amis himself says only, '[m]y impression is that the subject resists frontal assault. For myself, I feel it as a background . . . which then insidiously foregrounds itself' (pp.23–4). In allegorically reducing the superpower mentality to Bujak's mindset, Amis reduces the decision-making *scale* to the individual level. The point of unthinkability is further distanced by being deflected from the narrator, the speaking voice, to another character. The narrator himself fails to imagine his own family destroyed and concludes: '[b]ut in fact you cannot think it, you cannot go near it. The thought is fire' (p.48). Moreover, Bujak's reaction to the murderers is described and analyzed only retrospectively rather than by 'frontal assault' at the time he discovers them. By such narrative indirection, Amis keeps the event of nuclear holocaust remote, both temporally and spatially, while establishing correspondences between our present situation and the imagined future. If this story is 'only' about ordinary human criminality, it is also about the damage that humanity as a whole will do and suffer from in the event of nuclear war. The Glasgow youths who murder Bujak's family already represent, allegorically, the genetic mutations of a post-nuclear future ('"I saw that they weren't human beings at all . . . Terrible mutations, a disgrace to their human moulding'" (p.49)).

The possibility that the 'apocalypse', whenever it occurs, might throw time into reverse (as Einstein theorized happened at the beginning of the universe) is one that Amis explores at novelistic length in *Time's Arrow* and in short form in 'The Time Disease' . . . 'The Time Disease' . . . describes a world turned upside down by the effects of nuclear fallout, including distortions of the 'normal' temporal patterns. Survival here depends on doing nothing, so no one expends much emotional, physical, or mental energy. The ironic twist is that the 'time disease', a form of radiation sickness, does not accelerate the ageing process but the reverse; 'coming down' with 'time' here means dying of *youth*. Amis thus deploys the concept of time reversal to defamiliarize and satirize aspects of our present culture that reflect a time 'gone wrong' (fear of ageing, inability to distinguish real events from media fictions, etc.) . . . . . . The concept of time reversal receives its perhaps most lyrical and terrifying expression at the end of 'Bujak and the Strong Force', however (pp.49–50) . . . . . .

'Insight at Flame Lake' explores how the very existence of nuclear arms exerts an insidious psychological pressure on contemporary Western society. Here . . . the 'future' holocaust is projected onto present-day ordinary experience rather than vice versa. The narrative consists of a series of entries in Dan's notebook and Ned's diary during the course of a summer. From these stories, we piece together a 'sequence' in which Ned invites his nephew Dan to share a family holiday with his wife and child at their lakeside cottage. Dan, still recovering from the trauma of his father's suicide, has just been diagnosed with schizophrenia. He is determined to cure himself without the prescribed drugs, and his condition begins to worsen. This process goes unnoticed by his uncle, who continues to encourage the boy to play with the baby, Harriet, as a form of natural therapy. The double first-person narrative allows Amis to explore his notion of a pervasive cultural anxiety operating here upon two very different mindsets. Dan's imagination operates on both macro- and microcosmic scales. As the son of a nuclear physicist, he has a heightened awareness of 'subatomic' and 'superlunary' (p. 111) forces. Ned's concerns, by contrast, are all on a resolutely ordinary scale: daily newspapers, slightly paranoiac relations with a neighbor over his jeep, the growth of his baby. And yet both characters feel an 'exponential violence' building up in their world. Ned measures an increasing violence by reported instances of child abuse; Dan feels it in the 'bigger picture', the 'distortions and malformations' (p. 58) of nuclear power. For Dan, the lake *is* some kind of nuclear missile being fueled daily by the sun's heat pouring into the water . . . . . .

Dan's schizophrenic consciousness is manifested in a lack of connectives between his thoughts, passivity (Ned's diary records the way Dan sits for hours in one spot), and a heightened sensitivity both to physical pain (mosquito bites are 'exquisite' but also 'torture') and to communicative signals (Fran's glances are misread as sexual invitations, the baby's stare as an existential challenge). Temporal and spatial scales are schizophrenically skewed in Dan's imagination, as he himself is aware. He recognizes, for example, that when he perceives Harriet as growing to cosmically huge proportions, he is experiencing a routine symptom, *'size-constancy breakdown'* (p. 58). Tensions imperceptible to Ned mount up in Dan until he decides to 'foreclose the great suspense' (p. 65). Ned records finding the boy's room in chaos the next morning: '[t]he bedclothes and curtains had been torn to pieces, torn to rags. As I stood there and stared I had the sense of great violence, violence compressed and controlled – everything was scrunched up, squeezed, strangled, impacted, imploded' (p. 66). Up to this point, Amis has held the reader, as well as Ned, in suspense about the effects of Dan's illness. But a sense of foreboding has been instilled in the reader, who, unlike Ned, is made aware of Dan's worsening condition. The silent debates Dan holds with Harriet, together with a number of references to 'dead baby' stories in Dan's notebook and Ned's pervasive but unfocused anxiety about child abuse, all contribute to the reader's anticipation of Dan's killing Harriet. At this point, however, the reader discovers that Dan has killed 'only' himself. And the *actual* image of his frail body, seen through Ned's eyes, immediately cancels out the reader's *imagined* sense of the boy as threatening and dangerous: 'at once I saw his thin body, face down in the shallows'. Just before finding the body, Ned thinks to himself, 'so the lake was a dud, a fizzle – it never quite went off' (p. 66). At a symbolic level, then, Amis represents Dan's death as another act of disarmament, like Bujak's. Because the immanence of nuclear power is greater in this story, a more violent response is required from Dan to cancel out the threat of imminent explosion. In both stories, though, the fulfillment of expectation is blocked by an exercise of *choice* in an apparently determined sequence of events.

Again the textual chronotope is open-ended and invites active, 'writerly' reading. The text, consisting of fragmentary, nonconcurrent diary and notebook entries, must be assembled and interpreted. An overtly rationalistic reading is one possible way of interpreting Dan's death, for example, as suicide associated with schizophrenia and having nothing to do with Ned's family. This is clearly Dr. Slizard's interpretation. Read 'paranoically', however, the story might seem to suggest that, since there is more bufotenine [a chemical with hallucinogenic properties] in the boy's blood than is normal and his father's blood showed the same high levels, an inherited form of nuclear-aggravated schizophrenia led to Dan's death. While we might privilege the 'sane' voice of Ned's diary (reflections of a narrator expecting to return to his text and to a self coexistent with the person who wrote it) over the tentative and self-questioning voice of Dan's notebook, a *schizophrenic* reading yields a pattern of correspondences among different types of violence (child abuse, social violence, expansion of nuclear industry, the heat of the lake, mosquitoes biting, infantile growth, and female fat). It is after all this same notebook, written in the midst of Dan's illness, that gives us the clearest 'insight' into a possible connection between his own pathological condition and nuclear energy:

Dad was one of the fathers of the nuclear age. Then, when the thing was born, he became its son, along with everybody else. So Dad really threw an odd curve on that whole deal about fathers and sons. First he was the thing's father, then he was the thing's son. Great distortions and malformations should clearly be expected to follow on from such a reversal (p. 58).

This escalation of hostile energy may be insidiously related to a national increase in violence (i.e., more cases of child abuse and murder). If Ned remains perplexed, stating numbly, 'I don't know what is wrong' (p. 67 [This is the last sentence of 'Insight at Flame Lake']), the reader is nevertheless able to make connections, perhaps rational, perhaps schizophrenic, among the different types of actual and immanent violence.

'The Little Puppy That Could' takes place at some point following a nuclear holocaust when, 'after its decades of inimical quiet, the planet earth was once again an hospitable, even a fashionable address'. . . . Earth [now] seems to operate according to the laws of a contracting universe. Thus not only is chronology reversed, but our whole conception of time hangs in the balance between chronology and randomness. At first it would appear that the holocaust has unleashed countless genetic possibilities on the world, the current chaos of which also constitutes an opportunity for the surviving 'low-level' life-forms. 'In the deserts the lower forms flourished unchecked in their chaos: you could hardly turn your head without seeing some multipedal hyena or double-decker superworm pulsing towards you over the mottled sands.' Such scenes are common in science fiction and reflect the influence of con-temporary scientific thinking on the popular imagination . . . As Amis explores the implications of this world of seemingly endless potential, his style acquires a demotically liberating energy, as in this passage: '[n]atural selection had given way to a kind of reverse discrimination – or tokenism. Any bloody fool of an amphibious parrot or disgraceful three-winged stoat had as much chance of survival, of success, as the slickest, the niftiest, the most singleminded dreck-eating ratlet or invincibly carapaced predator' (p. 95). The linguistic inventiveness of this description, with its neologisms [newly coined words, for example, 'ratlet'] and internal rhymes, is proof enough that the narrator, despite his expressed disapproval, can be as exhilarated as any *Star Wars* fan by the idea of genetic mutability.

But more problematically, the survivors lack agency; even the survival-of-the-race instinct has become muted and ineffectual: '[d]own the soft decades they had lost the old get up and go – the know-how, the can-do. Predation and all its paraphernalia had quite petered out of their gene cams and pulse codes' (p. 101). Communal decisions (e.g., whether or not to 'move out and go nomad for a while') are made by genetic instinct rather than conscious thought: '[s]ite-tenacity was, alas, pretty well the only stable element in the local DNA transcription. How could you run when, in your head, this was the only place?'. Thus, rather than fight off the giant, ravenous dog that comes to prey on the village, they offer it a weekly human sacrifice. At the level of macrocosmic analogy, the dog signifies the last contraction of the universe to a crushing density of matter, for the animal has gravitas [solemn demeanour, seriousness] in its own right; heavy with the weight of its diseases and not so much evil as an instrument of the end, it inspires the reluctant respect of the villagers. ('[E]veryone was secretly impressed by the dog's asceticism in restricting himself to one human per week' (p. 105).)

The regular appearances of this new 'Natural Selector' (pp. 95, 107) help to establish a rhythmic, ritualized form of temporality. This scenario gives a sinister slant to Elizabeth Ermarth's celebratory concept of postmodernist 'rhythmic time', in which 'neither large-scale narrative sequence nor, indeed, coherent individual identities can be envisioned'.[11] Here the incoherence of individual identity opens the way for fascist-style ritual and religiosity: '[a]lthough the village was godless, the crater was agreed to be at least semi-sacred, and the people felt its codes, sensed its secrets with reluctant awe' (p. 103). While the present and future of the villagers may be described as overdetermined [that is, determined, in the sense of caused and/or constrained, by many factors], their sense of the past is comparatively open-ended. Revival of memory functions as a kind of future, such as when, toward the end of the story, Andromeda's name is drawn for sacrifice in the weekly lottery. Andromeda (for never explained reasons) still acts as an individual; she has named herself, for example, and has adopted a puppy that appeared (again, with no explanation) out of nowhere. Although the others want the puppy destroyed, Andromeda gets her way because of her exceptional status in the village. Even here, the narrator reflects, 'everyone has time for beauty, for art, for pattern and plan. We all come round to beauty in the end' (p. 102). Thus to the villagers, she clearly embodies some lost but remembered humanity – its art, beauty, youth, and agency. The prospect of her loss awakens a somnolent capacity for resistance in the villagers: 'on this night of sacrifice, of new nausea and defeat, the shouldered heads would not bow to receive their blows . . . Now you could feel the low rumble of hot temper, of petulant mutiny' (p. 108). Andromeda's puppy, the 'antimatter or Antichrist' of the dog, acts spontaneously where its counterpart does so by habit. But 'spontaneity' is associated here with instinct or genetic memory (i.e., as what 'puppies do'). The puppy's temporal universe retains its openness because it looks back, and here only the past provides any possibility of what we would recognize as a future. Thus the puppy wins its first victory over the dog when its memory is aroused, and, its 'inner templates shuffling and dealing', the dog searches 'for stalled memories, messages, codes' (p. 110).

The story's conclusion plays out an Einsteinian scenario where matter (the dog) and antimatter (the puppy) spiral toward a central gravitational point:

> For a time the puppy seemed freer than air, whimsically lithe, sub-atomic, superluminary, all spin and charm, while the dog moved on rails like a bull, pure momentum and mass, and for ever subject to their laws (p. 111).

Following up the nuclear analogy, the puppy tricks the dog into self-detonation, which leads to the destruction of both canines:

> With a howl of terror and triumph he hurled himself high into the flames – and the dog, like a blind missile, heat-seeking, like a weapon of spittle and blood, could only follow (p. 112).

Again, it is the genre that makes this juxtaposition of temporalities work. Generically speaking, the clash of values between puppy and dog is manifested as a contest between realism and romance, each with its own distinct chronotope. While the dog's weekly appearance imposes sequentiality on the villagers' lives, the puppy simply appears out of the blue and then stays, as is characteristic of events in the romance . . . In the romance chronotope, actions are not motivated or caused by preceding events but occur symbolically, allegorically. 'Where had the little puppy come from? Where was the little puppy heading?' asks the narrator. 'Of course, the little puppy had no idea where he had come from or where he was heading' (p. 87). From the romance perspective, the dog, with its calculating nature, its miasmic hide sporting a squad of post-Darwinian life-forms, its 'doggedness', is nothing but a freak, a monstrous anachronism; the puppy's conclud-ing metamorphosis as a boy (and a prince at that), however, is as unbelievable and symbolically apt as a romance ending should be (as well as suggestive of time's renewal with Adam and Eve's return to Eden). Many short story theorists have explored the genre's flexible allegiance to the traditions of fantasy and romance, on the one hand, and to those of realism, on the other.[12] Here the choice of romance over realism opens up a greater range of possible futures than those avail-able to 'Bujak'.

The last story of the collection, 'The Immortals', dramatizes a sig-nificant problem for the author/narrator: how to articulate the end of time. Strictly speaking, you cannot locate yourself within either a place or a time if both have become meaningless, while human history's value can only be assessed with critical distance, the very perspective that is then lost . . . Here, Amis invents a narrator who believes he is immortal and thus possesses that now impossible panoramic perspective on historical process. From this perspective, the narrator can induce a sense of pride in the implied reader over human-ity's historical accomplishments. The 'immortal' is impressed by 'our' efforts in the Renaissance, for example: '[y]ou really came through. To tell you the truth, you astonished me' (p. 122). He has to hurry to get there in time to witness it, though, before the whole thing is over. He can see patterns of destruction emerging in what seem to him just a few minutes of eternity: '[w]hat was the matter? Was it too *nice* for you or something? Jesus Christ, you were only here for about ten minutes. And look what you did' (p. 126). Although the narrator's position outside history enables him to discern its larger patterns, his macrocosmic perspective actually achieves the opposite result from the human perspective, reducing history to a few transient moments in the eternal existence of the universe.

The narrator thinks he is exempt from the general fate of humanity, including the apocalypse that is said to have happened in 2045, but, as the reader understands by the end of the story, he is one of the last human survivors of the nuclear holocaust . . . The immortal also stands for the contemporary postmodern observer, who, though perhaps possessed of an *abstract* knowledge of space, time, and history, lacks any sense of *personal* addressivity in time. The immortal catches glimpses of his own 'eventness', but dismisses them as delusory: '[i]t's strange how palpable it is, this fake past, and how human: I feel I can almost reach out and touch it. There was a woman, and a child. One woman. One child . . . But I soon snap out of it' (p. 126). Ironically, even with all the time in the world at his disposal, the immortal is the only protagonist in *Einstein's Monsters* who lacks any agency whatsoever. Not only does he fail to acknowledge his real world (if it can be called 'real'), but even in the world of his imagination he is an observer, someone who cannot afford to get too involved. Set in a post-apocalypse future, 'The Immortals' is the darkest story of the collection, not least because its chronotope is one in which agency seems to have been lost, and time to have been utterly foreclosed.

Here again, however, we find resistance to closure at the level of reader-text chronotope. As Amis remarks in the introduction to *Einstein's Monsters*, '[i]f we could look at ourselves from anything approaching the vantage of cosmic time, if we had any sense of cosmic power, cosmic delicacy, then every indicator would point the same way: *down*' (p. 24). This vantage point *is* achieved by the 'immortal' narrator, although he himself necessarily remains unaware of his pre-nuclear holocaust readership; his chronotope may be wrong for him while still working for us, including Amis, for whom 'the pessimistic view would seem . . . to be the natural one' (p. 21). As we have seen, the representation of contemporary culture in *Einstein's Monsters* is often a negative one. Most of the characters are victims who, lacking agency to various degrees, conform to [Fredric] Jameson's anatomy of post-modern culture as a whole.[13] At the same time, however, Amis suggests various ways in which value, weight, and space for individual agency may be acquired in the present, as is reflected by his own exercise of agency at the narrative level. Applying a puppyish 'spin and charm' (p. 111) to his plot development, Amis plants a surprise twist in each story: Bujak does not kill the murderers, Dan does not kill Harriet, the 'time disease' is youth, the puppy becomes a human being, the immortal is not so. This narrative 'lightness' of touch (in Italo Calvino's sense[14]) is in itself a deliberate gesture of defiance against the temporal determinism that spawned the nuclear arms race.

If this is so, there is still space, and a *need*, for the reader's agency in the reception of this collection of (post)holocaust 'postcards'. When these stories are read in order, an increasing 'unbelievability' becomes apparent at the level of technique. 'Bujak' opens the collection with an assured, third-person commentary on another's tragedy, and the suspense is manipulated with perfect control. The slippage in tone from satire to sentimentality becomes more ragged in 'Time Disease' with a more noticeable narrative strategy. The saccharine tone of 'Little Puppy' is difficult to take seriously, seeming strained, even gooey, while the suspense in 'The Immortals' falls a little flat, compared to its execution in 'Bujak': we know from the beginning that the speaker is deluded [not necessarily], since he calls himself the immortal (in the singular), while the plural title indicates otherwise. Although these may be technical lapses on Amis's part, as narratorial lapses of *insight* they paradoxically contribute to the effectiveness of *Einstein's Monsters* as a whole. An increasingly improbable narrative style corresponds to an increasingly improbable world. As is typical of contemporary short fiction, the collection unravels in its telling, then leaves it up to the reader to think through and discard each 'unthinkable' text.[15] □

Falconer's fascinating account demonstrates that *Einstein's Monsters*, slender though it may be in physical size, can bear sustained, serious critical attention, and prompts the thought that it would be rewarding to apply the same kind of close and theoretically informed reading to Martin Amis's full-length fiction – and, as this Guide shows, some critics have begun to do this. But the reactions to his next novel would give little time at first for close reading. Throughout the 1980s, the expectation had been growing that Amis would produce another book that would equal or exceed *Money*. It appeared in 1989, and, as the next chapter will illustrate, it would prove his most exciting, substantial and controversial work yet: *London Fields*.

CHAPTER SEVEN

Pity the Planet: *London Fields* (1989)

L ONDON FIELDS conveys a strong sense of impending apocalypse, of the end of the millennium and perhaps the end of the world: in these respects, it is a powerful and disturbing book. But it does not seem to have been primarily these portents of doom that debarred Martin Amis's sixth novel from the 1989 shortlist for England's best-known annual literary award, the Booker Prize. Amis was not the only well-known writer excluded that year – other 'remarkable omissions', according to the *Times*, were Peter Ackroyd, Julian Barnes, William Golding, Christopher Hope, Francis King and Iris Murdoch[1] – but he was the most conspicuous by his absence. As the novelist and TV presenter Melvyn Bragg remarked: 'Amis's exclusion from the Booker shortlist got him more column inches than most of those on it.' Bragg also referred to an article in the *Guardian* newspaper – he did not give its title – about the 'supposed sexist offensiveness' of *London Fields* that had 'set off an avalanche of correspondence'.[2] That article was Jane Ellison's 'Battle Fields', which asked pointedly:

■ So why isn't he on that prize list? . . . Perhaps the trouble is that Amis . . . writes about sex. Quite a lot about sex, as it happens. [*London Fields*] is awash with sex, sleazy, nasty sex, involving lots of black stockings, panties and things too dreadful to mention here . . . And this is where Amis starts to get into difficulties. His exclusion from the shortlist, it is rumoured, was insisted on by the two women judges on the panel, Maggie Gee and Helen McNeil.[3] □

After the Booker Prize had gone to Kazuo Ishiguro, 'the Japanese Englishman' on October 2 for his novel *The Remains of the Day* (1989),[4] the debate over the exclusion of *London Fields* from the shortlist – and the shortlist of the Whitbread Prize – continued to rage. A column in the *Liber* section, devoted to European literature, of the *Times Literary Supplement* reported on 15 December 1989:

■ After [Salman Rushdie's] *The Satanic Verses* (1989), the book most
argued over in Britain continues to be *London Fields* . . . . . . The talk is
about why the novel . . . has met resistance, and in particular the
reputedly decisive resistance of two women judges, the novelist
Maggie Gee (Booker) and a journalist, Val Hennessy (Whitbread).
Amis's fiercely comic fantasy about (among other things) environmental and moral apocalypse involves the enactment of some grotesque
sexual fantasies, in which she is seen conniving, of the central woman
character [Nicola Six] by the narrator [Samson Young]. Critics of the
book are accused of having mistaken satirical realism for moral turpi-
tude, of confusing the story with its narrator and of being blinded to
its merits by feminist or otherwise 'extra-literary' concerns.

To this, Maggie Gee – herself a powerful and distinctive novelist, and
by background a literary academic – replies that there is a strong formal, purely 'literary' case against *London Fields*, and that it was in these
terms that the Booker judges argued. She says, for example, that Amis
'has tried for effects that aren't quite worked out. There's a confusion
in the book about the function of the narrator. On the page where he
gives benediction to the child he seems a normative centre, but two pages
earlier he has bludgeoned Nicola Six to death'. She points out that
some male critics have disliked the book for similar reasons. On the
other hand, she wonders whether debate over the very notion of extra-
literariness has not gone to sleep in Britain, and concedes that matters
discounted by most of the critical establishment – sexual politics, for
one, and untutored, or anti-tutorial, gut reactions, for another – have an
inevitable place in judgements of taste . . . . . . Gee is a keen admirer of
much of Amis's work, and describes him as 'a very, very good comic
novelist'. All the Booker judges agreed that *London Fields* is very funny.
Another good reason, his supporters argue, for taking it seriously.[5] □

The debate remained active into the 1990s. Not all the Booker judges,
it seemed, had wanted *London Fields* excluded from the shortlist; as the
novelist and critic David Lodge wrote, in an essay published in 1992:

■ In 1989 I was chairman of the judges for the Booker Prize, Britain's
premier literary prize. We read, or at least scrutinized, over a hundred
new novels. The great majority of them were written within the conventions of fictional realism. I should say that it was a matter of great
regret to me that Martin Amis's *London Fields* was not shortlisted, due
to the strong objections of two members of the jury. Had it been, our
list would have looked somewhat different, for there are important
metafictional and fabulatory elements in this novel. None of the six
novels we ended up with could be said to deviate from the conventions of modern realistic narrative.[6] □

Lodge does not address the issue of sexism here, but back in 1989 Jane Ellison, in the article quoted earlier in this chapter, had offered a vigorous defence of *London Fields* against that charge, thus provoking the 'avalanche of correspondence' mentioned by Melvyn Bragg. Ellison's case is still worth hearing:

■ It is a shame that Amis has become the object of feminist outrage. It is also quite unfair on him. Why single him out for opprobrium? To claim that a work of fiction is 'sexist' is one of those tricky objections that tends to rebound on the critic. What about Updike? Lawrence? Tolstoy? Why stop there? You can see fiction itself as a great conspiracy of 'sexist' malignancy towards women . . .
   At its least, 'sexist' writing is not exactly monopolized by Amis. Women are expert practitioners in this field, too. Look at the work of Jeanette Winterson, a fashionable writer of contemporary fiction with a strong line on magic realism and gender-crossing. In her latest work, [*Sexing the Cherry* (1989)], not only does she make sledgehammer feminist jokes but – in the memorable words of the [*Sunday Correspondent*] – '[m]en get their willies bitten off'. Makes poor old Martin look pretty tame.
   But there is no need to plunder the pages of the 'literary' novel for the worst examples of sexist writing. Wander into any W H Smith and there are the shelves brimming with [*Ambition, Pearls, Destiny, Lace, I'll Take Manhattan*]. What do all these fat volumes have in common? Yes, lots of passages of pornographic sex. And they're all written by women . . . . . . Women cannot complain about their treatment in male fiction when it is women themselves who write these trashy, lurid blockbusters just to earn themselves a vast publisher's advance . . . . . .
   You may not like the sort of sex that Amis writes about, but it is not pornographic. It is not thrown into [*London Fields*] at a ratio of one paragraph to every five pages, it is not written purely to keep the reader salivating (it is far too nasty for that). For real pornography we must look instead to women like [Julie] Burchill and [Celia] Brayfield, the champions of real 'sexist' prose. History will judge whether the Booker judges were right about the shelf-life of their shortlist (in fact, prize-winners tend to become rapidly consigned to oblivion). But history may also judge that they kept Amis out for the wrong reasons.[7] □

Whatever the judgement of history, there can be no doubt that *London Fields* has proved it can continue to attract the serious attention of literary critics, both male and female. An excellent example is provided by Penny Smith, whose essay 'Hell Innit', published in 1995, considers the controversial representation of Nicola Six in the context of the presence of the millennium in three contemporary novels – *London Fields*, Alasdair

Gray's *Lanark*, and Shena Mackay's *Dunedin* (1992) – all texts in which, Smith suggests, 'there is a sense that as we approach the year 2000 we find ourselves looking not forward but back, to the catastrophe that has cast its shadow across the second half of the twentieth century, the Second World War'[8] – a particularly interesting comment in the light of the way in which the Holocaust becomes the theme of Amis's next novel, *Time's Arrow*. This is her insightful account of *London Fields*:

■ Where Alasdair Gray is a better writer than he sometimes seems, Martin Amis sometimes seems to be [a better] writer than he actually is. The most common criticism of Amis's work is that the parts are better than the whole, a contagious style ultimately failing to make up for lack of content. At the same time, there is no doubt that *London Fields* is both an indicator of the *zeitgeist* [spirit of the time], as well as an influence, and no discussion of the millennium in contemporary British fiction can afford to leave it off the list.

Amis's text shares *Lanark*'s sense of there not being much time left: 'Oh, Christ, no, the hell of time . . . Time *takes* from you, with both hands. Things just disappear into it' (p.239). As the Note to *London Fields* explains, an alternative title could have been *Millennium*. However, as 'M. A.' (the text is a prolonged tease and we're never sure whether we're in the hands of Martin Amis, real author, or Mark Asprey, fictional creation) explains: '*everything* is called *Millennium* just now'. So *London Fields* it is: 'This book is called *London Fields. London Fields* . . .' (Note, after Contents page).

Although the year is supposed to be 1999, 1989 is how it reads, with the bubble of the Eighties about to burst and recession immediately around the corner. London is at crisis point – although it is difficult to identify what form the crisis will actually take. Certainly the weather is behaving very oddly, there are cyclonic winds (killing 'nineteen people, and thirty-three million trees' (p.43). The animals are dying (p.97), and rumour has it that there is to be massive flooding, cosmic rays, and the Second Coming (p.118). The natural world is on fastforward, rushing toward catastrophe with the political situation racing to keep up. There's danger of '"[a] flare-up. A flashpoint somewhere"' (p.105). The international situation is mysteriously linked to the ill-health of Faith, the First Lady (p.207), and the 'new buzz word' is '[c]*athartic war*' (p.417). The sun is daily sinking lower as the earth tilts on its axis in anticipation of a full eclipse on November 5, at which point, so the rumours go, two nuclear bombs will explode, 'one over the Palace of Culture in Warsaw, one over Marble Arch' (p.394).

It's the end of the century and the planet is braced for impact (p.197) because while previous millenniums didn't really mean the end of the world ('Nobody had the hardware', p.369), this time things are different. But when November 5 does come around, there isn't a bang but a whimper. The comet doesn't hit, the bombs don't explode, the sun returns to its normal position. A woman, however, is murdered, and we are back with what we were promised on the novel's first page: 'This is the story of a murder' (p. 1).

London Fields is a murder story, popular fiction dressed up as high art, a text that functions as much as a textbook (designed for the undergraduate seminar requiring neat examples of the metafictional and postmodern) as a novel . . . *London Fields* is . . . multi-layered, the commentary of the narrator, Samson Young, sandwiching the fiction he is writing. The commentary, of course, tells us that this fiction is 'real' ('This is a true story but I can't believe it's really happening'): a woman – Nicola Six, 'the murderee' (p. 1), – dumps her diaries in a London rubbish bin (p. 26) and an author finds a ready-made story. At the same time Nicola Six finds her murderer. Or, rather, potential murderer for while, in Lawrentian terms, a murderee is always a murderee, '[t]he murderer was not yet a murderer' (p. 18) ['Lawrentian terms' refers to D. H. Lawrence's novel *Women in Love* (1921), in which Rupert Birkin, one of the main characters, says: '"[i]t takes two people to make a murder: a murderer and a murderee"'[9]]. A murderer has to be made, and so Samson Young describes how Nicola goes to work on Keith Talent who, although 'a very bad guy', working class, petty crook, wife-beater, rapist, is not yet 'the very worst ever' (p. 4). It is up to Nicola to turn him into that, and in order to transform Keith into what is required she plays him off against Guy Clinch – upper class, nice guy, handsome, rich (p. 27).

Nicola Six (a blend of sex and an Apocalyptic 666) has from an early age always known 'what was going to happen next' (p. 15), and in the case of her own murder is playing both prophet and author. Why she wants to die is another matter: '[i]t's what she always wanted' (p. 1). Nicola Six is a heart, and ball, breaker: '[s]he pauperized gigolos, she spayed studs, she hospitalized heartbreakers' (p. 21). For Guy, Nicola plays the virgin, teasing him into a state whereby he loses dignity, sanity, family. For Keith she's the whore. Nicola is all things to all men . . . . . . it is easy to see how the depiction of Nicola Six invites accusations of misogyny, even though Amis's apparent intention is for his female character to be read as a symbol of her age rather than a sign of her gender. Nicola is self-destructive, compelled not just to cancel love but to murder it (p. 21), a perversion of emotion which, according to this text, is reflected in a predilection for sodomy: '[i]t was the only thing about herself that she couldn't understand and wouldn't forgive'. But while Nicola can't quite comprehend her own desires she is aware that '[l]iterature *did* go on about sodomy, and increasingly' (p. 67). Joyce, Lawrence, Beckett, Updike, Mailer, Roth, Naipaul (p. 68), compiling her list of (male) writers she is tempted to see sodomy as a 'twentieth-century theme' (p.67), and Nicola 'would be perfectly prepared to represent her century' (pp.67–68). Sodomy, for Nicola, is about negation – *That's what I am*, she used to whisper to herself after sex. *A black hole. Nothing can escape from me* (p.67) – and that too is the motto of the suicidal last century of the second millennium.

The twentieth century has 'come along and after several try-outs and test-drives it put together an astonishing new offer: death for everybody . . . ' (p.297). At the end, however, death calls only for Nicola, who barely whimpers. This doesn't mean that the big bang won't happen, but is more a recognition that it has happened already. We've already seen the big one, and are living in its aftermath. The big one was the Second World War and what it unleashed, the possibility of nuclear holocaust. Just as Nicola has known since childhood what was going to happen next she's been accompanied by an invisible companion: ' . . . Enola Gay. Enola wasn't real. Enola came from inside the head of Nicola Six' (p.16). As part of her effort to humiliate Guy, Nicola extracts large amounts of money from him on the pretext of trying to save Enola Gay and her little boy, stranded in south-east Asia as a result of the Cambodian war. But just as Enola Gay isn't really a refugee in Thailand or Burma, she isn't a fantasy either:

> 'Enola Gay' was the plane that flew the mission to Hiroshima. The pilot named the aircraft after his mother. He was once her little boy.
> But Little Boy was the name of the atom bomb. It killed 50,000 people in 120 seconds (p.445).

Nicola has been able to con Guy because, like the vast majority, he hasn't known one of the most important facts in his sad century's history. Similarly, Keith has to be told that the bikini Nicola dons is named after the Bikini Atoll:

> 'What American men did there – one of the greatest crimes in human history. If you got the world's most talented shits and cruelty experts together, they couldn't come up with anything worse than Bikini. And how do we commemorate the crime, Keith?' She indicated the two small pieces of her two-piece. 'Certain women go about wearing this trash. It's very twentieth-century, don't you think?'
> 'Yeah. Diabolical' (p.127).

So diabolical in fact that it's as if the Second World War never really ended: ' . . . it seemed possible to argue that Hitler was still running the century – Hitler, the great bereaver' (p.395). History ended mid-century and what we are caught in in *London Fields* is the hell of the perpetual present.

Nicola Six, the murderee, walks in the shadow of Enola Gay, and so too does her murderer. When Nicola appears in the Black Cross pub Samson Young leaps to the conclusion that she's recognized her murderer in Keith. But this is one of those whodunnits in which the unwitting narrator turns out to be the 'who'. 'She leaned forward. "You," she said, with intense recognition. "Always you . . ."' (p.465). Nicola had known him from the start (p.466). And Young should have known too because he and Nicola are linked by the fact that they're both as good as dead already (p.260). However where Nicola, representative of a self-destructive century, wills her own death, Young has had his willed on him as a legacy of the work his father did, in London Fields, on High Explosives Research (pp.120, 161).

Samson Young is 'pre-nuked and dead-already' (p.323). So when Guy is about to kill Nicola, Young can make a deal with him and take his place because he has nothing to lose. '[A]fter the first blow she gave a moan of visceral assent' (p.467) and the narrator is left to take a suicide pill. A murder and a suicide and everything goes back to normal. Which is the problem with *London Fields* because, ultimately, any political message there is about the destructive temperament of the century, the madness of things nuclear, is lost as the skies clear and the novel, like other of Amis's novels, concludes by valorizing class and gender.[10] The woman gets what she's asking for and her death is, ultimately, engineered by Guy who beats up the already-humiliated Keith and reasserts himself as the dominant, upper-class male. The post-war, postmodern, postmillennial world gets back to normal.[11] □

The apocalyptic, millennial aspects of *London Fields* identified by Penny Smith are also discussed in Brian Finney's essay 'Narrative and Narrated Homicides in Martin Amis's *Other People* and *London Fields*' (1995). But as in his account of *Other People* in the same essay (see pp.49–54 of this Guide), Finney's major concern is murder and its relation to narrative. This extract starts by linking *London Fields* with *Other People*:

■ Both novels can be said to be centered on murderees – women who ask to be killed. In both the narrator turns out at the end to be the murderer. It is this responsibility of the narrator for the eventual elimination of the female protagonist that distinguishes and connects both books . . . Even the time scheme of *Other People* and *London Fields* turns out to be similar. *Other People* is about a timeless present – one reviewer suggested that 'perhaps everything happens in a single instant'.[12] So too, according to Amis, is *London Fields* a book 'about the present', despite its futuristic setting.[13]

By situating his novel at the end of the twentieth century, Amis is able to make overt many of the issues underlying contemporary life. Maybe he has made them too overt. But the imminent collapse of modern civilization, even the planet itself, what the book refers to as the Crisis, is an integral part of the fabric of the book as a whole. Nicola Six (pronounced 'seeks', but also misheard as 'sex'), the (anti)heroine, has decided to end her life rather than enter middle age knowing that love is dead for her – and soon for everyone else, Amis suggests. 'The death of God was possibly survivable in the end. But if love was going the same way . . . ' (p. 132). Nicola's death wish parallels that of the planet. As a *femme fatale* or 'Old Nick' (but a female devil) she opts for sodomy – the way of foolproof sterility. A personalized black hole, she draws men into her destructive magnetic field just as the black hole of physics threatens to swallow up our planet, our solar system, into its negative energy: '[s]he had the power . . . to receive [men's] love and send it back in opposite form, not just cancelled but murdered' (pp. 20, 21). So at the start of the novel she decides to have herself murdered either by Keith Talent, a working class yob (the English version of a jerk) and petty criminal whose only talent is for darts and pornography, or by Guy Clinch, a rich, nice but hopelessly romantic 'fall guy: fool, foal, foil' (p. 240). Keith represents 'reptile modernity'; Guy is handicapped by an 'archaic heart' (p. 192).

Unlike Prince, Samson Young, the narrator of and in this novel, appears to have none of his predecessor's godlike control over the actions occurring within the narrative. A Jewish American journalistic writer suffering from a twenty-year writer's block, he has come to London after answering an ad in the *New York Review of Books* for an apartment exchange. (It is typical of the strategy of this novel that he should have been drawn into the book by a literary artefact that is about books.) He finds himself occupying the palatial flat of a successful English playwright called Mark Asprey. Asprey's initials echo those of Martin Amis, so we have from the start the ghost of the author casting his enigmatic shadow over his fictional stand-in, the narrator. Sam, like the earth, is suffering from the final stages of a wasting disease ('"Radiogenic, naturally"' (p. 161)) that makes him almost impervious to the lure of sexual love. He is quintessentially one of life's observers, 'less a novelist than a queasy cleric, taking down the minutes of real life'. What he finds in the Nicola-Keith-Guy triangle is a ready-made thriller. 'Not a whodunit. More a whydoit' (p. 3). Thanks to Nicola's convenient ability to see into the future he can tell us exactly how and when she will die. Only who her murderer will be remains unknown.

So Amis sets up the novel in such a way that Nicola has to lure one of the men into murdering her while Sam has to worm his way into the main characters' lives (imaginatively as well as physically) in order to get his novel written before he dies himself. 'I'm on deadline too here, don't forget,' he writes punningly on the first page. The end of his novel has to be made to coincide with the end of Nicola's life on her thirty-fifth birthday and has to be finished before his own life is finished. We are forced to notice the artificial neatness of this entire construct in the opening pages. It is far too orderly to be true to life, although it qualifies as 'a true story' (p. 1), that is, a true fiction. At the beginning of the book Sam cannot understand this distinction. He sees himself as no more than a second-rate reporter doing 'fieldwork', incapable of 'improving on reality' (p. 39). He begins his researches in the spirit of a peeping Tom. Yet a crucial part of his initial raw material turns out to be not life in the raw but literature. He enters a web of intertextuality. He recovers Nicola's diaries that reveal among other things that she had had a torrid affair with Mark Asprey before his departure for Sam's apartment in New York. Keith gives him a brochure outlining the dubious services he offers. Guy reluctantly parts with two autobiographical stories he has written. Sam comments: '[d]ocumentary evidence. Is that what I'm writing? A documentary? As for artistic talent, as for the imaginative patterning of life, Nicola wins. She outwrites us all' (p. 43). She acts, that is, as Sam's muse. On his first visit to her apartment he pleads, '"Nicola, let me be your diary"' (p. 62). A diary might be a daily record, but that does not make it any more factual than other forms of writing.

The plot of the narrative is ostensibly being concocted by Nicola. She, not Sam, is in control of the *fabula* (story [the chronological events as they would occur in actual life]) although the *syuzhet* (or plot [the arrangement of events in the narrative, which may and usually does depart from strict chronology]) is necessarily in the hands of the story's narrator. As the novel progresses, Sam is drawn into the plot of the story he is telling, and not simply as a passive participant. At the end of Chapter 4 he stops Keith's narration of his first visit to Nicola's flat in mid-flight to go and see her himself to check out the accuracy of Keith's story that was being regaled to his mates at the pub and was in danger of turning fictional. Fictional! Sam should know better. When he arrives at Nicola's, she is reluctant to let him in. So he plays 'a mild hunch', and tells her that there is no need to dress for him. He scores a bullseye (to adopt Keith's darts lingo). She invites him up. 'That's what writing is, a hundred hunches . . . ' he comments (p. 60). Life and literature are becoming indistinguishable, even for the documentary narrator.

Gradually the scale of his interventions in the plot escalates. 'Guy asked my advice about Nicola. I gave my advice (it was bad advice), and with any luck he'll take it' (p. 101). He can't afford to have Guy see through her or his story will be ruined. But wasn't it Nicola's story? Sam does have moral qualms. He asks Nicola, "'Do you really need Guy? Couldn't you just edit him out?'" (p.119). Amis here is simultaneously sharing the author's dilemma with his readers. Sam also tries to get her to pay off Keith's gambling debts to prevent Keith's having his darts finger broken in retaliation. Next he traps Nicola into revealing her earlier affair with Mark Asprey. (How can Nicola be said to be in control of this part of the story?) Forced to try and fly back to New York for a week, Sam asks her to "'keep activity to the minimum'" while he's gone (p.235). On his return, after discovering the cigarette burns on Keith's daughter, whom he has grown to love, and thinking that Keith may have caused them (having misread one of Keith's diary entries – another instance of the unreliability of journal writing), he pleads with Nicola to lure Keith away from his home as much as possible and keep him happy so as to minimize the possibility of his hurting his daughter again. "'There go my unities,'" Sam remarks (p.388). Ostensibly he is referring to the Aristotelian unity of place. More important, he is drawing attention to the multiplicity of narrative voices in the book. Sam might be the designated narrator, but Nicola is meant to appear to control the plot, and M.A. lurks just off stage reminding us that both Sam and Nicola are narrative mouthpieces with limited autonomy. There is no escaping the problematics of the narrative act in Amis's fiction.

As the interventions by the narrator in the events that he is narrating grow in importance, instances proliferate in the narrative of the dependence of narrative, not on life, but on other narrative. Take the case of Keith. Even more than John Self in *Money*, he is the typical product of what [Jean] Baudrillard has called the age of simulation. Simulation, according to Baudrillard, is opposed to representation. In an age of simulation it is no longer possible to distinguish between the image as representation of a reality outside it and the simulacrum, 'never again exchanging for what is real, but exchanging in itself, in an uninterrupted circuit without reference or circumference'.[14] Keith has been educated by the popular media. His idea of authenticity and his expressions and vocabulary all derive from the tabloids and television. Initially, Sam makes the mistake of thinking that the string of clichés that Keith employs when he describes a football match he has attended are 'just memorized sections of the tabloid sports pages'. Then with a shock he realizes that they are *what he actually sees* (pp.97, 98). Similarly Keith's attitude to women and sex is entirely conditioned by the media, especially the porn industry. Nicola comes to understand that, if it were possible to make a taxonomy of it, '[h]is libido would be all tabloid and factoid' (p. 202). He actually prefers sex on video, which is where he acquired a taste for it in the first place.

Video allows him to fast forward the uninteresting bits and to freeze frame the most salacious glimpses of female flesh. Nicola, who understands the power of simulacra, capitalizes on this by seducing Keith on screen, making pornographic videos of herself for him to watch in solitary, onanistic pleasure.

Keith is an extreme example of the general truth that, as Amis says, 'our sex lives are mediated by images from elsewhere that we now all have in our heads'. Nicola equally manipulates Guy with 'ads for love' in which, 'like advertisements for menthol cigarettes, they walk through the corn hand in hand'.[15] Guy's sister-in-law Lizzy's love life reduces itself to a series of capitalized media clichés – 'He Refuses To Make A Commitment. She Has A Problem Giving Him The Space He Needs . . . ' (p.281). Even Sam is not immune. 'I too,' he writes, 'have need of the Fast Forward' (p.40). Sam's na[i]ve attempt to keep life and fiction separate from each other is undermined in numerous ways throughout the novel. He is forced to admit the extent to which the demands of narrative form compel him to tone down Marmaduke, Guy's horrific baby, a caricature that Amis calls entirely 'essayesque',[16] or to exclude important material from the book. Missy, for example, Sam's American girlfriend, 'had to go. For reasons of balance. Reasons of space' (p.435). . . . 'The form itself is my enemy,' Sam realizes. 'In fiction (rightly so called), people become coherent and intelligible – and they aren't like that' (p.240). What Sam fails to see is that he, too, is writing within a narrative genre, the thriller, which he is simultaneously subverting by turning it into a 'whydoit'. Amis uses Sam's literary na[i]veté to demonstrate the inescapability of the poststructuralist assumption that all forms of narrative belong to the democratic state of textuality.

Not only does Amis totally undermine Sam's claim to factual reportage in his narration; he also problematizes the distinction between life and literature. Literature insists on spilling over into life in a hundred different ways in this book. When Guy, stifled by his expensive domestic life, tells his wife he's going out, she asks him what for. '"See some life,"' he shouts back. '"Oh. Life! Oh I get it. *Life*"' (p.86). That confusion between Life and *Life* is necessary for the novel to work. In a letter in which Mark Asprey tells Sam he should try writing fiction, he also recommends Sam read his novel, *Crossbone Waters*. The book, an adventure story with a love interest, turns out to be 'an *awful* little piece of shit' (p.389). Next Sam discovers some old magazines in which it turns out that the heroine sued Mark Asprey for her portrayal in the book and the entire novel was a thinly disguised slice of life. Finally, in his last letter to Sam, Mark Asprey admits that virtually all of his book including the heroine's magnificent breasts was a figment of his imagination. Asprey's justification: '[i]t doesn't matter what anyone writes any more. The time for it mattering has passed. The truth doesn't matter any more and *is not wanted*' (p. 452). We are thrown back into a Baudrillardian world where images no longer represent anything beyond themselves. In this fictional world in which Keith and everyone else cheats in one form or another, in this apocalyptic fable about our postmodern condition, *Life* is Life.

Who then is making whom up? Who is in control of this narrative? Is it Sam? Is it Nicola? According to Sam she 'outwrites us all' (p. 43). Yet even here Sam is employing writing as a figure of speech. Certainly she outacts them all. She is also aware of the power writing can exercise over life. She starts off dropping her diaries in Sam's sight. She uses a book to reveal to Guy the fact that she had guyed him all along about her invented friend, Enola Gay, the name of the plane that delivered the first atom bomb, Little Boy (implying that guys like Guy ought to be better read in the history of the discovery of thermo-nuclear fission). She knows how to really revenge herself on Mark Asprey – by locking herself in a room and burning the manuscript of the only novel he ever wrote from the heart . . . But what about her own status within the novel? This is problematic, to say the least. One reviewer called her 'a masturbatory figment of male imagination, not really a woman at all'.[17] Sam worries about this:

'Nicola, I'm worried about you, as usual . . . I'm worried they're going to say you're a male fantasy figure.'

'I *am* a male fantasy figure. I've been one for fifteen years. It really takes it out of a girl.'

'But they don't know that.'

'I'm sorry, I just *am*' (p. 260).

. . . Amis is covertly offering an ironic defense within the novel of his penchant for female characters like Selina [in *Money*] and Nicola. 'I'm writing comedies. Vamps and ballbreakers and golddiggers are the sort of women who belong in comedy'.[18] Such women are types, the subjects of fictional narratives, genre-specific. Nicola herself begins to question her own reality status within the novel when she gets into a conversation with Sam about when it is acceptable for fictional characters to vacillate. She agrees that characters subject to sexual vacillation are permissible:

'They *are* the story. With the other stuff there's no story until they're out of the way.'

I said uneasily, 'But you're not in a story. This isn't some hired video, Nicola.'

She shrugged. 'It's always felt like a story,' she said (p. 118).

Amis is constantly playing metafictional games of this kind with his readers, and nowhere more than in the surprise ending. The narrator replaces Guy at the last minute to become what? The one to bring Nicola's life within the narrative to an end? Or the real fall guy whom Nicola had set up from the start? 'She outwrote me. Her story worked. And mine didn't', Sam writes after taking the pill that will end his life (p. 466). But it is his story of her story. He has outlived her. He has contained her within his larger narrative.

But Amis has not finished playing metafictional hide and seek with the reader. How does Mark Asprey, or rather M. A., come into all this? Because the whole novel only works on the premise that the reader is aware of the author's playing games with his na[i]ve narrator who is nevertheless given all the linguistic sophistication of Amis's developed narrative style. Amis is constantly playing implicit jokes on the narrator. For one so earnestly bent on adhering to the facts, for example, he shows a tremendous unconscious talent for fictional allusion. On reading the contents of Nicola's diary, he comments that it 'was . . . just a chronicle of a death foretold' (p. 17). At the end of the book he leaves Mark Asprey his 'confession', saying that '[p]erhaps it is also an elegy to the memory of an unfortunate lady' (p. 468). Unwittingly he transforms factual diaries and confessions into fictional fables by [G]arcía Márquez and Pope. [The allusions are to the title of Gabriel García Márquez's novel *Chronicle of a Death Foretold* (1981) and Alexander Pope's poem 'Elegy to the Memory of an Unfortunate Lady' (1717).] Only in the Endpapers, Sam's two last letters to Mark Asprey and Kim Talent, does Sam begin to suspect that he is himself the victim of fictional invention. His letter to Mark ends with a PPS: '[y]ou didn't set me up. Did you?' (p. 468). And in his letter to Keith's daughter he feels himself succumbing to the pill he took: '[b]lissful, watery and vapid, the state of painlessness is upon me. I feel seamless and insubstantial, like a creation. As if someone made me up, for money. And I don't care' (p. 470). He might have been responsible for bringing Nicola's life to an end. And she might have ensured that he brought his own life to an end. But at the last minute he realizes that both of them have been given life and deprived of it by the ghostly M. A. The narrator is and always has been as much of a fictional instrument as the characters in the hands of the author. The author. Not Mark Asprey. Because authors can never enter directly into their own narratives. They are compelled to invent alter egos, Sams or Mark Aspreys, who, by the essential nature of fictional narrative, are held at a distance from their creators who are themselves locked in their solipsistic state of non-narrative being.

If, as Amis maintains, the bleak facts of contemporary life can only be rendered comically, that is with black humor, then it is essential that readers be induced to identify with the author rather than with the objects of his creation whom he seeks to mock with his dark laughter. To effect this the author has to introduce a narrative alter ego in the person of the narrator, someone who can both enter the action and control it and us, the readers. But the narrator is not the author. In both *Other People* and *London Fields* Amis explores the ambiguous position that the narrator of postmodern fiction such as his must occupy. Simultaneously he must be both an instrument for the author and as much a victim of the author's capricious will as any of the other characters. Similarly readers are made to see their active implication in the sadistic treatment met out to characters by narrator and author, and yet to be themselves subject to the wayward will of the author.

In fact, Amis goes out of his way to detach his readers by the end of each book from the narrator who has acted as their Virgilian guide through the inferno of contemporary civilization. Having encouraged the narrator to do our dirty work for us, we ultimately find ourselves victims with him of the author's covert manipulation. By killing off the narrator at the end of both books, Amis is abruptly distancing us from the narrative, compelling us to take an extranarrative perspective, to share with the author his murderous act of closure. *London Fields* is a 'whydoit' in more senses than one. It investigates why eventually it is the narrator who murders Nicola. It also investigates why we as readers want Sam (or one of Amis's fictional characters) to murder her. What is this rage for form? Why do we derive enjoyment in proportion to the ingenuity shown by the author in plotting the murderous end to his characters' fictional lives? The appeal of fiction has always been the clarity it offers us by its orderly rearrangement of life. What postmodern writers such as Amis have done is additionally to draw our attention with various metafictional devices to the artistic ingenuity entailed in transforming life into *Life*, anarchy into order, homicide into harmless pleasure, and readerly into writerly narration.[19] □

The issue of 'writerly' narration, of the role of the author, is taken up and explored by Frederick Holmes in his intriguing 1996 essay, 'The Death of the Author as Cultural Critique in *London Fields*', which sees the characters of the novel as would-be authors of stories who are really being written by the intertextual web of broader cultural codes:

■ Martin Amis's *London Fields* both comically illustrates Roland Barthes's thesis about the death of the author and parodies it by rendering it literal. The novel self-consciously dramatizes a contest for authorship; all of the characters are 'authors' of one sort or another who are vying with each other to shape events into the form of a story that will count as authoritative. None, however, is the real originator of the plots, which issue from the intertextual web formed by the various codes operative in the culture at large. The narratives that supply the subjectivities of the characters are all prefabricated and clich[é]d. They certainly corroborate Barthes's contention that 'the writer can only imitate a gesture that is always anterior, never original. His only power is to mix writings, to counter the ones with the others, in such a way as never to rest on any one of them. Did he wish to *express himself,* he ought at least to know that the inner "thing" he thinks to "translate" is itself only a ready-formed dictionary, its words only explainable through other words, and so on indefinitely.'[20] The most successful surrogate authors in *London Fields*, the collaborative team formed by the narrator, Samson Young, and the controlling figure, Nicola Six, recognize the received character of their materials and accordingly are able to muster sufficient detachment to deploy them successfully to manipulate others. (Art, in Amis's world, is a thoroughly impure affair, a surprisingly direct source of power.) But paradoxically, the end which they are working toward is her literal death, since she has assumed the role of 'murderee' in the 'snappy little thriller' (p. 3) which she has concocted and which Samson transcribes.

This aimed-for and ultimately achieved death is a postmodernist parody of the deconstructionist position on language and meaning. The murder is a way of supplying closure and generating a teleological structure which confers the extra-textual meaning denied by post-structuralist theory. Nicola, as the satanic *femme noire* [woman in black] or *la belle dame sans merci* [woman without mercy], the killer of love and her own ultimate victim, is a construction designed to provide an inverted, nihilistic significance – a master narrative of dark destiny which trumps the contingency and debasement of mass culture and signals the larger apocalypse towards which the planet is moving in Amis's futuristic dystopia. She is explicit that her demise, predestined as it is, needs to be significant: '"Of course it could be managed. Easy. A bungled rape, strangulation . . . The time [Keith Talent] followed me home I could have managed that. But what do you think I'm after? A 'senseless killing'?"' (p. 119). The perverse significance which she seeks consists of the destruction of love, and this necessitates the unwitting participation in her plot of Guy Clinch: '[s]he had always been sure . . . that Guy contained a strong potentiality of love, which she needed, because the equation she was working on unquestionably needed love in it somewhere' (p. 132). In Nicola's plan the death of the author becomes a paradoxical assertion of the power of the author, an attempt to reinstall her in a position of authority as one capable of using the available cultural codes to make a purposeful design, if not of creating ex nihilo [out of nothing] in some godlike, Romantic fashion.

But is Nicola actually in control, and is her death really an exit from the labyrinth of the text? As Mick Imlah notes,[21] there is a suggestion in the ambiguity of the initials M. A., which appear at the end of the novel's introductory Note, that Nicola/Samson might be the fictional creation of the writer Mark Asprey, Samson's shadowy nemesis who never appears 'in the flesh' and who might exist on a higher ontological plane as the author of the other characters. The suicide letter which Samson leaves for Asprey concludes with the question '[y]ou didn't set me up. Did you?' (p. 468). And in the following letter to Kim Talent, Samson adds, 'I feel seamless and insubstantial, like a creation. As if someone made me up, for money' (p. 470). In the final analysis, though, Asprey, too, is just another character, behind whom is Amis. While eschewing originality in the absolute sense and embracing a parodic, postmodernist intertextuality, he nevertheless puts his own individual stamp on *London Fields* with a cynical sensibility and an intrusive, highly metaphorical, hard-boiled style which, while nominally that of his fictional narrator, is unmistakably his own.[22] I would argue that he performs the paradoxical feat of nihilistically denying the possibility of meaningful creation while simultaneously creating a memorably corrosive, if somewhat compromised, satire of contemporary culture.

As mentioned, *London Fields* is a metafiction which flamboyantly parades its own artificiality. Although its narrator disavows the power of invention and claims a factual status for the events which he says he records directly from life or copies from Nicola's diaries (p. 42), his many confidences about the process of writing the book only have the effect ultimately of highlighting its fabricated nature. So does the fact that all of the other major characters, as authors of one sort or another, focus our attention on the medium, on the process of writing rather than the finished product (even the semi-illiterate Keith is a writer whose struggles with his 'book', his darter's diary, are unintentionally risible). Samson's constant allusions to the literary works of others and comparisons of his own work in progress with them also contribute to the foregrounding of artifice, as do the implausible, highly stylized names of the characters: we have, to provide a few examples, Guy Clinch, Chick Purchase, Analiese Furnish, Trish Shirt, and Dink Heckler. The characters themselves behave like the one-dimensional cartoon figures that their names suggest. The actions in which they are involved are too bizarre and extreme to seem verisimilitudinous according to the standards of Jamesian realism, but, as Luc Sante states, to call the plot of the novel mechanical 'would be to belabor the obvious. It *is* a mechanism, the way a Tom and Jerry escapade is a mechanism, only in this case every pratfall is informed by rich sociological context. It *is* a panoramic cartoon that takes in a whole world of culture and custom and speech.'[23]

What Sante implies, and what I would like to argue overtly, is that the novel's self-reflexive dispelling of fictional illusion does not signal the unreality of the text in relation to the 'real' world. It bespeaks, rather, a mimetic intention to reflect, with a good deal of parodic and comic exaggeration, the culturally constructed nature of what we conventionally think of as psychological and social reality. In the *fin de siècle* climate of Amis's London (which seems as much a satiric comment on present-day London as an admonitory prophecy of its future), the only available narratives for constructing the self and interacting socially are either debased and shallow or hopelessly anachronistic. They are the products of mass consumerist culture and the remnants of older patterns of behaviour which no longer have currency in the society which Amis depicts.

Keith Talent's identity as a womanizing petty crook and darts enthusiast is entirely the construct of the narratives disseminated by television, movies, and the gutter press. The very social milieu which he inhabits, the violent, misogynistic one of dingy pubs and after-hours drinking clubs, where stolen property is fenced and sexual conquests are bragged about, operates according to the not-always-compatible codes which structure advertizing, action movies, television dramas, pornography, tabloid gossip about celebrities, and sportswriting and broadcasting. The stylistic disjunction which can occur when the habitu[é]s of the Black Cross pub shift from one set of codes to another is a source of the novel's comedy. When the subject of conversation turns to soccer or darts, the demotic Cockney and West Indian dialects of the speakers suddenly give way to the more literate, but heavily clich[é]d, argot of sports reporting . . . perhaps because he is blind to the contradictions apparent in his presentation of himself, Keith does not recognize the manufactured character of his own identity and perceptions. He mistakes culture for nature, and accordingly he fails to notice the illusory cast of the images which constitute his reality. His ludicrous readiness to accept the fictions promulgated by the mass media as unquestionable realities is shown in the difficulty which Nicola has in convincing him that his virile movie idol, Burton Else, is actually a homosexual (pp. 189–90). Keith assumes that television discloses a real, attainable world that transcends the poverty and shabbiness of his own: '[t]elevision was the great shopfront, lightly electrified, up against which Keith crushed his nose' (p. 8).

He not only mistakes its illusion for reality; he is also unequipped to recognize the moral contradictoriness and crassness of what he values. Pornography alone, to which he is addicted, engages his aesthetic faculty. His finer emotions attach, in just the way that advertisers intend, to material objects, or rather to the status associated with them, rather than to people. His neglected dog Clive elicits an inconsequential sentimentality, but he is incapable of loving his wife, Kath, or of recognizing how brutally he treats her. When Nicola, who has invaded his council flat masquerading as a social worker, complains about the unhealthy condition of his home and accuses Kath of child abuse, it is the insult to his dog and his smoking that triggers his ire: '[h]is protective instincts were stirred. Loyalty: it was a question of loyalty. Nobody talked that way about Keith's dog – or about his cigarettes, which were superkingsized and had international standing' (p. 258). In actuality, Keith is incapable of loyalty or honesty, but what is significant for my purposes here is that by selectively invoking an ersatz and hackneyed ethic of male heroism Keith is able to ignore his perfidies and inconsistencies and to see himself as noble. Owing to the parodic style in which the narrator enters into Keith's emotions, however, the reader has quite a different perspective:

> Tears at the dartboard, lachrymae at the oché [the line behind which a player must stand when throwing]: this was Keith's personal vision of male heroism and transcendence, of male grace under pressure. He remembered Kim Twemlow in the semi of last year's World Championship . . . . . . Kim and Keith: they were men. Men, mate. Men. All right? Men. They wept when they wept, and knew the softnesses of women, and relished their beer with laughter in their eyes, and went out there when it mattered to do what had to be done with the darts. Take them for all in all (p. 314).

Cast by Nicola into the role of Keith's foil, Guy is equally the product of his culture, but in this case the formative narratives are those of an antiquated gentility which are no longer honoured or even widely understood in Amis's London. As one critic succinctly states, 'Guy enacts the literary code of a romantic hero who is absurdly out of context'.[24] His displays of magnaminity and gentlemanly fair play are ruthlessly seized by the other characters as opportunities to trick and exploit him. The epic extent of his credulousness, in conjunction with the fact that he alone is capable of selfless actions, supports Bette Pesetsky's charge that Amis 'seems unable to equate goodness with anything other than a gullibility bordering on imbecility'.[25] Guy's devotion to high culture, which Nicola pretends to share in order to inspire his love for her, is shown to be ineffectual and irrelevant in a society too decadent to be morally improved by art. Guy's high-minded short stories rest unpublished, and the people around him remain unaffected by the refining sentiments which art breeds in him. His wife Hope, who bullies and deceives him shamelessly, clearly believes that his idealism is foolish. And Keith, to provide a second example, simply subsumes the little he knows of high culture into the tawdry narratives which fuel his fantasy life. Television dramas of the artistically ambitious, Masterpiece-Theatre sort are just another source of porno-graphic images for him; he finds, to his surprise, that they are more likely to contain nudity than seemingly more risqu[é] fare (p. 165). After feigning to be Nicola's student in a literary session on Keats, which Nicola videotapes in order to prove to Guy that Keith's frequent visits to her flat are innocuous, he has the following thoughts:

> John Keith . . . [t]op wordsmith, and big in pharmaceuticals. Books: one way to make a fast quid. Breakfast by the pool. Wife in good nick. 'Really, dahling, I got to stop writing them Hollywood scripts and get down to serious writing.' Fucking great study full of leather. Snooker! Jesus. Lady Muck with the schoolmarm skirt round her waist. Wasn't bad. No. In the end I thoroughly enjoyed it . . . Keith wondered, parenthetically, if Keats had ever played a form of darts (pp. 356–7).

What Keith is referring to about Nicola is the fact that, by sitting with her back to the camera and letting her skirt fall open, she had secretly turned a tutorial on the exalted theme of Keats's yearning for immor-tality into yet another of the many pornographic sessions which she arranges for him. This is clearly not *Educating Rita* (1981) with gender roles reversed. In the postmodernist context of *London Fields*, high culture is not set above mass commercial culture in hierarchical fashion, as it typically is in modernist works, but is assimilated paro-dically into mass culture. Another example involves Lawrence's *The Rainbow*, which is one of the monuments of the past discussed with exaggerated reverence by Nicola and Guy. The following description of Keith by the narrator is a close parody of the famous, emblematic opening of Lawrence's novel, which celebrates the participation of the Brangwen men in the rhythms of nature:

> He sensed the pulse and body of the street-trade and heard the cars lowing in the furrows. Like new corn the young Swedes and Danes formed lines at his stall, and were reaped . . . The hot macadam pulled on his shoes, like desire, and he had the surety a man knows when there is a sickly Saudi Granny in the back of the Cavalier. He harkened to the chirrup of fruit-machine and the tolling of pinball table, humped the dodgy goods and defrayed life's pleasures with sweat of brow and groin and armpit, knew also the firm clasp of Analiese's ankles around his neck, the coarse reassurance of Trish Shirt's hair in his fist. And ever dazed from staring at the sun, the source of all generation. Heaven and earth was teeming around him. And how should this cease? (p. 114)

How are we to interpret this parody in particular and the diminishment of high culture generally in the novel? Has Amis inherited the notorious philistinism of his father's *Lucky Jim*? Or is high culture, in fact, not being levelled at all in *London Fields* but rather being used as a standard of value? Is it Lawrence who is being ridiculed, or is it, rather, Keith and his unwholesome way of life? It might be possible to affirm the latter possibility and say that the function of the parody is to satirize the debased condition of contemporary society, to show, for example, the falling off of urban life from Lawrence's pastoral ideal (this could explain the significance of the title *London Fields*). Amis's method in this regard could be said to resemble the use of classical or biblical stories and allusions in Dryden's or Pope's satires or even the use of the cultural and literary past in Eliot's poetry.

The difficulty with this reading, though, is that the novel does not really seem to allow for the existence of a base outside mass culture from which it could be repudiated. All of the narrative patterns which comprise this culture are parodically exaggerated, it is true, but so are those which might otherwise be held to transcend it. To treat Keats as pornography or Lawrence as a joke or as bait in a sordid trap is to forfeit the potential to see them as a real alternative to the ephemeral and demeaning narratives of the commercial media. It is tempting to apply Fredric Jameson's general thesis about postmodernism to *London Fields* and to conclude that it manifests the aesthetic logic of late capitalism in which '"culture" has become a product in its own right; . . . modernism was still minimally and tendentially the critique of the commodity and the effort to make it transcend itself. Postmodernism is the consumption of sheer commodification as a process'.[26] In support of this position, we could note, in company with Mark MacLeod,[27] that the motives of all the characters in the novel who perform as author-figures (with the exception of the ineffectual Guy) are mercenary and venal. Nicola is an inverted author-god who is incapable of original creation and whose literary efforts serve the end of destruction. Samson is willing to deceive and even to murder in order to complete what he expects to be nothing more significant than a 'pretty saleable' thriller (p. 1). (He does not seem bothered by the irony that he will not live to enjoy the proceeds.) The wealthy pulp novelist and playwright Mark Asprey enunciates the literary credo of a society in which aesthetic experience has no other function than as a commodity: '[i]t doesn't matter what anyone writes any more. The time for it mattering has passed. The truth doesn't matter any more and *is not wanted*' (p. 452).

The problem with viewing the novel in the terms explained immediately above is that they cannot account for what readers sense to be the novel's intention to lament the very cultural sickness in which it participates. Samson may, as I just stated, treat his novel-in-the-making as nothing more lofty than a potentially lucrative commercial venture, but he also insists throughout, in contrast to what Asprey says, that it must express the truth about its subject (pp.43, 240). However paradoxical such an aim might be in a metafictional context in which no narrative has a foundational reality, Samson shows that he wants something more than money. And ultimately he condemns his project, which suggests that he can stand apart from it morally: '"[i]t's a wicked book. It's a wicked thing I'm doing . . . "' (p.435).

Perhaps the most satisfactory way to make sense of the ambiguous quality of *London Fields* is to invoke another theorist of postmodernism, Linda Hutcheon, who opposes Jameson's position and argues that postmodernism's complicity in the capitalist process of commodification does not negate, although it does compromise, its political critique of that same process.[28] According to Hutcheon, such doubleness is an inherent feature of postmodernist parody, which is defined by 'repetition with critical distance that allows ironic signalling of difference at the very heart of similarity'.[29] This idea explains our uncertainty about how to react to Amis's parodic representations of the images and narratives which circulate in mass culture. It also accounts for the dissatisfaction of those who would like Amis to separate himself unequivocally from and repudiate points of view and behaviour which they find retrograde or offensive. Consider Pesetsky's objection, for example, the tentative language of which suggests that she is not quite as certain as she claims that Nicola should be read as evidence of Amis's sexism and not as a negative comment on the culture at large: 'Nicola is a problem, though; she makes us yield to a sneaking suspicion that a misogynist lingers here somewhere. She is not truly satisfying as character or caricature. She seems to be another of Mr. Amis's plastic women'.[30] One could accuse him in a similarly hesitant way of racism or of class prejudice, owing to the presence in the novel of black, working class, and upper class characters who conform to derogatory stereotypes. This sort of charge is understandable because, if Amis does not seem directly to endorse such oppressive categorizing, he seems unwilling or unable to privilege as authoritative any other discourses, including those which could contest it.

It is interesting that Nicola may be viewed as a postmodernist author who ultimately finds the doubleness of which Hutcheon writes intolerable, in a way that Amis seems not to. She, too, confronts the crisis of legitimation which, according to Jean-François Lyotard, is an effect of the 'incredulity toward metanarratives' that characterizes the postmodern condition.[31] This incredulity is shown by her refusal to equate the narratives current in contemporary society with reality. Unlike most of the other characters in the novel, she is acutely sensitive to the baselessness of these messages: '"[t]hey believe in each other's lies just like they believe in television"' (p. 342), she says contemptuously of Keith and his cronies. In contrast, she knows that the roles which she plays and the scenarios which she skilfully improvises have no underlying reality. A trained actress, she is also the most intelligent and successful of the author-figures who are competing to dictate the narrative shape of the novel which they inhabit: '[s]he outwrote me,' writes Samson after completing the plot which she has designed by murdering her (in his unrealized version, Keith, not he, is to be the murderer). 'Her story worked. And mine didn't' (p. 466). She has more power and freedom than any of the other characters in manipulating and revising the ready-made scripts of society, but paradoxically the exercise of this freedom entails her own oppression . . . the plots which she orchestrates necessitate that she enact and parody the very roles which feminists have rejected as limiting and destructive: those of Madonna and whore, which she plays for Guy and Keith respectively. Her detached awareness that these roles do not express her essential identity and her cold-blooded ability to use these parts for an ulterior purpose do not, when all is said and done, liberate her from them. She exaggerates the two personas to such an extreme extent that she manages to heap parodic scorn on them, but she embodies them nevertheless. The only escape from this doubleness is death, not as meaningless extinction but as narrative closure, the ineluctable conclusion of a self-fulfilling prophecy of doom: '[i]t was fixed. It was written. The murderer was not yet a murderer. But the murderee had always been a murderee' (p. 18).

Amis is open to criticism for limiting Nicola's options so radically. If the self is a social construct, why – in a time when women are struggling to fashion new, fulfilling identities for themselves – is Nicola restricted to only two unpalatable choices? It is true that the novel recounts formative childhood experiences which predispose her to choose these roles (pp. 15–21). But this simply raises another question: why did Amis decide to motivate her in this way and not some other? Perhaps this is tantamount to asking more generally why his point of view on humanity has to be misanthropic, why the novel's vision has to be so thoroughly nihilistic. I cannot answer these questions, but I do contend that the bleakness of *London Fields* subserves a carnivalesque comic and satiric energy which, however, is implicated in the culture which it ridicules and attacks.[32] □

Where Holmes relates the concern with murder in *London Fields* to the notion of the 'death of the author', Peter Stokes's 1997 essay 'Martin Amis and the Postmodern Suicide' contends that the problem at stake in the novel is 'of larger proportion than the death of the author or the formlessness of the subject. Here those threats are compounded by others – the possible destruction of the literary archive, and possibly the destruction of the world.'[33] In the following extract, Stokes ingeniously argues that in *London Fields* the death of the author (Samson Young), his book, and Nicola Six represent 'a simulated apocalypse in microcosm', a sacrifice by Samson that supplants 'global nuclear apocalypse':

■ The narrator of *London Fields* is a failed American writer named Samson Young. Sam has arrived in London at the end of the millennium after securing an apartment swap with a successful English novelist, Mark Asprey, who signs his welcome note to Sam, M. A. Sam, who can't – as he explains again and again – make anything up and thus flounders as a writer, soon grows jealous of the many trophies and awards decorating the Asprey home. Reading an Asprey text found around the apartment, Sam becomes demoralized by the incredible success a hack novelist like Asprey enjoys. Sam's own writerly luck changes, however, when he chances upon a true story unfolding before his eyes. He uncovers some diaries that predict the end of the world. He then searches out the diarist and watches as the predictions unfold – and that story, which he records, becomes the narrative of *London Fields*. The story is, Sam assures his readers, a 'true story', but 'unified, dramatic and pretty saleable' (p. 1). At the novel's end, after taking a fatal dose of pills, Sam reports feeling – much like John Self at the end of *Money* – 'seamless and insubstantial, like a creation. As if someone made me up, for money' (p. 470). Believing that he has once again failed as a writer, Sam appoints his rival, Asprey, as his 'literary executor', believing that Asprey will honor his deathbed request to destroy the manuscript, to 'throw everything out'. And yet Sam goes to his death with a nagging uncertainty, and thus his suicide note to Asprey concludes with the question: '[y]ou didn't set me up. Did you?' (p. 468). Asprey is, Amis explains to Will Self, 'an anti-writer', successful but terrible – 'really', Amis continues, 'a deflected parody of the hatred I feel aimed at me'.[34]

The answer to Sam's question then, of course, is yes. The ruse of *London Fields* is that it appears to be an appropriation – not merely plagiarism, but out-right theft – of another author's work. As Amis's remarks to Will Self indicate, Asprey is another version of himself, another M. A., and Amis has indeed set Sam up – and Sam is indeed a creation, made up, for money. At a variety of levels, then, *London Fields* works as a kind of joke about plagiarism, or *text-theft*. Amis, disguised as Asprey, appears to have stolen the novel from Samson Young. In *London Fields*, then, as in *Money*, Amis attempts to problematize the credibility of narrative authority en route to suggesting that such authority is essentially formless, insubstantial. As with *Money*, though, in *London Fields* that formlessness is once again valued positively. The text is free to travel, surviving even its author's suicide. Because the author function is transfigured here as a composite author, the text is offered other means of finding its way into circulation, into print. Amis's novel thus plays with the notion of text-theft in such a way as to suggest that disconnecting a text from its author is the best way to keep it moving, to get it read. Indeed, those disconnections take place at several levels in the novel.

. . . for example, Sam has in fact stolen the narrative from someone else's text – the diarist's. In that way, the novel underscores the significance of this multi-authoring from the very start. The novel begins, then, in 1999 when Sam arrives in London where he fortuitously happens upon his true story – fortuitous because Sam, who has not written anything in years, assures his readers that he cannot write fiction. Staring out the window of his London apartment, Sam happens to see a woman – whom he had just seen earlier that day, for the first time in his life, in a pub called the Black Cross – throw out a bundle of diaries. Intrigued, Sam recovers the diaries, which turn out to be the property of Nicola Six, a mysterious woman living in London. As her diaries indicate, since childhood Nicola has had visions. In those visions she knows what's going to happen before it happens. Or so it seems. Ever since she was a little girl, Nicola has seen visions of London with rings circling outward from the center – ground zero. As the novel begins, however, *that event* at least has not come to pass. Nicola's life takes a new course when she has a vision of her own death. She ceases to record any more visions in her diaries and even throws the diaries away. Through the last of her recorded visions Nicola comes to know the minute, hour, and date of her death, as well as how it will be carried out – murder, involving a car, a car-tool and a dead-end street. Yet Nicola does not know who the murderer will be. She knows the certain end of her life's story, but she does not know how her life will arrive at this end – just as she envisions the destruction of London by bombs without knowing how that end will be achieved. Her vision, ultimately, is one of her own mortality coupled together with the end of the world. Entering the Black Cross one afternoon, Nicola encounters Keith Talent, a kind of over-grown Dickensian street urchin, a professional cheat and darts champion. Later that afternoon Nicola writes in her diaries, for the last time before throwing them away, that she has found her murderer: "'I've found him. On the Portobello Road, in a place called the Black Cross, I found him'" (p. 22).

As Amis describes it to Self, '*London Fields* began life as a novella. It was going to be a sixty-page story called "The Murderee". There was going to be a Keith figure and a Nicola figure, just moving towards each other and then the deed would occur'.[35] . . . Given the environmental and nuclear catastrophes threatening the world at the close of the 1980s, Amis began to wonder, '[i]s the planet the murderee?'.[36] *London Fields*, then, is a meditation on the possibility that the world – in an anthropomorphized sense – *wants* to die, with Nicola representing a kind of suicidal earth-figure, but a suicide in need of assistance. Originally Amis conceived of this assistance coming Nicola's way through Keith. But as the story developed, Amis explains to Self, more characters were added, including, as Amis puts it, 'the narrator' – Sam – 'who became a kind of actor'.[37]

After discovering Nicola's diaries, Sam begins writing out her prophecy-in-progress – indicating already that his authorial voice is a composite one. As the novel begins, the coming end of the millennium, a vague but quickly developing world crisis, as well as a fast approaching total eclipse, and Nicola Six's self-prophesied murder all converge in one critical mass of apocalyptic suspense. As a low-life – if somewhat failed – street tough, Keith makes for a near perfect murderer. Coincidentally, Keith has the most prestigious darts final of his career on the same evening as Nicola's prophesied murder, the eclipse of the sun, and the end of the world. By now the thoroughness of those metaphorical substitutions ought to be clear. As Sam writes, to Keith '[t]he whole world was darts' [in the text, this is immediately followed by a qualifying statement: 'well, maybe'], but then, as Sam also notes, 'the whole world – on certain screens, in certain contingency plans – was definitely a dartboard' (p. 396). It makes sense then that Nicola, upon entering the Black Cross and seeing Keith for the first time, should feel that she had found her murderer. As Sam later emphasizes, however, Keith was not alone in the Black Cross that day. Sam was there, too. Nicola was right, she had found her murderer, but it was Sam, not Keith – Sam, who, as Amis indicates, entered the story to become a kind of *actor*. 'Always me', Sam writes at the close of his narrative, 'from the first moment in the Black Cross she looked my way with eyes of recognition. She knew that she had found him: her murderer' (p. 466).

Yet Sam undergoes great struggles on the way to becoming an actor within his own narrative. Like Nicola, he knows how the story is meant to end, but he does not know – anymore than Nicola – how the story will get there. He is, of course, ambivalent about helping to bring the story any nearer its inevitable end by his own hand. He feels certain the world will end, but with his own health waning too, his patience begins to run out: 'I'm not one of those excitable types who get caught making things up. Who get caught improving on reality. I can embellish, I can take certain liberties. Yet to invent the bald facts of a life (for example) would be quite beyond my powers' (p. 39). As a result, the development of Sam's story, of his documentary – as he decides to think of it – is stalled:

> I guess I could just wing it. But all I know for sure is the very last scene. The car, the car-tool, the murderer waiting in his car, the murderee, ticking towards him on her heels. I don't know how to get to the dead-end street. I close my eyes, trying to see a way – how do writers *dare* do what they do? – and there's just chaos. It seems to me that writing brings trouble with it, moral trouble, unexamined trouble (p. 117).

Finally, Sam recognizes that if Nicola's prophesy is going to come off, he will have to act himself, he will have to invent – to save his story. But the entrance of the author into his own apocalyptic narrative changes the course of everything.

The eclipse comes and goes; Keith loses his darts final, and Nicola is murdered. But Sam has taken Keith's place as the murderer. The car is Keith's, the car-tool is Keith's, but it is Sam who is waiting at the dead-end street. By appropriating Keith's authorship of the murder Sam has changed the course of events – the course of the novel he is writing. Writing and invention are simply, despite Sam's protestations to the contrary, the same thing. And when the future has to be written, when the future awaits being written, then the future is no done-deal but simply the blank space at the end of the page awaiting new inscriptions. The future, after all, like nuclear war, like the apocalypse, is a literary event – an ellipsis, a potential, a not-yet waiting to be written into existence. Sam recognizes that at the end of his narrative: 'I'm in it' (p. 464), he remarks, more than a little surprised at the obviousness of the fact. Writing is an act of complicity, and in writing there are no safe spaces from which one may merely observe. In this action then – murdering Nicola and taking enough pills to end his own life – Samson, as his name suggests, pulls down the roof on himself and all that he has come to perceive as the enemy of his story: the future prophesied by Nicola Six.

Rather than a global nuclear apocalypse, then, *London Fields* delivers a simulated apocalypse in microcosm – represented in the deaths of Nicola, the author, and his book. Thus Sam's re-authoring of Nicola's premise and his rewriting of her apocalyptic plot have the effect of supplanting global destruction with his own Samson-like sacrifice. Sam undertakes that sacrifice because he has learned over the course of the novel that Nicola's inevitable end, and even his own inevitable end, are not the same as the end of the world. Before his suicide, then, Sam assembles his 'Endpapers' (p. 468) and leaves two suicide notes: one, to Mark Asprey asking him to destroy all records of these events and another to Kim Talent – the infant daughter of Keith and secret heroine of the novel who slowly comes to represent for Sam a hopeful alternative to the apocalyptic teleology [ending] of his own story – asking her nothing more nor less than to outlive him. And so the story ends, much as Sam imagined it would from the beginning, with himself and Nicola dead. Yet the story of *London Fields* survives him, because Asprey turns out to be Sam's executor in several senses. Asprey does function as Sam's literary executor, but he evidently acts against Sam's instructions – he does not destroy the text, otherwise there would be no way to explain the existence of a document called *London Fields*. But Asprey is Sam's executor in a second sense, in that he does seem – as Sam suspects before his death – to have set Sam up to die. Ultimately, Sam – like John Self in *Money* – turns out to be the dupe of an authorial conspiracy he had not foreseen.

The conspiracy against Sam appears to have been co-authored by Asprey and Nicola. In the course of *London Fields* Sam learns to his surprise that Nicola is an acquaintance of Asprey's – and a former lover. That fact more than any other exacerbates Sam's jealousy of Asprey. His jealousy is somewhat assuaged when Nicola admits that Asprey's writing is terrible – and she even confesses to having recklessly destroyed one of Asprey's novels. At the close of London Fields, however, it becomes apparent that Asprey, Nicola, and Sam have all come to rely on one another in some rather complex ways. And it appears that an elaborate deal has been struck, one that necessarily includes setting Sam up. Nicola needs Sam for a murderer. Sam needs Nicola for her story. And Asprey needs the two of them to replace his destroyed novel. It seems, then, that Asprey agrees to provide Nicola with a murderer by swapping his apartment for Sam's, so long as Nicola provides him with a replacement novel, to be produced by Sam. That arrangement explains why Nicola, after spying Sam for the first time in [the] Black Cross, throws away her diaries outside Asprey's window – where she knows Sam is watching. The destruction of one book, then, produces another. And the destruction of one story does not mean that it cannot be replaced by another. Nicola's vandalizing of Asprey's text obligates her to replace it. Asprey provides Sam, who will produce the book that Asprey – as a disguised Amis – will later pass off as his own. Thus the novel survives the death of its author, and circulates wherever it may.

In this way *London Fields* carries on the work begun by Amis in *Money* of problematizing the authority and fixity of the author figure. In both novels Amis values that problematization positively – and thus, by transfiguring the author as a composite, the text is offered other means of finding its way into circulation, of being disseminated. Disconnecting a text from its author, then, appears to be one strategy for making sure that the death of an author need not require the death of the narrative. The novel functions as a critique of the easy equation between personal catastrophe and global catastrophe, between an apocalyptic mood and an apocalyptic catastrophe, between a discursive agent and discourse as an agent. *London Fields* is, after all, a novel with an argument. It argues that literary discourse has a part to play in redirecting the future of nuclear and apocalyptic discourse alike. It is important, then, that an argument such as that survive its author – and be thought of apart from the authority of the author figure – in order to emphasize that such authority really resides in discourses such as those that hold the power of scripting the future.

As Foucault asks at the close of 'What Is an Author?': '[w]hat difference does it make who is speaking?'. And as Foucault argues, questions other than the identity of the author need to be asked: '[w]hat are the modes of existence of [a] discourse? Where has it been used, how can it circulate, and who can appropriate it for himself?'.[38] Like Foucault's essay, Amis's fiction suggest that discourses need to be thought of in terms of their social function – as means of agency. Amis's novels argue that postwar nuclear discourse has changed fundamental social relationships in important ways. Rather than try to halt that change, Amis's work tries to operate within that apocalyptic discourse in order to redirect it. Thus at the end of *London Fields* the roof is indeed brought down upon Samson and Nicola, but all the novel's other characters survive – and those that survive carry on with their lives, informed by that apocalyptic experience in miniature. What Amis's recent fiction underscores, then, is the power of discourse, rather than the power of the author. And as postnuclear subjects everywhere learn to write about nuclear weapons, that discourse will be redirected toward new ends.

In a recent interview with Graham Fuller in the Spring 1995 issue of *Interview*, Amis reflected on the changes within the discourse of apocalypse in the half dozen years since *London Fields*: 'the big question of the second half of this century was, What are we going to do with nuclear weapons? Now that we've got out of the emotional idea that it could all end tomorrow, we can look at other things'.[39] A feeling of suspense continues to insinuate itself within all manner of public discourses as the twentieth century comes to a close, but Amis argues that a kind of corner has been turned, and that those who have been learning how to write about nuclear weapons are also learning how to act – how to become actors in the endless unfolding of that discourse on the end . . . now, postmodern fiction pushes literary discourse beyond the apocalyptic horizon – to a place where the future awaits being rewritten, with new endings.[40] □

But if, as Stokes suggests, *London Fields*, for all its apocalyptic quality, finally implies, optimistically, that the future can be rewritten, that apocalypse can be avoided, what about the past, where the script of history, like a pact with the devil, is written indelibly in blood, where, in Heidegger's famous phrase, 'the dreadful has already happened'? The past can be rewritten, it can be relived, but it cannot be changed, ever: this is the theme of Martin Amis's next novel, which takes on that most harrowing and highly-charged of twentieth-century topics: the Holocaust.

CHAPTER EIGHT

Wrong in Time: *Time's Arrow* (1991)

MARTIN AMIS was well aware of the dangers of taking on the Holocaust in *Time's Arrow*, particularly for a novelist with his reputation. In an interview with Christopher Bigsby, published in 1992, he said:

■ When you start a book like this you are terrified by what George Steiner is going to think of you [George Steiner is a prominent literary and cultural critic who is much possessed by the Holocaust and has himself written a short, powerful novel, *The Portage to San Cristobal of A.H.* (1981) about Hitler's reasons for perpetrating it[1]]. I was astonished that this was my subject. If you had asked me two years ago whether I could write about the Holocaust, something I had long been interested in, I would have said that I was perhaps the least qualified living writer to do it. But once you have got over that you have to say to yourself, very early on, that I bring what I bring to this subject. I can't become another kind of writer because of the subject.[2] □

In a later interview in the USA with Eleanor Wachtel, first published in 1996, Amis expands on how *Time's Arrow* came about:

■ I was thinking of writing a story of a man's life backwards in time and then I read a book by a friend of mine, Robert J[ay] Li[f]ton's *The Nazi Doctors* (1986) . . . after a couple of days of reading Li[f]ton's book, I saw that in fact I was going to write about [the Holocaust]. I thought if you did this world backwards, there would be a real point – the inversion is so complete. And the inversion that Li[f]ton talks about is 'the healing-killing paradox'.

I felt I was in a forest of taboos throughout writing this book. This is the most difficult and sensitive subject ever, I think, but I do believe, as a writer, that there are no No Entry signs. People say, legitimately in a way, what am I as an Aryan doing with this subject? But I'm writing not about the Jews, I'm writing about the perpetrators, and they are my brothers, if you like. I feel a kind of responsibility in my Aryaness for what happened. That is my racial link with these events, not with the sufferers but with the perpetrators.[3] □

In his remarks to Wachtel, Amis identifies three important aspects of *Time's Arrow*: its concern with the responsibility of the perpetrators of the Holocaust; its reverse narrative technique; and the influence of Lifton's *The Nazi Doctors*. All of these aspects will be further explored in the critical extracts in this chapter.

The initial review response to *Time's Arrow* suggested that Amis had brought it off. For example, the distinguished critic Frank Kermode, writing in the *London Review of Books*, affirmed: '[f]or the author it was an extraordinary feat – for readers it is a genuine test – of imagination',[4] while in the *Times Literary Supplement*, M. John Harrison declared that 'as an act of imagination, *Time's Arrow* has the hallmark of something earned, struggled for, originated'.[5] This time a Martin Amis novel did make the Booker Prize shortlist,[6] although the award went to Ben Okri's *The Famished Road*, a decision denounced by a writer who – as Martin Amis might once have seemed the least likely living author to tackle the Holocaust – might similarly have seemed the least likely person to approve of a Martin Amis novel: the conservative philosopher and polemicist – who has also himself written two novels – Roger Scruton. Selecting *Time's Arrow* as one of his 'International Books of the Year' in the *Times Literary Supplement* of 13 December 1991, Scruton complained of the relative lack of objectivity with which English writers had been treated in that year:

■ Apart from the award of the Booker Prize to the fey and pseudo-sensitive Ben Okri, we have witnessed the slovenly butchering of Martin Amis on grounds of immorality, despite (or maybe because of) the fact that *Time's Arrow* is the first Martin Amis novel to contain the faintest hint of a moral idea. It is also, in my view, brilliant.[7] □

Scruton's surprising endorsement epitomised the way in which, as a result of *Time's Arrow*, a sense was starting to develop that Martin Amis had sustained and developed his stylistic and structural brilliance while moving into a new area of seriousness and responsibility.

In the years since its first publication, *Time's Arrow* has continued to earn critical respect and attention. A sustained and insightful example of this is provided in Donald E. Morse's 1995 essay 'Overcoming Time: "The Present of Things Past" in History and Fiction'. Morse begins by addressing what he calls 'the age-old human fantasy of beginning again, living life again, or of being given another life to live'[8] and points to a variety of forms in which this desire emerges in contemporary popular culture in English, from past regressions to films about vampires who continue to haunt and drain the living. Morse then moves on to offer a perceptive exploration of *Time's Arrow* as one example[9] of a novel 'which address[es] the problem of representing the no longer perceivable past within the present':[10]

■ In *Time's Arrow* as the river of time flows forward the main character Odilo Unverdorben . . . moves backward [and] a nameless narrator . . . puzzles over both the movement and nature of time as well as his own nature and identity. Knowing only duration and mistakenly assuming that he has just commenced rather than re-commenced life, the narrator continually misreads signs and misinterprets events including such decisive ones as death and birth and essential distinctions such as backwards and forwards . . . . . . The narrator's ignorance of time's direction creates irony in the novel in much the same way that Oedipus's ignorance of his past creates irony in *Oedipus Rex*. In Sophocles's play the king laudably tries to rid his land of a plague by banishing whomever is responsible but discovers to his horror that the source of the country's illness lies in past events of which he himself was the cause but which he is now powerless to change. Similarly Odilo in *Time's Arrow* condemned to replay his life – for like Oedipus it is far too late for him to change events – runs backward on his timeline until the moment when he anticipates '[[m]y father] will come in and kill me with his body'. After that he will divide into sperm and ovum which in turn will be re-absorbed harmlessly into his parents' bodies. His awareness of the end – in much the same way as Oedipus's dawning awareness of the truth – adds to his torment: 'Odilo knows this [that he will perish upon his father entering his mother] and feels this too' (p. 172) . . .

At the beginning of the novel Amis capitalizes on the comic effects created by treating literally a life being lived backwards: 'it is the garbage people [moving backwards] who bring me my reading matter' (p. 20). The first human conversation in the novel is printed in reverse:

'Dug. Dug,' says the lady in the pharmacy.
'Dug,' I join in. 'Oo y'rrah?'
'Aid ut oo y'rrah?'
'Mh-mm,' she'll say, as she unwraps my hair lotion (p. 14).

Readers will quickly reconstruct the conversation as '"Gud".' or good; '"harr'y oo"' or how are you?; '"Aid ut oo y'rrah?"' Harr'y oo tu dia or How are you today?

Amis does not continue using reverse spelling – the joke might quickly wear thin – but continues to indicate time's reversal by inverting the order of sentences within each conversation. This technique forces the reader to participate in this backwards running world since only by reconstructing the conversation in reverse can the reader affirm the normal temporal order. The words themselves which Odilo speaks backwards are all predetermined because he has said them all before. But then everything in his world – gesture, emotion, action – is completely and fully determined. 'I speak without volition', says the narrator, 'in the same way that I do everything else' (p. 14). For humans, as [J.T.] Fraser maintains: '[e]xpectations, memory and conscious experience – elements of the mental present working together – make us aware that our potentialities are greater than our possibilities. This awareness is manifest in a feeling that has a special name: it is called free will or human freedom'.[11] Odilo surrendered his free will and relin[q]uished any claim to human freedom in order to serve evil more fully as a Nazi doctor in the death camps, especially 'fiercely coprocentric' [centred on faeces] (p. 132) Auschwitz.

Amis suggests that choosing to do such evil negates the possibility of other choices making negation the essence of evil . . . As Erich Kahler notes: those Nazi doctors such as Odilo 'professionally attending to the most gruesome activities, seemed to act only with a certain part of their being, while another part was left behind, remained in the background . . . ';[12] the Nazi 'split in the personality reaches into unfathomable depths, it is total, it is consummate schizophrenia . . . The part that commits atrocities seems wholly impersonal and, accordingly, in-human in the literal sense of the word; indeed, we should rather call it a-human.'[13] In *Time's Arrow* the part left behind was the conscience, soul, or animating principle which Odilo's action negated – what remained was inhuman or a-human. Such negation as he practiced involves surrendering human freedom and ultimately hope. As Dante emphasized in the motto he chose for hell's gate 'Abandon All Hope / Ye Who Enter Here' those who forfeit all choice and freedom in effect choose hell – where by definition there can be no further choice. This utter lack of choice becomes Amis's theme, while his narrative method of moving literally backward through Odilo's life allows him to 'attend to the most gruesome activities' of this 'life that is unworthy of life' (p. 154) . . . . . .

[The twentieth century has witnessed both] the increasing scope and efficiency of destruction [and] increasingly widespread state sponsored torture that aims 'to coerce the personality of the individual into submission, to destroy self-worth'.[14] . . . Under the Nazis this purpose of 'mass dehumanization' was carried out with inconceivable efficiency using all the resources available to the modern highly industrialized state, yet with the chilling anonymity of the equally efficient modern bureaucracy . . . Moreover, as David H. Hirsch maintains in *The Deconstruction of Literature: Criticism After Auschwitz*:

The inescapable essence of Nazism lies not alone in its methods of mass killing nor in the bureaucratization of mass killing (though such monstrous inventions are not to be overlooked) but in its racist ideology, which led all too many of the German people to believe they were a superrace and the SS to believe they were gods ... This may be the reason that the SS had not only to kill their victims but to kill them mercilessly and to strip them of all human dignity before destroying them ... ... the SS men's belief in themselves as gods who not only enjoy the power to decide who will live and who will die, but who can also enjoy toying with their victims.[15]

It is this set of values that Amis mirrors when he models the traditional ruler of hell on the SS. Customarily, the devil meets people in their own image of him ... In *Time's Arrow* the towering nightmare figure who presides over hell proves a distorted image of Odilo clothed in a doctor's 'white coat (a medic's stark white smock)', the black jackboots of the SS, 'and a certain kind of smile'. He 'was ... a male shape, with an entirely unmanageable aura, containing such things as beauty, terror, love, filth, and above all power' (p. 12). Clearly this personage enjoys power, smiles while torturing victims – as did the SS 'who enjoy[ed] toying with their victims', and is in every way a monstrous perversion of the image of the helpful healer.

For the doctors of the deathcamps, such as Odilo, human beings were so much garbage to be disposed of during and after diabolical experiments in camp hospitals. It is, therefore, doubly fitting in his reversed hellish life that the narrator describe him and his fellow humans as 'kings of crap and trash' (p. 51); first: because hell is filled with excrement – Dante, for example, pictures Hell's inhabitants as not only existing in utter darkness but as themselves being only so much cosmic waste or garbage – and second: the death camps as described by most commentators were 'deliberately organized to become monuments to filth and excrement'.[16]

This reversed world perspective of *Time's Arrow* yields irony and comedy, while allowing Amis to confront the horror of the a-human:

[People] say hello when they mean goodbye. Lords of lies and trash – all kings of crap and trash.[17] Signs say No Littering – but who to? ... Government does that, at night, with trucks; or uniformed men come sadly at morning with their trolleys, dispensing our rubbish, and shit for the dogs (p. 51).

That last telling detail – 'and shit for the dogs' – convinces the reader of Amis's fictional reality ...

Everything of worth in Odilo's world – 'all sustenance, all meaning (and a good deal of money) issues [most appropriately] from a single household appliance: the toilet handle' (p. 18). He asks rhetorically: 'Where would Tod [one of Odilo's several false identities] and I be without the toilet? Where would we be without all the trash?' (p. 40). But the fullest irony derives from the worst events: after encountering the 'new smell in the air. The sweet smell [of the crematoria]' (p. 127) and observing 'the evening sky, hellish red with the gathering souls' (p. 128), Odilo begins the process of creation:

> It was I, Odilo Unverdorben, who personally removed the pellets of Zyklon B and entrusted them to the pharmacist in his white coat . . . . . . Entirely intelligibly, though, to prevent needless suffering, the dental work was *usually* [emphasis added] completed while the patients were not yet alive (p. 129).

* * *

> I am not 'in it' for the gratitude. No. I am 'in it' . . . because I love the human body and all living things . . . It is a war on death that now comes in many forms. As well as phenol we are obliged to extract prussic acid and sodium evipan (p. 144).

* * *

> I now extract benzene, gasoline, kerosene and air . . . Twenty cubic centimetres of air . . . with a hypodermic almost the size of a trombone and my right foot firmly stamped on the patient's chest, I continue to prosecute the war against nothing and air (p. 145).

His is truly, if ironically, 'creation' *ex nihilo* out of the nothing of trash, excrement, and ashes.

Bereft of choice, a king of crap flung backwards through time, Odilo himself in his torment will experience the privative nature of evil as he arrives at his early months ' . . . the world of an infant [where] before-and-after relations have no meaning'.[18] . . . As Odilo moves literally and physically from after to before his memories are erased along with that much consciousness . . . During his hellish trip to nonexistence Odilo encounters neither understanding nor possibility.

The soul's futile attempts to make sense out of experience fail, therefore, because without the crucial knowledge that time is running in reverse all of its theories or perceptions prove incorrect except the final one achieved in the very last moment of existence:

Look! Beyond, before the slope of pine, the lady archers are gathering with their targets and bows. Above, a failing-vision kind of light, with the sky fighting down its nausea. Its many nuances of nausea. When Odilo closes his eyes I see an arrow fly – but wrongly. Point-first (p. 173).

Intuitively, the soul realizes the implications of this wrong-headed arrow – the arrow of time of the book's title: 'Oh no', he says, 'but then . . . ' (p. 173). And the unfinished sentence tells all: Odilo's closed eyes and contentless dreams indicate how close he is to obliteration. The narrator this 'passenger or parasite' (p. 16), this conscience or soul, this spirit or essence, this 'I within' realizes at last the awful truth: 'I within, who came at the wrong time – either too soon [if life is lived backwards], or after it was all too late [if life is lived forwards]' (p. 173).[19] Thus at the end of the novel all illusions of benevolent good will shatter violently upon the soul's apprehension of the true direction of time's arrow. The truth about the direction of time and time's truth about Odilo's life also dissolve the dramatic tension between the soul – which Odilo long ago jettisoned – longing for redemption and the person actively choosing ruin. Stephen Donaldson contends 'it is the responsibility of every human being to create the meaning of his/her life' and the action of *Time's Arrow* implies that the large choices for such meaning will be either 'redemptive [or] . . . ruinous'.[20] The parasitic soul might still wish for redemption, but Odilo long ago chose ruin for them both . . . . . .

[L]ike virtually all of the Nazi death camp doctors and guards Odilo was as impotent morally and spiritually as he was impotent sexually. He traded his personal potency for omnipotence over others – 'I am omnipotent. Also impotent. I am powerful and powerless', he boasts and laments (p. 148). Rather than inviting his soul to travel the road with him, he rejected it. Only at death did the forgotten soul appear flung back out of 'the blackest sleep' (p. 11) forced to re-enter the corpse, to re-animate it until both could be safely dissolved into sperm and egg.

Amis says he borrowed this reverse movement for his plot from [Kurt Vonnegut's novel] *Slaughterhouse-Five* (1970) where Billy Pilgrim watches films backwards of World War II bombing raids over Germany. Each film ends happily with all the fire and destruction safely packed up into the bombs which then disappear into the bellies of the planes and are subsequently returned first to the factories to be taken apart and their components disposed of harmlessly in the earth.[21] . . . . . . Unlike Vonnegut . . . , Amis directs the focus of his novel not upon the innocence of those who suffer, but upon the diabolical psychology of those sworn to heal who volunteer as SS to torture and destroy systematically in clear violation of their Hippocratic oath, their common humanity – which they then forfeit – or any least dedication to the healing arts. But the atrocities committed by these Nazi doctors of which Odilo is the example are so mind-numbing, so brutally inhuman, as to appear almost beyond the reach of imaginative representation 'in either consciousness or discourse'.[22] As Hirsch summarizes:

> The futility of all attempts at [such] representation was encapsulated in Theodor Adorno's famous dictum (which he later recanted), that it is not possible to write poetry after Auschwitz.[23] . . . Basically, Adorno raises the issue that any literary representation of Nazi atrocities would aestheticize, and thus make acceptable, the horrors and cruelty.[24]

Amis's solution to this problem lies in following Vonnegut's model of the bombs which suck up fire and inventing a life lived in reversed time which in turn creates the almost diabolical illusion of accomplishing good works. Thus Odilo *removes* gas pellets from the death camp showers and returns them to the camp pharmacy, 'knock[s] together a human being out of the unlikeliest odds and ends' (p. 142), or most spectacular of all 'make[s] a people from the weather. From thunder, and from lightning. With gas, with electricity, with shit, with fire' (p. 128). Readers encountering such images but knowing however dimly or in whatever repressed fashion something of the historical truth, must then actively and painfully reverse them. By so involving the reader Amis insures that far from aestheticizing the atrocities or providing aesthetic pleasure from the misery and pain of the victims as Adorno feared,[25] this process renders them part of the reader's immediate experience since in re-reversing time as read the reader must impel time forward towards the full banality of its horror, for of all the potentialities which become possibilities, only one will be actualized. Thus historical reality is brought back to consciousness through imagination.

Amis achieves in *Time's Arrow* exactly what Adorno despaired of poetry or any imaginative literature accomplishing for as the reader goes through the novel inevitably, inexorably, the full awful truth of this evil with attendant horrors and cruelty strikes home. Far from being 'the native medium of evil . . . [which] obscures things'[26] time in Amis's novel serves to unmask evil. The reader is left confronting the debris of the past – the mud mixed with ashes . . .[27] ☐

Morse suggests how *Time's Arrow* avoids aestheticising Auschwitz by forcing its reader to re-reverse fictional time and thus imaginatively re-enact real history. The important issue of the way in which Amis's novel involves its readers is valuably developed further by Neil Easterbrook in his 1995 essay "'I know that it is to do with trash and shit, and that it is wrong in time": Narrative Reversal in Martin Amis'[s] *Time's Arrow'*. Easterbrook examines how Amis's novel explores evil-doing in such a way as to implicate the reader and thereby shake his or her complacent assumption that s/he would not perpetrate such crimes. His essay is also valuable because it takes up Amis's acknowledgement, in his 'Afterword' to *Time's Arrow*, that the novel 'would not and could not have been written without' Robert Jay Lifton's *The Nazi Doctors: Medical Killing and the Psychology of Genocide* (1986), and draws extensively and illuminatingly upon Lifton's and Eric Markusen's *The Genocidal Mentality Nazi Holocaust and Nuclear Threat* (1990) in analysing Amis's anatomy of evil.

■ Martin Amis's short but tremendously moving *Time's Arrow, or The Nature of the Offence* (1991) traces what Hannah Arendt once named 'the banality of evil', which the novel names as the protagonist's 'quiet dedication' (p. 142) to the Nazi cause. Although late in his life he is deeply critical of those who lack 'initiative', actually he was one who 'just follow[ed] orders' (p. 17), emphasizing for us the troubling fact that horrors such as Nazism and the death camps were possible only because of the massive scale efforts of ordinary, unremarkable 'people very much like ourselves'.[28] Rather than exculpating the Nazi protagonist, Amis'[s] genius is to excoriate complacent readers by crafting uncanny patterns so seductive readers can't help being drawn in, and thereby be implicated in the crime.

In *Time's Arrow* time itself runs backward, rendering the narrative 'a ghost-negative' that gradually unfolds his buried secret – that he had once assisted 'the worst man in the worst place at the worst time' (p. 12). We finally meet that man 114 pages later (and fifty years earlier) at Auschwitz: 'Uncle Pepi', the infamous Josef Mengele. As its plot moves backward in time from death toward birth some seventy-five years earlier, the story moves forward toward a reconstruction of a personal and political history hidden, obfuscated, and concealed by the 'sacred efficacy' (p. 130) of cash to erase memory and efface truth. Vladimir Nabokov once remarked that '[c]uriously, one cannot read a book: one can only reread it',[29] an especially apt description of literary dynamics where plot and story reciprocally reverse one another. Since the novel's 'film is running backwards' (p. 16), such narrative anachrony compels us to begin any exposition with the plot's conclusion, the narrator's birth.

'Odilo Unverdorben' (which in certain respects might translate as 'Adam Innocent') is born in 1916 in Solingen, coincidentally the birthplace ten years earlier of Adolf Eichmann (p. 170), the Gestapo overseer directly responsible for deporting and then murdering Jews at concentration camps. Odilo's father, wounded and 'ruined' (p. 172) by [t]he Great War, soon dies, leaving him to be raised by his mother, a nurse, who inspires Odilo's early interest in medicine. On a camping trip at thirteen, Odilo visits the site that will later become Auschwitz (p. 170). The only other remembered events of his youth concern rejection by women, homoerotic repression, and abuse by bigger boys: 'Odilo is innocent. Odilo is, it turns out, innocent, emotional, popular, and stupid' (p. 157). Stupidity doesn't stop him from entering medical school, where he marries Herta, a young secretary (all of his affairs with women will concern either immediate subordinates or prostitutes). But '[w]hat could appear to be stupidity', as Robert Jay Lifton reminds us in *The Genocidal Mentality . . .* 'is better explained as an - ideological constellation',[30] which must be the reason for Odilo's matriculation. Once married, however, he finds himself impotent and subjects his wife to a series of beatings and eroticized humiliations (pp. 157–9); they eventually have a child (Eva), although Odilo will abandon both.

After graduation, he goes to work at *Schloss Hartheim* (p. 152), a Renaissance castle converted to medical laboratory[31] where doctors experiment with the techniques later fully developed in the death camps, as Odilo discovers in his first posting at Treblinka (p. 151). Commissioned as an officer, he then serves a stint in the Waffen SS. In 1942, at age twenty-five, he joins the Kat-Zet (K Z) and becomes assistant to 'Uncle Pepi' (the name always appears within scare quotes) at Auschwitz (p. 142). By 1944 he is helping kill 'the Hungarian Jews, and at an incredible rate, something like 10,000 a day' (p. 137).[32] The slaughter accelerates until, just before Russian troops arrive, Odilo escapes (p. 124), eventually making his way to Rome, where in exchange for some gold an Irish emissary of the Vatican helps him obtain a new identity (pp. 110–21). The gold, of course, 'came direct from the *Reichsbank*' (p. 130), as extracted from the pockets and wrists and even the teeth of its Jewish victims. These 'fruits of [his] meticulous vandalism' (p. 26) both enable his escape and act as the very agency of amnesia, its instrument of historical erasure.

Taking the first of his 'pseudonyms . . . noms de guerre' (p. 110), in 1946 Hamilton de Souza is in Portugal, comfortably ensconced within a rich villa (pp. 110–17); in 1948, he sails for America (p. 98) as John Young (pp. 76–110), who, aided by another Nazi taking the alias 'Kreditor' (p. 79), finds work in a Manhattan hospital. At some point in the '60s, Kreditor discovers accusations have been made against Young, who then becomes Tod Friendly and flees New York (p. 76), ending up a wealthy senior doctor at an HMO [Health Maintenance Organization] in a prototypical American suburb exemplifying

'America's pretty pluralism' (p. 25). Although he retreats into 'watery oblivion' (p. 69) and a 'muffled self' (p. 92) as 'Friendless Friendly' (p. 71), in his 70s he dies a quiet death – of a heart attack (p. 11), an ironic commentary on the Nazi euphemism *Gnadentod* ('mercy death') that Nazis held they brought to Jewish misery. In German, *tod* means 'death'; 'Tod Friendly' then explicitly suggests *Gnadentod*, just as 'John Young' earlier signifies his renewed potency.

Devoted to exploring the central conceit of time reversal invariance[33] and establishing the pattern of identification which will eventually implicate readers, the novel's first sixty pages slowly unveil the wholly unremarkable, mundane, and trivial life of Tod Friendly. Beyond the promise that readers will uncover Tod's hidden secret, what is fascinating about the opening pages is how Amis works through the occasionally comic reversal of time's arrow. . . . If time runs backward, then the most quotidian events have an altogether different cast: mail arrives not from the postman but from the trash can (p. 135); food flows from stomach to plate to carton to grocery shelf (p. 19); twice a week housemaids enter a sparkling home, 'dirty all the dishes', then drop money on the counter before leaving (p. 102). Comic reversals find their tragic complement in more subtly allegorical events: '[w]ith one fierce and skilful kick of his aching foot, he will mend a deep concavity in the refrigerator's flank. With a butt of his head he will heal the fissured bathroom mirror . . . ' (p. 63) . . .

. . . [T]he narrative serves as the reader's double, an 'I' who comes to consciousness in Tod's journey backward into history. This 'I' has 'no name and no body' (p. 155), has 'no access to his thoughts – but I am awash with his emotions' (p. 15). It begins as the Nazi doctor's alter ego, but just as the reader's initial identification with the protagonist is gradually estranged and defamiliarized, it eventually 'slip[s] out from under him' (p. 155); produced by a 'parallax' of perspective (p. 57), it is 'nauseatingly sundered' (p. 100) by the sheer weight of bearing witness to the unconcealment of Tod's history.

While this observing 'I' is the eye-witness, it is not a conscience or a soul; in fact, as one of Tod's lovers rightly observes, Tod 'has no soul' (p. 62). So the narrator-witness hovers above events, experiencing them with precisely the distance of the narratee, thereby doubling readers' experience. Yet this bifurcation or sundering is true of Tod/Odilo himself: '[h]e sheds the thing he often can't seem to bear: his identity, his quiddity . . . ' (p. 57). As estranged from himself as from all humanity, his 'search for invisibility' (p. 71) is 'evasive action . . . flight' (p. 108) from moral consciousness, which he finds 'weary, multiform, intolerable' (p. 78), rendering him more 'like a brilliant robot' (p. 127) than human being. This heterodiegetic defamiliarization follows the conventions of the central narrative trope and identifies the

Nazi rationalizations for genocide: 'I immolate myself in denial' (p. 96). [Easterbrook's endnote (p. 60, note 6) is inserted here for convenience: 'Heterodiegetic' denotes a narrator divorced or absent from his own first-person narrative; see [Gérard] Genette's *Narrative Discourse* [(New York: Columbia University Press, 1980), trans. Jane Lewin]. The sense of 'defamiliarization' I have in mind is developed, in variously differing ways, by Viktor Shklovsky and Walter Benjamin.] Odilo, however, moves backward from disavowal to reality. Consequently, he passes through one 'deracinating spectacle' (p. 125) after another, uprooting and replacing a sense of self articulated only by its ability to forget and to erase and to evade the real meaning of events. While he has no difficulty recognizing human agency, the essence of human subjectivity eludes both Tod and the narrator. For while Odilo and Herta's baby 'exerts colossal power *as a subject*' (p. 135), Odilo cannot comprehend, cannot countenance this moral and ontological power. The narrator finds this disjunction between human subjectivity and its articulation especially pronounced in German, where for an English audience the pronoun 'I' is divorced from its transparency: '"*Ich*". Not a masterpiece of reassurance, is it? *I* sounds nobly erect. *Je* has a certain strength and intimacy. *Eo*'s okay . . . But *Ich*? It sounds like the sound a child makes when it confronts its own . . . Perhaps that's part of the point' (p. 134; second ellipsis is original). In fact, the narrative is the story of Odilo's confrontation with his own ordure.

Who this narrating 'I' is necessarily never finds exact articulation, but its insistent movement remains absolutely clear. Together, they are headed somewhere: '[p]arasite or passenger, I am travelling there with him. It will be bad. It will be bad, and not intelligible . . . I will know the nature of the offence. Already I know this. I know that it is to do with trash and shit, and that it is wrong in time' (pp. 72, 73). Their journey is to '[a] place without depth. And a place without time': Auschwitz, where time has 'no arrow' (p. 151).

Because the narrator moving forward remains always distanced from the events unfolding backward, there exists a bitterly ironic disparity between the memory of events and their revisionary interpretation. In almost every respect, Odilo's pathology parallels the psychological profile of the Nazi doctor outlined by Lifton, who names the Nazi doctors' two m[o]st notable traits 'doubling' and 'psychic numbing':

'Psychic numbing' is a form of dissociation characterized by the diminished capacity or inclination to feel, and usually includes separation of thought from feeling. 'Doubling' carries the dissociative process still further with the formation of a functional second self, related to but more or less autonomous from the prior self.[34]

What Amis does is manifest these traits in Odilo, whose disavowal is precisely the one Lifton identifies: 'repudiation not of the reality itself but of the meaning of that reality'.[35]

As Odilo, the narrator radically misreads every event at Auschwitz. For instance, he thinks himself an angel, a god, a creator restoring dead Jewish bodies to life: '[i]t was I, Odilo Unverdorben, who personally removed the pellets of Zyklon B and entrusted them to the pharmacist in his white coat' (p.129); who then moves on to return glasses or gold fillings, reunite husband with wife, usher prisoners to trains bound homeward, channel repatriated Jews 'back into society' (p.149). Each physical transformation is miraculous, but utterly unremarkable: 'stunning successes were as cheap as spit' (p.132). Unlike the empirical reversals marking the novel's early pages, none of these ironies is presented as humorous; instead, their shocking misreadings continually bespeak the barbaric cruelty and ruthlessness of systematic massacre. Gassing, for example, was actually selected because it was 'humane',[36] even though Himmler admired its efficiency . . . . . .

Such potent, virulent absurdities are at the core of *Time's Arrow*. Amis vividly articulates a consciousness that could so divorce itself from humanity as to serve as a guard, doctor, or officer at Auschwitz. Here, where 'there was a sadistic irony at work' (p.163), names are always *pseudonyms, noms de guerre*: the officer's quarters at Auschwitz is 'our *clubhouse*' (p.127 [Easterbrook's italics]), the ovens '*Heavenblock*', the sprinkle room 'the *central hospital*', and an officer's tour '*Sommerfrische*', fresh summer air (p.133). And . . . the protagonist's several names offer thinly disguised commentaries on his ideology, beginning with innocence and ending with death.[37]

The disparity between Odilo and his narrator-witness models the doublings and reversals that characterize Odilo's identity as a Third Reich physician. 'I am omnipotent. Also impotent' (p.148), he remarks, underscoring one curious 'characteristic of Nazi doctors' [identified by Lifton], their 'mixture of omnipotence and impotence'.[38] This mixture was produced, Lifton argues, by the 'Auschwitz self' – defined by

> reversals of healing and killing, the operative Nazi biomedical vision, the extreme numbing that rendered killing no longer killing, struggles with omnipotence (deciding who would live or die) and impotence (being a cog in a powerful machine), maintaining a medical identity while killing, and somehow finding meaning in the environment.[39]

The 'Auschwitz self' structured the transformation of morality by logistics ['logistics' is, strictly speaking, the 'art of moving, lodging and supplying troops and equipment' but takes on here a wider (and darker) meaning, applying to the skills of organising the Nazi concentration camps]; as Odilo comments, 'the triumph of Auschwitz was essentially organizational' (p. 132). Amis has closely followed Lifton's profile of the genocidal mentality, right down to the detail that Odilo, who has 'a modest talent for neuropsychiatry' (p. 149), should therefore find himself delivering the Zyklon B, for the gas chamber doctors were most frequently psychiatrists.

But the Nazi doctors also displayed traits Lifton doesn't emphasize, such as their lust for wealth and, when apprehended, their 'chronic diffidence' (p. 115). Refusing to take responsibility for their actions, they instead incessantly whined about their own suffering,[40] nicely represented when Odilo shifts emphasis away from his own incredible evasion of responsibility to the 'incredible invasion' (p. 62) of his privacy, which of course is the narrative itself. Since the narrator has no access to Odilo's thoughts, we only get glimpses of his rationalizations and moral equivocations; *awash with his emotions*, however, the narrator does witness to the experience of the place.

And indeed creating analog[ues] of that experience is what constitutes the novel's brilliance. *Time's Arrow* contains several image clusters and recurrent motifs that disclose Odilo's Auschwitz self. I mention only one: '[t]he Auschwitz universe, it has to be allowed, was fiercely coprocentric. It was *made* of shit' (p. 132). While at the beginning of the novel the central conceit of recursive temporality [that is, of reversing time] produces merely scatological humour (pp. 18–19), it quickly takes on allegorical resonance – the Nazi doctor gradually expels nourishment to *ingest* shit: '[t]his stuff, this human stuff, at normal times (and in civilized locales) tastefully confined to the tubes and runnels, subterranean, unseen – this stuff had burst its banks, surging outward and upward on to the floor, the walls, the very ceiling of life'. Amis drags us through such '[o]rdure, ordure everywhere' (p. 125). The obvious, telling trope reveals the Nazi cognate of *order* as *ordure* ['cognate' means 'of [the] same linguistic family; representing [the] same original word or root'] and Nazi deity the apotheosis of defecation: '[w]hen he swears, Odilo invokes human ordure, from which, as we now know, all human good eventually emanates' (p. 123).

The novel's treatment of psychic time makes it a parable of what Freud called *Nachträglichkeit*, the revisionary retroactivity that belatedly recasts the past as a repetition of the present; it is the rereading or reinterpretation of past events that then structures 'primary revision' in the return of the repressed: '[s]omewhere in the severe dance of this roiling sleep I can sense the beginnings of a profound rearrangement, as if everything bad might soon be good, as if everything wrong might soon be right' (pp. 115–16). It is *Nachträglichkeit* which directly structures the sort of revisionary history that would obscure or deny the Holocaust.

In fact, the ethical problems produced by reversing time parallel ironies predicated entirely by the novel's textuality: '[l]ike writing, paintings seem to hint at a topsy-turvy world in which, so to speak, time's arrow moves the other way. The invisible speedlines suggest a different nexus of sequence and process' (p. 95). The narrator, everywhere present but nowhere visible, as in Flaubert's famous phrase,[41] allegorizes a Jewish double: the narrator literally reads backward (p. 51). What this self-reflexive textuality represents, I think, is the total inability of National Socialism to understand the Other as another Self in the reciprocal relation of intersubjectivity, which Emmanuel Levinas has named 'being-for-the-other'. We see this denial throughout the novel, beginning with Tod's refusal to look in the mirror (p. 17). Belatedly, readers recognize the banalization of evil effected by an affected amnesia.

In the novel's final paragraphs, Odilo confronts the inevitable, his own dissolution because of his father's toxic potency. Father erases son by impregnating his mother (p. 172), a hard joke about original sin and the causes of Nazi genocide, a sort of Oedipal double reversal. All of these passages compel readers toward reflection – however banal evil may really be, the most trivial individual, innocent and aimless, perhaps even like ourselves, may one day *quietly dedicate* himself to genocide.

Amis superbly realizes Arendt's declared purpose – to focus our attention on the utter barbarity of the crime – Odilo's whining sentimentality of his own suffering, his greed, his sadistic cruelty, his 'coprophagic smile' (p. 161), his envy and jealousy, his lust for power, a lust that finds exact expression in Amis'[s] phrase which allegorizes the entire Nazi movement: 'erotic revanchism' ['revanchism' means a 'policy of seeking to recover lost territory']. As Amis comments in the novel's 'Afterword', the Nazi 'offence was unique, not in its cruelty, nor in its cowardice, but in its style' (p. 176). Odilo's 'above all *thorough*' style (p. 94) leads him to perform his duty 'with impeccable ovinity' (p. 157 [in a sheep-like way]) – without the slightest shred of integrity even for his own beliefs. (Before the *Kristallnacht* he claims to have been 'one of nature's philo-Semites' (p. 160).)

All of us dream of turning back the clock to change events. Instead, Amis turns us to remember how events were and to say again, with [Paul] Celan, *Never*.[42] □

Paul Celan (1920–70) was a German poet who was sent to a forced labour camp and whose Jewish parents were murdered in a concentration camp. He was much preoccupied with the Holocaust in his poetry, which has been seen as the 'most outstanding' to have emerged in Germany since 1945.[43]

Easterbrook's concerns with the psychology of the Nazi doctors and with Amis's use of Robert Jay Lifton's studies are among the topics that Richard Menke explores in his 1998 essay 'Narrative Reversals and the Thermodynamics of History in Martin Amis's *Time's Arrow*'. Menke traces the phrase 'time's arrow' to A. S. Eddington's *The Nature of the Physical World* (1928), where it is used in relation to the second law of thermodynamics; the second law of thermodynamics, Menke contends, constitutes the field of metaphor active in the novel's title and its view of the Holocaust. His essay offers a fascinating account of how certain ideas drawn from popular understandings of modern science can illuminate *Time's Arrow*:

■ ... *Time's Arrow* [is a] postmodern *unbildungsroman* [a *bildungsroman* is a novel that shows the formation, or education by life, of its central character] ... What provides the crucial twist in Amis's scheme is the first-person voice that supplies the novel's retrograde narrative: although from Tod's point of view life presumably proceeds normally, to the unfortunate and impotent narrator trapped within him everything happens in reverse, a fact that quickly dawns on the reader but only becomes apparent to the narrator slowly and confusedly. The novel sets forth a life, a traditional project of fictional realism but, by an act of authorial fiat [decree], 'the film is running backwards' (p. 16). Instead of providing the seamless transparency attempted by more orthodox realisms, the reversed narrative *willfully* obtrudes between the imaginary life and the account that constitutes it, occupying an uneasy middle ground between mimesis [imitation, 'showing'] and diegesis ['telling'], between representation from within the action and commentary from without.[44]

Against Tod Friendly's sometimes brutal, often banal life history, the narrative provides the filigree of art, a stream of ironically inverted meditations, brilliant *aperçus*, and time-reversal set-pieces. And along with the satisfactions of this showy (and often very funny) literary artistry, the narratorial voice – which is only a voice, a 'passenger or parasite' (p. 16) in Tod's body with access to his emotions and dreams but not to his thoughts – offers the principal source of humanity among the human shapes that hurry backward through *Time's Arrow*, their eyes focused on what they have just left, their blind steps leading them ineluctably into the past. For the nameless inner *doppelgänger* who narrates the events of Tod's life from finish to start turns out to be more or less Tod's vestigial conscience or soul, abandoned during the pivotal experience of Tod's life (indeed, of the twentieth century), or so dislocated by its experience of the Holocaust that it must reverse the sequence of Tod's biography in order to make sense of his life at all.

Interpreting life backward, this fictional soul is a supremely reliable narrator; he may be relied upon to get things diametrically, and often poignantly, wrong. The scheme allows not only for powerful art but also for a more humane artistic vision than Amis's usual murderous satire. But at what price? *Time's Arrow* presents the act of narrative as the soul of fictional art, with its task of recounting, reordering, and reinterpreting history. Yet, ironically, this extraordinary act of narrative can itself only reimagine history by conceding its powerlessness before it. The novel's narrative reversals, which present literary art as history's double, ultimately ratify the one-sidedness of the relationship between the two.

This pessimistic conception of the relationship between literature and history centers upon the field of metaphor tacitly at work in both the novel's title and its vision of the Holocaust: thermodynamics, the physics of heat and its relation to other forms of energy. The physicist and science writer A. S. Eddington coined the phrase 'time's arrow' to denote the directionality of time that follows from the second law of thermodynamics, which describes the inescapable increase in entropy in closed physical systems.[45] Because this law alone sets the direction of time's arrow, Eddington accorded the second law of thermodynamics precedence among the laws of physics. The narrative of *Time's Arrow* reverses the arrow of time but paradoxically awards the law of entropy an even higher place than Eddington does [entropy here means 'the measure of the degradation or disorganisation of the universe']: for all its comedy, artistry, and surprising humanity, *Time's Arrow* offers a darkly thermodynamic vision of history . . . . . .

Narrative Reversals

The local reversals of *Time's Arrow* range from the jocular to the portentous. A Hollywood movie is a machine for dismantling a couple. 'Work liberates' people: as they prepare to begin the week on Friday evenings, 'they laugh and shout and roll their shoulders' (p. 57). Indeed, the novel's backward point of view completely recasts production and consumption, getting and spending, creation and destruction. 'Creation . . . is easy, is quick' (p. 23); objects emerge intact and ready for use from the 'industrial violence' of the incinerator, the car crash, and the garbage truck, whose 'monstrous jaws' bring Tod trash bags filled with his favorite tabloid paper (p. 20). 'Destruction', on the other hand, 'is difficult. Destruction is slow' (p. 26). As the narrator sees it, Tod spends years ripping up his garden until only the weeds remain.

What the narrator finds most striking about the processes of destruction and creation is the human body's role in them . . . After his retirement ends, Tod's profession involves methodically mangling the human body just as he has demolished his garden: Tod turns out to be a doctor. As far as the appalled narrator can tell, doctors spend their time wounding patients' bodies until they are healed by the violence of accident or disease. 'You have to be cruel to be kind', he concludes (p. 41). Tod seems unfazed by the practice of medicine, but the narrator feels 'harrowed by it, . . . curled up within, feebly gagging, and trying to avert [his] eyes' from the damage doctors do (pp. 33, 34).

But there would seem to be worse to come. As novel and narrator hurtle into the inevitable past, the narrator senses that they are moving toward the root of Tod's iciness, his unease, what his most devoted lover identifies as his lack of a soul (at first, admits the narrator, 'I used to take it personally, and I was wretched' (p. 62)). Tod's secret 'will be bad, and not intelligible' (p. 72), but the narrator knows one thing about it: 'that it is to do with trash and shit, and that it is wrong in time' (p. 73). As Tod's interest in articles about Nordic super-races and multiple births has hinted, with an irony that links tabloid fantasy and Nazi atrocity, the secret hinges on his involvement in the Holocaust. In fact, Tod turns out not to be the middle-aged, middle-American Tod T. Friendly at all. After seeing Tod through several incognitos, the reader and the narrator learn that Tod once had the identity, and the narrator now occupies the body, of Odilo Unverdorben, one of the Nazi doctors at Auschwitz.

Making Sense of the Holocaust

As Tod/Odilo awaits escape to postwar America (from his point of view) or immersion in the Second World War (from the narrator's), he suffers a recurrent dream that the narrator reads as an omen of 'a profound rearrangement, as if everything bad might soon be good, as if everything wrong might soon be right' (pp. 115–16): '[h]e dreams he is shitting human bones' (p. 116). We have no information about the time sequence of the dreams that are the only form of consciousness the narrator shares with his host; we cannot know whether Odilo dreams he is voiding bones forwards or backwards, creating them or consuming them. And we must guess whose bones they are: the victims of Odilo's malignant medicine, of course – but Odilo's bones, as well, or Odilo's soul? The dream offers an image of self-evacuation as well as of cannibalism, of expelling one's own insides as well as of ingesting the Other.

The dream remains mysterious, but the clarity that the narrator giddily anticipates finally arrives as Odilo moves through a ruined Europe that awaits the violent restorations of war: '[t]he world is going to start making sense . . . / *Now*', declares the narrator, as the novel strains the limits of prose typography to proclaim the change. The narrator announces himself as 'I, Odilo Unverdorben', without the pronominal distinction that has marked his separation from Tod, for although time still flows backwards for him, he and his host are 'one now, fused for a preternatural purpose'. At first this purpose seems less than obvious in the chaos attending the Russian liberation of Auschwitz (or, as the narrator experiences it, the 'Bolsheviks['] . . . ignoble withdrawal' (p. 124)). But the walls of a hospital at the camp present a sight that, like Odilo's dream, portends lucidity if only it is read aright:

> marks and pfennigs – good tender – stuck to the wall with human ordure. A mistake: a mistake. What is the *meaning* of this? Ordure, ordure everywhere . . . Naturally, I didn't immediately see the logic and justice of it. I didn't immediately see this: that now human shit is out in the open, we'll get a chance to find out what this stuff can really do (p. 125).

Money has become worthless, but the essence of creation remains intact; in the 'fiercely coprocentric' universe of Auschwitz, the toilet, font of all life and meaning, has spilled over to fill the world (p. 132). The officers call Auschwitz 'Anus Mundi', observes the narrator, '[a]nd I can think of no finer tribute than that' (p. 133).

The toilet is the site of a daily miracle of creation, and Auschwitz starts performing a roughly analogous marvel as, under the directorship of 'Uncle Pepi', a fictional double for Joseph Mengele, its real work begins. 'Enlightenment' – surely the term quietly recalls Adorno – comes to the narrator the day he sees 'the old Jew float to the surface of the deep latrine, how he splashed and struggled into life, and was hoisted out by the jubilant guards, his clothes cleansed by the mire' (p. 132). Like the latrine, the camp is unsightly and inelegant, the narrator admits, but '[c]reation' can be 'ugly': the 'preternatural purpose' he shares with Odilo is '[t]o dream a race . . . ' (p. 128). The work of Auschwitz, as the narrator sees it, is nothing short of the creation of the Jews.

Auschwitz produces whole trainloads of Jews – and a doctor like Odilo presides over each step in this mass production, from the ovens whose fires assemble human bodies from smoke and ashes, to the 'Sprinkleroom' where the Zyklon B that will vivify them is infused, where life arrives with convulsions of pain. '[W]e cry and twist and are naked at both ends of life . . . while the doctor watches', the narrator concludes. And no doctor has a more central place in this nativity than Odilo, for Odilo himself 'personally remove[s]' the pellets of poison gas (p. 129). Tod's secret indeed has to do with trash and shit, but the narrator's point of view gets time wrong to make Odilo's crimes look right, to render the violent creation of a people easier than its brutal decimation. At the expense of the intelligibility of everything else, the narratorial soul of Odilo has made sense of the Holocaust, reliteralizing Nazi eugenics as good birth, recasting genocide as genesis.

Provided with clothes that fit perfectly, with spectacles and other personal effects, the nascent Jews are united with their loved ones in tearful instant 'familial unions and arranged marriages' (p.131); just as Hollywood dismantles fictional couples, Auschwitz manufactures real ones. When the camp is broken up, the next job of Odilo's unit is to 'deconcentrate' the Jews, to disband the ghettos and diffuse their occupants throughout Europe. '[T]his was our mission after all: to make Germany whole. To heal her wounds and make her whole' (p.149). The narrator has even appropriated the rhetoric of Nazi militarism to explain the task of creating a middle-European Jewry and integrating it into the society of which it would for so long form a part. Poignantly and pointedly, his inverted prescription for restoring Germany's wholeness makes far more literal and logical sense than the Nazis' [prescription].

As the flames of the Holocaust wane, Odilo ends up creating more people from the violence of fire. But now the process goes awry, for Odilo and his fellow doctors now create not Jews but the physically and mentally impaired – and, as the months roll back, the patients who emerge from the eugenic fires become more and more tragically disabled. Disenchanted with the project, separating from Odilo again, the narrator reconsiders the work he and Odilo have performed:

> [c]alling on powers best left unsummoned, he took human beings apart – and then he put them back together again. For a while it worked (there was redemption); and while it worked he and I were one, on the banks of the Vistula. He put *us* back together. But of course you shouldn't be doing any of this kind of thing with human beings . . . (p.156)

Such scruples arrive too late or too early, for the Final Solution is over or has not yet begun. Odilo has not yet taken part in the Holocaust, has not yet lost his soul, and the narrator now feels as aloof from him as he had felt from Tod. 'The world has stopped making sense again [. . .]' (p.157).

Double Vision

Time's Arrow achieves its sometimes facetious but ultimately tragic vision by means of an unwavering irony born of its intertwined characterological and narrative doublings. Odilo's nearly palindromic first name [that is, it is nearly the same name if spelt backwards – Olido] recalls both St. Odilo of Cluny, who established All Souls' Day to honor the departed spirits of the faithful, and St. Odilia, patron saint of the blind; both would seem appropriate allusions in this treatment of the willful moral blindness and well-intentioned misperceptions of a Nazi doctor and his estranged sense of decency or long-fled soul. His surname, Unverdorben ('uncorrupted, unspoiled, innocent' in German), records with irony what Odilo has lost so irrevocably, describing the misapprehending narrator he unknowingly harbors within him. With its implicit, structural antithesis (*unverdorben* means 'not *verdorben*', 'not polluted or corrupt'), the name encapsulates the dual structure of the narrative, which opposes the life history of Odilo (hideous and banal, lived forward) to the narrative of his *doppelgänger* (striking and scrupulous, lived backward) . . .

. . . [T]he central paradigm *The Nazi Doctors* employs to discuss this psychology is the idea of 'psychological doubling'[46] . . . . . . 'Indeed', asserts Lifton, 'Auschwitz as an *institution* – as an atrocity-producing situation – ran on doubling',[47] which Lifton defines as 'the division of the self into two functioning wholes'.[48] . . . According to Lifton, the Nazi doctors, above all those of Auschwitz, had to develop a murderous self to carry out the day-to-day atrocities required for a genocidal project, in order to allow these mundane individuals to function properly as systematic killers. Lifton points out that their very profession might well have rendered them unusually susceptible to doubling, even to a doubling that inverted their avowed aim of healing; doctors must cultivate a clinical manner, must learn their trade by opening up corpses without becoming sick, must often indeed 'be cruel to be kind'. During the Holocaust, Lifton argues, a terrifying and extreme form of this psychological doubling became 'the mechanism by which a doctor, in his actions, moved from the ordinary to the demonic'.[49]

In his extensive use of Lifton's historical and psychological accounts, Amis makes much use of this grotesque paradox, that the very techniques of the self that help doctors become healers could be mobilized and extended in the service of genocide. After all, from the narrator's point of view, standard medical practice appears heartless, while the work of the concentration camp seems lifegiving. 'Put simply, the hospital is an atrocity-producing situation' (p. 102), writes Amis, borrowing a term directly from Lifton and applying it not to Auschwitz but to Tod Friendly's ordinary clinical practice. And in the hospital the doctor becomes a 'biological soldier' (p. 36) – a description silently borrowed, via Lifton, from a Nazi manual on eugenic sterilization.[50] Whether in medical practice or medicalized mass murder, it seems to be 'the same story. Render up your soul, and gain power' (p. 58).

The loss or impotence of Odilo's soul as a result of his genocidal doubling, and the radical reversal of time that alone can make sense of the Holocaust, constitute the novel's diegetic account of its own being . . . . . . The dual vision that results from the absolute division of Odilo as actor in the plot and Odilo as narrated subject contrasts history and narrative with an ever-present irony, and it is this ironic principle, along with the narrator's occasionally sardonic judgements about the world he sees, that aligns *Time's Arrow* most closely with the vein of satire in Amis's earlier work. But now irony becomes the essence of narrative technique; readers of the novel must translate the backward processes, plotlines, and conversations into normal time, pressing the audience into the very creation of this irony. After all, the book cannot simply be read backward, as the narrator sees the Japanese and observant Jews doing; the narrator's flawless English syntax and complex trains of thought still work in the normal order. Neither the narrator's thoughts nor his words are written from back to front. Consequently, with the exception of the relatively few conversations (which we learn to read by skipping ahead and reading the lines in reverse), . . . the technique of the narrative forces readers into many of the same misperceptions the narrator makes, except that we are familiar with the forward passage of time and so can always recognize them as misperceptions. Again and again surprised by sequence, as it were, a reader of *Time's Arrow* must reassemble history from the literary narrative that imagines it.

Against the now sordid, now monstrous realities of history, the narrator of *Time's Arrow* will always misunderstand, although his misinterpretations will often be painfully preferable to history and always rendered in the splendidly wrought prose of Martin Amis. That *Time's Arrow* considers potential contrariness to the timeline endemic to the work of art seems clear; visiting the Metropolitan Museum of Art, the narrator notes that he can read visual art and texts in a way that harmonizes with his own view of time, that they offer a solace against the jarring movements of life and history as he experiences them:

> Like writing, paintings seem to hint at a topsy-turvy world in which, so to speak, time's arrow moves the other way. The invisible speedlines suggest a different nexus of sequence and process . . . I wonder: is this the case with all the arts? (p. 95)

Whether in the form of a painting or of a novel narrated backward, art can represent a world contrary to the arrow of history. In relation to life and history (and, in the case of Odilo, to lifehistory), art provides the aesthetic – if not quite the political – unconscious, an unconscious that *Time's Arrow* imagines as wholly bereft of agency in or access to

147

history. And this is in part because the novel's understanding of history in general and the Holocaust in particular is, as its title hints, a thermodynamic one . . .

The Thermodynamic Nature of History

Classical physics (along with many fields of twentieth-century physics, for that matter) describes a universe in which phenomena are in principle reversible. One body collides with another, say, and forces are redistributed; run the events backward and the collision is equally obedient to the laws of classical physics. Yet this temporal symmetry contradicts our human experience of a universe in which things happen forward, in which events do not seem reversible. To cite several of the customary examples: an egg never unscrambles, a cold cup of coffee never regains the heat it has lost to its surroundings, a shuffled deck of cards never returns to its original order by means of any amount of subsequent shuffling, the scattered balls on a pool table never triangulate themselves back into the shape of the rack. Whence, then, arises the apparent directionality of time?

Nineteenth-century physics traced the problem to thermo-dynamics, the study of heat and energy transfer. According to the first law of thermodynamics, the total amount of energy in a closed system is invariable; energy is conserved. However, according to the second law of thermodynamics, heat will flow from a warmer region to a cooler one, but not *vice versa*; therefore, in a closed system the amount of energy that is unusable (having already flowed to the cooler region and unable to flow back) will always tend to increase. After the cup of coffee cools, the air around it and the table under it contain much of the energy that once warmed the coffee; the total amount of heat in the room has not changed (if we neglect the fact that the room is not truly a closed system), but the energy is so scattered that it is not recover-able for use. In 1865 the German physicist Rudolf Clausius termed this unusable energy *entropy*, borrowing the same root as *trope* ('turn-ing, transformation') to devise a neologism in analogy to *energy*. In its best-known form, the second law stipulates that the entropy or dis-order in a closed system will always increase as time passes.[51] For the Victorians, this law bespoke the tragedy of the inevitable 'heat-death' of the universe, a time when all energy would be dissipated into entropy and all order into anarchy, when all energy transfer, all work, all life would become impossible.

It is the second law of thermodynamics that describes the asymmetry of time, the fact that past does not simply mirror future as left mirrors right; the inescapable increase of total entropy in a closed system marks the direction of time. In *The Nature of the Physical World*, the

British astrophysicist A.S. Eddington awarded the second law of thermodynamics 'the supreme position among the laws of Nature'[52] since it alone was responsible for what he was the first to call 'time's arrow':[53]

> I shall use the phrase 'time's arrow' to express this one-way property of time which has no analogue in space. It is a singularly interesting property from a philosophical standpoint. We must note that – . . . . . . (1) it is vividly recognized by consciousness. . . . . . . (2) It is equally insisted on by our reasoning faculty, which tells us that a reversal of the arrow would render the external world nonsensical. . . . . . . (3) It makes no appearance in physical science except in the study of organization of a number of individuals [that is, individual molecules, objects, or pieces].[54]

The directionality of time that results from entropy's increase, Eddington points out, is intimately installed in our awareness of ourselves in the world, confirmed by human reason, and dependent upon the fact that there are multiple parts to be organized or disordered.[55]

Eddington, always mindful of the philosophical and psychological (and elsewhere to the theological) aspects of physics, is here especially sensitive to the intimate connection between time and consciousness. Again and again Eddington's writing stresses the way in which 'nearly all our knowledge of the external world' is in fact 'indirect', 'a matter of inference and interpretation'.[56] Gillian Beer emphasizes Eddington's desire to foreground epistemological questions in her account of the relationship of his popular science writing to the literary modernism of writers such as Virginia Woolf.[57] Yet in contrast to his assiduous qualification of our knowledge of space, Eddington claims that 'we have direct experience' of time,

> of the time-relations that we ourselves are traversing – a knowledge of time not coming through external sense-organs, but taking a short cut into our consciousness. When I close my eyes and retreat into my inner mind, I feel myself *enduring*, I do not feel myself *extensive*.[58]

Our experience of it as internal and personal is 'peculiarly characteristic' of time. As opposed to our fallacious perception of space as stable and solid, our very intimacy with time renders it (properly, in Eddington's view) essentially 'mysterious'.[59]

In singling out 'time's arrow' as a site for exploration, *Time's Arrow* seems to affirm Brian McHale's overly sweeping but influential thesis that the move from modernism to postmodernism in fiction represents 'the shift . . . from an epistemological dominant to an *ontological one*'.[60] For Eddington, questions of space are broadly epistemological (how can we know about the universe when our knowledge of it is so oblique and uncertain?), while questions of time are ontological (what is the nature of our sense of endurance in time?). Eddington hails 'time's arrow' as the link between temporality and subjectivity, physics and consciousness; as Amis writes, '[t]ime [is] the human dimension, which makes us everything we are' (p. 76). Writing a novel in which 'time's arrow moves the other way' (p. 95), Martin Amis ratifies the relationship between time and consciousness even as he reverses the arrow: fundamental to the scheme of *Time's Arrow* is the revolt of the narrator's consciousness and his reason against the nonsense of the ordinary world seen chronologically backward.

As it emphasizes the connection between time and consciousness, *Time's Arrow* also incorporates what Eddington identifies as the third element of this relationship: entropy. For it is the apparent reversals of everyday thermodynamic activities that provoke many of the narrator's disquisitions on the remarkable properties of the world he sees, including his Swiftian (and very Martin-Amis like) attention to the grotesque reversed thermodynamics of the body. The body adds caloric energy, forges higher-energy molecular bonds, to make food out of excrement. The violence of accidents restores smashed cars or maimed patients to their proper order. Factories collect streams of pollution from the skies. A fire organizes ashes, smoke, and flames into letters, fingernails, people. All of these interactions bespeak the spontaneous organization and decrease in entropy that characterize the reversal of time's arrow. Eddington argues that our sense of time's arrow has fundamentally to do with thermodynamics; Amis's novel not only borrows Eddington's phrase as its title but takes this hypothesis for granted and awards the second law of thermodynamics precedence in its gallery of virtuoso inversions.

It is hardly surprising, then, that the novel's backward understanding of Nazi genocide should also turn out to be a thoroughly thermodynamic one, as if to affirm the grim aptness of the term *Holocaust*. From end to beginning, *Time's Arrow* treats the Holocaust as a consummately thermodynamic event. Reducing entropy right and left, the thermodynamics of Auschwitz pieces together Jews and Gypsies out of scattered molecules of haze, sorts stashes of clothes and dental work, assembles perfect families out of a human chaos. The narrator's mission is 'preternatural' in precisely this respect: it contradicts the ordinary rules of life, history, thermodynamics, and nature more thoroughly than anything before or after it in the novel. The final deconcentration of Central European Jews from the ghettos offers another thermodynamic allegory, although not now a reversed one;

created from the violence of fire, the Jews are dispersed through the rest of society, their ethnic or cultural 'difference' no longer recapturable as the fuel for Nazi rhetoric and the occasion for systematic genocide. Even *'Arbeit macht frei'* ['work liberates'], the infamous Auschwitz inscription echoed in the narrator's interpretation of TGIF [Thank God It's Friday] – has a certain thermodynamic plausibility; doesn't 'work' (the transfer of physical energy) liberate electrons, molecules, and potential energy in a way that occasions entropy in the first place?

The Holocaust realizes *in extremis* [at an extreme] the tragically thermodynamic nature of history in *Time's Arrow*, for history becomes tragedy when it is dreadful and unpreventable: '[w]hat goes around comes around. 1066, 1789, 1945' (p. 16). As one of the most horrifically irreversible processes of the twentieth century, the Holocaust crystallizes Amis's idea of a backward narrative, especially when coupled with Lifton's attention to the Nazi doctors' part in genocide, a role imbued with [a] specifically medical irreversibility . . . 'Time is now heading on towards something', proclaims the narrator as he begins to move from private life in America into the monstrous history of Nazi Germany; '[i]t pours past unpreventably, like the reflections on a windscreen as the car speeds through city or forest' (p. 67). Transitively as well as intransitively, history 'pours past' in *Time's Arrow*: it both streams by the narrative and extrudes the ineluctable past as a series of half-shocks to the narrating subject. Reversing chronology, *Time's Arrow* depicts a world in which, instead of one thing leading to another, everything leads to one thing: the past. The past is unchangeable and, for its part, '[t]he future always comes true' (p. 162). Once history becomes thermodynamics in *Time's Arrow*, it becomes as inescapable as the second law.

Only viewed in reverse does the second law of thermodynamics appear unambiguously deterministic, for it actually describes the calculably large probability that entropy will increase, not necessarily the specific way in which this increase will happen. In fact, more recent philosophical investigations based on theories of chaos and complexity have stressed the way in which the statistical nature of thermodynamics allows the unpredictable appearance of local pockets of order, dubbed 'negentropy', even as the total entropy in an entire system increases; consequently, '[t]he future does not derive from the past in strict linear fashion'.[61] Postmodern historical fiction is similarly supposed to reject understandings of history as deterministic and stable in favor of treatments of history as ambiguous, textual, aleatory.[62] Yet *Time's Arrow* sets up the relationship between literature and history as divorce rather than dialectic, leaving no place for their synthesis as historiography. Its carefully constructed narrative, almost impeccably mimetic, even carefully 'realistic', within its *donnée* of temporal reversal and narratorial powerlessness, treats history as the atrocity-producing situation that narrative, passenger or parasite, can only view as an image on the windscreen: outside, overhead, upside-down.

. . . [An] apt image of the narrative of *Time's Arrow* is provided by a famous passage in the field whose metaphorics, as I have argued, underlie the conception of the novel. The second law of thermodynamics, pointed out the Victorian physicist James Clerk Maxwell,

> is undoubtedly true as long as we can deal with bodies only in mass [that is, *en masse*], and have no power of perceiving or handling the separate molecules of which they are made up. But if we conceive a being whose faculties are so sharpened that he can follow every molecule in its course, such a being . . . would be able to do what is at present impossible to us.[63]

Take, in Maxwell's example, a closed container full of air; even at a uniform temperature, it will be full of molecules with varying amounts of kinetic energy, which is to say, traveling at different speeds.

> Now let us suppose that such a vessel is divided into two portions, A and B, by a division in which there is a small hole, and that a being, who can see the individual molecules, opens and closes this hole, so as to allow only the swifter molecules to pass from A to B and only the slower ones to pass from B to A. He will thus, without expenditure of work, raise the temperature of B and lower that of A, in contradiction to the second law of thermodynamics.[64]

This hypothetical 'being', soon christened 'Maxwell's Demon', would apparently violate the second law of thermodynamics by transferring heat from a cooler region to a warmer or (what is the same thing) by producing order without work, decreasing the entropy of a closed system, reversing Eddington's arrow of time. If *Time's Arrow* offers a thermodynamic vision of history, it is a vision in which narrative occupies the place of that most famous of thermodynamic personages, Maxwell's Demon . . . . . .

In *Time's Arrow* . . . Maxwell's Demon becomes the muse or presiding spirit of the art of postmodern fiction. History in this novel, like the Holocaust that represents its cruellest and most inescapable productions, is a supremely thermodynamic phenomenon. Like Maxwell's Demon, Amis's narrative reverses these thermodynamics to generate a new order counter to the inevitability of the tragic narrative of thermodynamics, of heat-death or Holocaust: heat flows backward, entropy decreases, human bodies are created in the violence of fire, wry comedy and a sort of piquant pathos swamp tragedy and banality. But against the sparkle and spectacle of the narrative flows history, brutal, banal, unchangeable, Other. *Time's Arrow* never lets us forget that its narrative, like Maxwell's Demon, is only a thought experiment . . . . . . Although the Maxwell's Demon of Amis's narrative imaginatively restarts the motor by moving backward and decreasing entropy, it nevertheless offers a metaphorics in which the consumption of human lives in the Holocaust may be considered along the same thermodynamic lines as the consumption of goods in contemporary America. *Time's Arrow* itself, then, betokens a certain postmodern falling-off of distinctions. Indeed, the very logic of postmodernism, like claims that at the end of the millennium we have reached the end of history, may postulate a thermodynamics of history in which entropy now predominates. After the portentous and apocalyptic millennial murder-mystery-*cum*-snuff novel *London Fields* – for which Amis had considered the title 'Time's Arrow' (*London Fields*, 'Note' after Contents page) – *Time's Arrow*, Amis's first post-Cold War novel, might well be taken as an emblem of the heat-death of history.[65] □

Menke's concluding comparison between *London Fields* and *Time's Arrow* implies the superiority of the latter work and reinforces the widespread view, amply demonstrated by the critical material in this chapter, that Martin Amis had achieved a new stature with his seventh novel. It might have seemed, even from the initial review responses, that *Time's Arrow* had at last established him as a serious writer who combined dazzling stylistic and structural skills with profound moral, social and historical concerns. But then came *The Information* – and, as the next chapter will show, Amis was once more embroiled in controversy, this time of an especially vicious kind.

CHAPTER NINE

That Comes at Night: *The Information* (1995)

IN DISCUSSING Martin Amis's eighth novel, *The Information*, it becomes very difficult – at times, virtually impossible – to separate strictly literary criticism from an analysis of 'Martin Amis' as a cultural phenomenon, a highly public player in the field of literary success and fame. It is not only that the appearance of *The Information* was preceded by much publicity, and vehement controversy, about Amis's apparent pursuit of a half-million pound advance for the novel, and his oral and marital difficulties as he sought expensive dental treatment and his first marriage broke up, but also that the novel itself takes literary success and failure as a key theme, further blurring the boundaries between fiction and reality, literature and life. Two detailed and fascinating reviews, however, did succeed in discussing *The Information* as a literary work rather than a publicity phenomenon. The first appeared in the *Times Literary Supplement*, by Adam Mars-Jones – whose account of *Einstein's Monsters*, and attack on Amis's style, was quoted in chapter six of this Guide. Mars-Jones does not mention the real-life publicity but sets the novel in the context of Amis's previous work, offers a complex verdict on the strengths and weakness of *The Information*, and provides a more general analysis and appraisal of Amis's writing:

■ Martin Amis's new novel has everything in common with *Money* . . . and *London Fields* . . . in terms of tone and territory. Without continuous characters or an overarching structure, the three books can't really be said to form a trilogy, but they certainly make up a mighty triptych, a love poem to West London from which love is excluded. There is no character in the new book with the brute stature of a John Self or a Keith Talent, and even the surnames of the main characters have lapsed into realism (Tull, Barry [but see John Nash's comment later, p. 169, on the surname 'Barry']), but it would be impertinent to imagine that Amis had mellowed.

If the reader senses exhaustion in the author as well as the characters by the end of the third volume (it is a characteristic of Amis that he doesn't develop his characters so much as wear them out), there is no loss of performance page by page. It's more a sense that the glittering steely nets Amis throws around the world are tightening around him. Disconcerting to encounter new notes of desperation in an author whose subject has always been precisely that: desperation.

Amis's originality as a stylist has been to separate verbal beauty from the cause it has traditionally served, to detach lyrical language from the lyrical impulse. Why should intense verbal music be the privilege of those who love life in however contrary a fashion, the Nabokovs, the Updikes? The closest Amis has come in his literary persona to *joie de vivre* was a disillusion crackling with scorn, and that was not recently: there was a time when he scowled more brightly on the world. *Life is low*, he sings, *all life is low-life*, and this is not what we are accustomed to call a song . . . . . .

Much of the new novel is structured around . . . the trope of rancorous twins. The protagonist and his antagonist are two talentless novelists, one of them (Richard Tull) hyperliterary and caricaturally unsuccessful, the other (Gwyn Barry) subliterary and caricaturally successful. Richard and Gwyn were born a day apart, and the novel opens on Gwyn's fortieth birthday, the eve therefore of Richard's. This pattern is repeated with almost suspicious obligingness by Richard's two sons, Marius and Marco.

The strangest pairing, though, is of hero and narrative voice. In Amis's last novel, *Time's Arrow* . . . , the disjunction between the describing presence and the experience described was the whole subject and method of the book [see previous chapter of this Guide], but when your hero is a literary man, there seems no reason to double the point of view . . . . . . Richard is rendered in the third person, where traditionally there can be free play and fertile overlap between creature and creator, but here the distinction is strongly defended, and a first person keeps butting in.

The trope of rancorous twins creates a polarized world based on the exaggerated differences between two essentially similar characters (untalented, heterosexual, white British male novelists of forty), and this disguises or compensates for the absence of what is for many people the essential business of the novelist: the finding of common ground in the apparently dissimilar . . . . . .

The Information is full of sentences that are compulsive hostages willing to die for their author's sake, pressing their pleading faces against the paragraph windows and crying, 'Take me, I saw it all. I can explain.' One particularly insistent passage proposes that the four principal literary genres (tragedy, comedy, romance and satire) have by now all bled into each other. Amis himself, however, is locked into satire, the only genre which invites and requires negative emotion, the one in which empathy is dilution and blunder.

Humour in satire is based on exaggerating differences, while in comedy it moves towards recognizing affinities, and this suits Amis well. Only in satire, above all, could he write so many pages (the London triptych runs to well over a thousand) full of commandingly vivid detail, none of it sensuous. Not a sensation enjoyed, hardly even a tune heard with pleasure, no food taken into the body without latent or patent disgust. The only activities in the three books that are genuinely identified with are smoking and drinking – pleasures that punish. Food and sex are tolerated and even craved when they approximate to this mortificatory condition . . . . . .

Satire is pre-eminently the mode of diminishing returns, and Martin Amis has been practising it longer than most. In the literary typology that he proposes, satire corresponds to winter, but he came to it in spring. As a writer, he has always looked on the blight side.

His persona has been the malcontent, regarding vigour as incipient decay and life as a special case of death.

A writer who in his twenties considers the body a site of embarrassment and humiliation will have much to write about in his forties. The only surprise about this is that Martin Amis seems surprised by it. It's as if he made a bargain that by not identifying with his youth, by affecting to despise it, he would be spared the indignities of ageing. When the hero of *The Information* launches the familiar agonized tirades against his hair and skin, tirades that for consistency's sake are yet more hyperbolic with every book, the reader may be tempted by a rebellious interior murmur of *Martin, when you told us the body was a bad joke, remember? Weren't you listening?*

The Information has a plot, but as with its predecessors it isn't the sort that drives its sap through every sentence and makes every phrase, however flowery, align itself with an unseen sun. As the plot impinges on the reader, it can be summarized like this: things can't get any worse, and then they do. Amis is canny enough to winch Richard up a little bit from time to time, thus enhancing the impact of his next fall, but any bungee rope attached to his ankles is guaranteed to be that little bit longer than the drop.

Amis shies away from a more ambitious reversal of the plot's depressive current. After almost 400 pages of continuous immersion in Richard Tull's hysterical rancour, the point of view shifts to his nemesis Gwyn Barry. It would be both shocking, after so much demonizing, and shapely as a piece of narrative construction, to make Gwyn at this point less than a monster, merely mediocre. The Amis of *Success* . . .

might have enjoyed that, but the Amis of *The Information* makes him more smugly appalling than his enemy could dream, with the strange result that he seems worthy of Richard's tedious hatred.

Comic set-pieces suffer from the same reflexive hyperbole. It's as if Amis has lost the knack of going just too far enough. Richard's novel *Untitled* turns out to be so unreadable that it breaks the health of anyone who attempts the task, which means that every time the book acquires a reader we brace ourselves for a more extreme diagnosis. Infinitely better are passages that remember to cut overstatement with understatement, like a description of a car accident retailed so offhandedly it sounds like good news.

When mechanical comedy is combined with a female character, the book is at its weakest, as it is with long passages about Richard's wife Gina and her love life before their marriage, when she slept her way through the literary establishment of London. Satire is always cartoony, but Amis's satire operates a discriminatory cartooniness, making men huge and absurd, women absurdly diminished.

If Nabokov did, as Richard Tull reports, describe himself as '"frankly homosexual"' (p. 29) in his literary tastes (a man who read men), then Martin Amis is that mythical beast, the man who makes women lesbian. There is nothing for women in *The Information* beyond the prose masterclass, the lessons in how to make a verb curdle or an adjective explode. Gina may be the hero's wife, but everything she does is generic and labelled as such. On page 1, '[s]he was a woman. She knew so much more about tears than he did.' She is sympathetic as a fact of gender. It is no credit to her. On page 85, Richard says that without his fiction-writing all he would have would be life. 'And this was a disastrous word to say to a woman – to women, who bear life, who bring it into the world, screaming, and will never let it come second to anything.' Women's reproductivity is their essence, they love life as a fact of gender.

You could learn more about women from reading Genet, for whom at least femininity is an important and sometimes a coveted category, than you can from *The Information*. Much is conceded to woman – emotional responsiveness and love of life – but the gifts are invariably poisoned. The world is reformulated right away to downgrade the yielded territory. In the area of the emotions, it's as if women have pulled a fast one: by feeling more they suffer less, and as for love of life, doesn't that prove they're shallow? Life? Who'd love *that*?

It is bizarrely easy to take Amis's female characters more seriously than he does himself. When Richard's impotence is described in inverted romance terms, for instance ('[i]n the last month alone, he had been impotent with her on the stairs, on the sofa in the sitting-room and on the kitchen table' (p. 90)), we know how he feels about it, but how does Gina feel? Does she even notice? This reviewer, being homosexual, has a sentimental respect for the Other Persuasion, and likes to think that two people are present in a marriage, or even a coupling. In a first-person or virtual first-person narrative, the exclusion of Gina's responses might be pointed or strategic, but Amis has made the choice of the rancorous-twin point of view. And on the irrelevance of Gina to her own sex life the twins agree.

In the whole book, Gina's head contains only one thought not expressed in dialogue, and that turns out to be something about Richard, not something about herself (she knows he will never turn his verbal violence on her). His unlikely attractiveness to her, current or past, remains unexplored, but perhaps love too is generic and female. We know that Richard married her not out of love but sexual obsession, on the advice of a man who said this was the thing to do. The marriage-crisis strand of the book ends with a single sentence more appropriate to a short story than to a 500-pager: '[b]ecause if he forgave her, she could never leave him now' (p.494). The key to the marriage's survival is in one partner's hands only.

Within the negatively defined world of his fiction, Martin Amis has all the time been reaching for a positive, that is, a double negative. Looking for an Unholy of Holies, a big No to say No to, he has been drawn to the Bomb (*Einstein's Monsters*) and the Holocaust (*Time's Arrow*). He has also been drawn to ways of looking at the universe that don't put human beings at the centre of it – nuclear physics in *London Fields*, and now astronomy in *The Information*.

These rhetorical moves have had different degrees of success. The borrowing of imagery from physics for *London Fields* sometimes made it seem that he was using a black hole as a paperweight, particularly as it was combined with a fear of environmental collapse. In private life, Amis may be the largest single contributor to Friends of the Earth, but a literary persona incredulous of purity and reassured by adulteration makes him an unlikely ecologist in his fiction. His urban portraiture, for instance, which must be some of the best ever written, comes into its own at precisely the point where the city ceases to be a nice place to live, becomes soiled and inhumane.

The attraction of the astronomical digressions in *The Information* is presumably their distance from the human, but they are given explicitly to the author himself . . . In *The Information*, Richard Tull is in the third person, and 'Martin Amis' occupies the first . . . Nothing that 'Martin Amis' says about himself clashes with what we know of our author, and some of it – about the awfulness of being a short teenager, for instance – would be touching in another context, but this solution to the negativity problem is a problem in its own right . . . . . . The separation of 'Martin Amis', with his astronomy and his literary theory, from the world he describes breaks down before too long. He starts describing people he sees on the street in astronomical terms (a 'yellow dwarf' (pp. 124, 125, 280, 282), for instance), and before you know it Richard is comparing his family to the solar system.[1] □

Some of Mars-Jones's criticisms of *The Information* – for example, of its stereotyped representations of women – are echoed by Julian Loose in the *London Review of Books*, but on the whole Loose is more sympathetic, and he particularly applauds what he sees as Amis's stylistic inventiveness, especially his 'epic, frothing digressions'. Like Mars-Jones, Loose is able to set his appraisal of *The Information* in the context of Amis's other writing; in contrast to Mars-Jones, however, he does allude, if discreetly (the reference in brackets to 'publisher's advances', for example) to the controversy preceding the novel's publication and to the real-life Martin Amis.

■ Clearly, for Martin Amis, enough is nothing like enough. To read him is to discover an author as voracious as his characters . . . Amis goes to any length to remind us of our whole-hearted addiction to the unwholesome – to alcohol, say, or nuclear weapons. The central character in his new novel, *The Information*, is so committed to smoking that he wants to start again before he's even given up . . .

In *The Information*, a pitilessly professional literary agent explains that nowadays the public can only keep in mind one thing per writer. Authors need definition: '"[l]ike a signature. Drunk, young, mad, fat, sick: you know"' (p. 130). Amis's handle could well be: insatiable. And not just because he has become such a Post-Modern operation that, as we used to say of Madonna, even his publicity gets publicity. One of his favourite metaphors – for accumulating phone-calls, deals, anxieties – is of jets stacked in the sky above some fogbound airport (perhaps 'Manderley International Junk Novel Airport') (p. 318), a consummate image for contemporary over-stimulation and over-supply, for what can barely be accommodated and yet won't nearly suffice. Amis once proposed 'never being satisfied' as Philip Roth's great theme (*Moronic Inferno*, p. 44) but it is the boundless nature of need that he, too, endlessly celebrates and satirizes. And if Amis is the poet of profligacy, the expert on excess, it is because he is himself full of what he might call male need-to-tell, what John Updike has diagnosed as an urge 'to cover the world in fiction'.[2] *Money* may have been the definitive portrait of Eighties materialism, but Amis has a sly suspicion that we haven't yet tired of reading about the things we cannot get too much of – like fame and money, sex and information.

Amis's latest anti-hero suffers from too much information, and not nearly enough fame, money or sex. Richard Tull, a '"charisma bypass"' (pp. 172, 174, 449), lives on the obscure margins of the literary world

. . . Richard's lot goes beyond the common unhappiness of the mediocre. The morning post brings demands from his publishers for the return of advances on unwritten books, and a solicitor's letter from his own solicitor; he is acutely impotent, and – plagued by intimations of his own mortality (having just hit 40) – cries to himself in the middle of the night. What twists failure's stiletto ever deeper is the corresponding success of his only friend, Gwyn Barry. Gwyn has written a blandly accessible novel about a New-Age utopia and, inexplicably, become an international bestseller. Richard is more than bitter: he is consumed beyond all reason, 'exhaustingly ever-hostile' (p. 103). And so, in the best tradition of Amis characters, he formulates a plan, a mission: 'to fuck Gwyn up' (p. 38).

Of course, Richard proves no better at revenge than at anything else . . . . . . As [his] strategies variously fizzle out or detonate in his face, the narrative takes the form of one of the many books he's failed to write: 'The History of Increasing Humiliation' (p. 129). We soon realize that all plot lines, all other characters exist only in so far as they serve to detain Richard in a never-ending '*Mahabharata* of pain' (p. 41). If Gwyn never quite seems a worthy subject of Richard's outsize fury, it is because he never carries much conviction as a subject. Similarly, the women in the novel remain mere objects of desire and disappointment. They may know all about tears (a woman crying is 'make-up in melt-down' (p. 291)), but they don't get to read Proust, write books or take any decisions: Amis frankly gives up on the attempt to make them more than two-dimensional, acknowledging 'difficulties of representation' (p. 256). He also reminds us more than once that literary genres are in a muddle, now that '[d]ecorum is no longer observed' (p. 53), but perhaps another decline is unintentionally mapped in this novel, a descent from black comedy to mechanical farce. For despite the ever-entertaining wit, the only twist is that there is no twist, and a terrible predictability sets in, as though Richard's chronic habit of failure had consumed the novel itself.

The Information makes much of rivalry and hatred between authors, but to describe the book's subject as literary rivalry seems a category mistake . . . Rather, *The Information* is a study of envy and egomania that happens to play itself out in the world of publishing . . . there is no sense of one writer warding off another's potentially crushing influence, or of the fragile accommodations made between near-equals . . . If *The Information* has anything to say about literary rivalry, it is because, for Amis, writing is an activity as inherently confrontational as tennis, or tag wrestling . . .

If *The Information* fails to induce apocalyptic awe, it may be because, apart from the droll sketches of literary circles, this new novel is a very familiar Amiscellany. There's too much of the same: male envy, not least between authors and near twins; furious games of tennis . . . ; alcohol-fuelled trips to America, empire of trex [rubbish, junk];[3] sad men staring disgustedly in bathroom mirrors at faces blasted with age and ridden with 'bigboys' (p. 197); villains who speak a post-Yardie patois and believe in getting their retaliation in first; talk of 'batch' [batchelor] (pp. 36, 78, 166, 264 – see also *Money*, pp. 63, 171) and 'spinst' [spinster] (pp. 36, 37, 78, 165, 264, 269), and orthodontic descriptions of urban decay ('the sound of fiercely propelled metal as it ground against stone . . . the whole city, taking it deep in the root canal' (p. 67)). The cosmological interludes of *London Fields* return with a vengeance: '[t]he quasars are so far away and getting further away so fast. This is to put Richard's difficulties in context' (pp. 163–4). This is also to risk a sense of fatigue, for over-use can make such astronomic comparisons seem all too dull and sublunary, perhaps prompting us to recall the Total Perspective Vortex featured in *The Hitchhiker's Guide to the Galaxy* (1979), that exquisite torture which does nothing more than show you your ultimate significance in relation to the rest of the universe.

Yet the loss of all sense of proportion is, of course, why Amis is so enjoyable to read . . . we may feel that with *The Information* Amis has ended up down a cul-de-sac, but his writing is still fantastically rich. There is no better place to find the spot-on perception: Americans call everybody '*sir*' but manage to make the word sound like '*mac* or *bub* or *scumbag*' (p. 323); people's mouths 'nuzzle the necks' of cellular telephones (p. 105), and bike messengers wear 'city scuba gear' (p. 102); a flock of birds rears up 'like a join-the-dots puzzle of a human face or fist' (p. 103); in pre-natal classes, adults sit around on the floor and gaze up at teacher 'like the children they would shortly bear' (p. 164).

The offbeam precision of the Martian poet is only one of Amis's modes, but it lends his writing such casual authority that frequent assumptions of the first person plural are unusually persuasive, even when 'we' would rather be included out: '[b]itter is manageable. Look how we all manage it' (p. 42). 'We may think we are swearing at others, at traffic. But who *is* the traffic?' (pp. 466–7). Hungry for the universal, and attentive to the vagaries of excess, Amis will go places other writers won't: '[i]f we think about it, we all know the sneak preview of schizophrenia, with the toilet paper, those strange occasions when there seems to be no good reason to stop wiping' (p. 236). Often, though, Amis's imagined reader seems more specific, a product of what Richard's son calls '"male-*pattern* boldness"' (p. 66): '[t]he sense of relief, of clarity and surety a man feels, at the prospect of temptation, when he knows he has washed his cock before leaving the house' (p. 175).

In his earlier novels, a more-or-less recognizable 'Martin Amis' might appear and make playful remarks, such as: '"I really don't want to join it, the whole money conspiracy"' (*Money*, p. 262). Martin Amis's presence in those books modishly alluded to Heisenberg's principle (an observed system interacts with its observer) and dramatized the unequal, even sadistic relationship between author and creation. *The Information* features more of 'Martin Amis' but less of the playfulness. Richard can't seem to decide if our present ironic age ends up with stories about writers, or with stories about 'rabble, flotsam, vermin' (p. 129). Certainly it is the latter which allowed Amis and 'Amis' to come into their own. Where in *London Fields* we learn that Keith Talent went through his mid-life crisis at the age of 19, or read that '[i]n common with Leo Tolstoy, Keith Talent thought of time as moving past him while he just stayed the same' (p. 172), the gap between the protagonist's low-life awareness and the author's cruelly superior understanding was the joke, the ironic motor for the fiction. But *The Information* is dominated by Richard Tull, a figure who (success and readability apart) is much like Martin Amis. Admittedly 'Martin Amis' tells us about the very specific perils of teenage dating when you stand only 5-feet-six ('or 5' 6½", according to a passport I once had' (p. 281)), but he, too, takes his kids to Dogshit Park, shares many of Richard's thoughts, and would seem to know what it is to experience a mid-life crisis – or, rather more grandly, 'a crisis of the middle years' (p. 62).

That crisis finds narrative expression in a kind of theatrical throwing-up of hands: 'how can I ever play the omniscient, the all-knowing, when I don't know *anything*?' (p. 63). Amis-the-narrator keeps reminding us that he doesn't control his own characters ('To be clear: I don't come at these people. They come at me. They come at me like information formed in the night' (p. 260)). Where the unstoppable John Self knew he had our sympathy (even if he wanted 'much, much more of it' (p. 29)), 'Amis' makes a show of interrupting himself, dismissing language and fiction as inadequate to the task, losing his patience like a harassed teacher: '[w]e are agreed – come *on*: we are agreed – about beauty in the flesh' (p. 15). But this forsaking of authority is everywhere betrayed by flexes of authorial muscle ('I think we might switch for a moment to the point of view of Richard's twin sons' (p. 43)), and by the sheer virtuosity of the writing. No one since Sterne has described impotence with such relish, even summarizing the theme in literature ('as for Casaubon and poor Dorothea [in George Eliot's novel *Middlemarch* (1871–72)]: it must have been like trying to get a raw oyster into a parking meter' (p. 168)). Perhaps the one thing Amis cannot do, we realize, is communicate a Beckettian sense of exhaustion, or a feeling that he is no longer in control. When he declares that 'the information is telling me to stop saying *hi* and to start saying *bye*' (pp. 124, 282), we can't help but note that only Amis would say it that well, with that vernacular spin – and, of course, want to say it at such length.

Redundancy is integral to the Amis project. Richard Tull delights in the self-defeating way in which abbreviations – MW for micro-wave, FWD for Four Wheel Drive – contain more syllables than the words they represent. Similarly, Amis flourishes three dazzling simi-les when one would do, or conjures up the perfect image, only to take it one step further: '[i]f the eyes were the window to the soul, then the window was a windscreen, after a transcontinental drive; and his cough sounded like a wiper on the dry glass' (p.46). Amis likens the beer-sticky streets of Ladbroke Grove to the darkness and fire of Pandemonium, and indeed his similes are increasingly Miltonic, always threatening to detach themselves from the main narrative and strike out on their own. Thus Richard, about to enter Gwyn's large and lavish house:

> Gwyn's set-up always flattened him. He was like the chinless cadet in the nuclear submarine, smalltalking with one of the guys as he untwirled the bolt (routine check) on the torpedo bay: and was instantly floored by a frothing phallus of seawater. Deep down out there, with many atmospheres. The pressure of all that Gwyn had. (pp.17–18).

The primary pleasure of reading *The Information* is that of being regu-larly swept up in these epic, frothing digressions. The effect is like the description of an American interviewer Richard encounters, whose superficial 'warmth' and 'niceness' (p.295) have been turned up on the dial 'as if these qualities, like the yield of a hydrogen bomb, had no upper limit – the range had no top to it – and just went on getting bigger and better as you lashed them towards infinity' (pp.295–6). Such passages are so enjoyably overwhelming, so addictively all-consuming, that you feel you want to read a novel by Martin Amis even when you are reading a novel by Martin Amis.[4] □

The responses of Loose and Mars-Jones are part of the process by which the reputation of a novel, the reputation of a writer, are formed, and John Nash's essay 'Fiction May be a Legal Paternity' considers *The Information* in relation to issues of critical reception, academic syllabi, and 'canonization' – the admission of a text to a 'canon' of works which are held to have 'literary value':

■ The recent publishing and journalistic excitement surrounding Martin Amis's latest novel, *The Information*, is a timely addition to the critical debate over the canon. It raises the issue of the necessity of judging contemporary writers while simultaneously revising the criteria of the literary . . . . . . In interview, Amis has explicitly raised the question of literary status as regards his own writing, and it is the subject-matter of *The Information*. An important issue raised by the novel is that of a reader's responsibility when faced by a fictional text that asks the question of value, and in doing so values that very question. In valuing the question, then, any answer remains only tentative. This novel proposes the necessary inevitability of a judgement that is at once invoked and left open, along with the question of how to value. In *The Information* Amis relates this question to genre and style, and to the question of canonicity, as well as raising the issue of our own responsibility towards current 'serious' writers. The novel is a timely reflection that anxieties over the canon may themselves be canonical for academic literary studies.

Amis has said that his latest novel is based around the problem that there are no demonstrable means of distinguishing good writing from bad (yet the distinction is still operative), and that one must simply place faith in one's talent.[5] Time, we are often told, will tell. In *The Information*, the principal protagonist, Richard Tull, repeats these lines with specific reference to the institutionalization of the problem within English studies:

> you cannot demonstrate, prove, establish – you cannot know if a book is good . . . The literary philosophers of Cambridge spent a century saying otherwise, and said nothing (p. 136).

We are then offered one-sentence summaries of the work of I. A. Richards, William Empson and F. R. Leavis.

There has indeed been a certain obfuscation of the boundary between author and character. A recent interview with the *Guardian Weekend* displayed a forlorn-looking Amis on its front page, head encircled by a background dartboard, with the title, 'An Interview with Mr Talent', a seemingly deliberate evocation of the arrows-artist Keith Talent from *London Fields*.[6] Most obvious in such journalism, of course, is a certain glorification of the writer, which invites confusion only to reinforce the singular talent of the author. This will be particularly important for *The Information*.

Behind Amis's questioning of literary value is a belief in its ultimate possibility, in what he calls (in a piece on Bellow) 'the luck of literary talent itself' (*Moronic Inferno*, p. 9). In *The Information* the sympathetic Richard is a critic more than a writer, someone whose value system more or less accords with a literary establishment or syllabus, at odds with the short-term values of a world that praises the prize-winning *Amelior*, written by his rival and oldest friend, Gwyn Barry. Richard works at a smalltime publishers, the Tantalus Press, home to the talentless. This is how the relationship between the two writers is described:

> The unspoken wisdom was that Richard . . . reserved the right to keep it clear that he thought Gwyn's stuff was shit . . . Oh yeah: and that Gwyn's success was rather amusingly – no, in fact completely hilariously – accidental. And transitory. Above all transitory. If not in real time then, failing that, certainly in literary time (p. 112).

Writing in this conceptualization operates on a dual temporality: as a commodity in 'real' history and autonomously in a . . . 'literary' dimension in which 'Shakespeare is the universal' (p.253). At the intersection of the two is the manifestation of talent, a sort of ur [primitive, original, earliest]-literature. However, it is often difficult to recognize that talent because of our local temporal horizons . . . . . .

[I]n *The Information*, . . . Richard's interior voice has been dislodged, which he blames on Gwyn's easy success. 'He wants to do to Gwyn what Gwyn has done to him. He wants to assassinate his sleep. He wants to inform the sleeping man; an I for an I' (p.91). Richard's desire for repose has been terminally disrupted: good cannot be told from bad and voice has also become indistinguishable. Traditions of the literary and the marketplace become commensurable discourses.

Amis's characters include varieties of the self-referential. There are the writer Martin Amis in *Money*, another writer, M.A., in *London Fields*, and I in *The Information*. Notably, the degree of explicit authorial intrusion has steadily diminished over the course of these three novels. At the same time that Amis writes his name out of these novels, the topic of writing and value becomes increasingly important for their plot and structure. In *Money* the literary value of writing is associated only with the character Martin Amis; writing is here much more about other denominations of value. In *London Fields* the quality of the written is a vehicle of exasperation for the narrator, jealous of the apparent success of M.A. By the time *The Information* is with us, however, literary value is the thrust and point of the book, and here Amis shows himself only in silhouette: in sign-language initials to a nameless child, in physical description.

Yet there is an I voice for *The Information* which is associated with Amis. And this voice worries too about its reception:

> In a million millennia, the sun will be bigger. It will feel nearer. In a million millennia, if you are still reading me, you can check these words against personal experience . . .

Later still, the oceans will be boiling. The human story, or at any rate the terrestrial story will be coming to an end. I don't honestly expect you to be reading me then (p. 114).

The Amis figure thus places himself in the literary timeframe, which is metaphorically also that of universal explosion.

Richard's restlessness is also that of the mid-life crisis (MLC), post fatherhood, and the information that comes to him at night, with '[i]ntimations of monstrousness' (p. 64), is the knowledge of his mortality. Amis's own MLC has been well-publicized in interviews. For this is the occasion when one first views the intersection of real time and literary time. For [Harold] Bloom, literature is itself a form of MLC: '[a]ll that the Western canon can bring one is the proper use of one's own solitude, that solitude whose final form is one's confrontation with one's own mortality'. Bloom is no longer in the spring of life and a certain morbidity creeps into his polemic. 'The canon' we learn 'is the minister of death'. It is, however, itself a rather aged minister not up with our times. 'We possess the canon because we are mortal and also rather belated.'[7]

However, the death may be other than human, it may also be literary (as Bloom's remarks on the inability to subsume tradition might imply). Not content with remarking on the apocalyptic tone of recent philosophy, Derrida has also described as 'literary' those texts 'which are very sensitive to this crisis of the literary institution . . . to what is called "the end of literature"'.[8] By inviting the impossible question – is this literature? – Amis's novel is a self-conscious symptom of the crisis Derrida mentions; and for Amis it is apocalyptically associated with the end of the world, with dying, and with the very notion of the ending. This is also generic, in two domains: such crises are part of literature (or reading) in an institutional frame (where does this course end?); and the endings of Amis's novels, although sometimes courting death and dissolution, attempt a generic openness.

Tragicomedy, the narrator of *The Information* tells us, is 'a genre which literature finds hard to do and rarely attempts' (p. 271). However, that is not quite the genre Amis is working in. Much of Amis's writing project has been to find and express the tragic, the romantic and the satiric within comedy (or is it the other way round?). The weather has altered the pattern of seasons, and the genres previously associated with them are similarly indistinct. But this is not tragicomedy. We are left with 'anti-comedy' (p. 491): the seasons are out of sync. Having done 'satire in summer, and comedy in autumn, and romance in winter' the spring beckons tragedy. 'But comedy has two opposites; and tragedy, fortunately, is only one of them' (p. 479). So what we are left with is a cycle – natural, generic – in disarray. The final page of *The Information* gestures towards this anti-comedy:

> Soon the apple blossoms were everywhere, as an element.
> And that was the blossoms gone for another year. But for a little while longer they flew in festive and hysterical profusion, as if all the trees were suddenly getting married (p. 494).

As with the ending of *Money*, the comedy that closes *The Information* is not tragic but melancholic.

For Amis, the information (it comes with the MLC) is apocalyptic: it's about death, local and universal. It is monstrous, the *telos* [end, final goal] of life. The end of 'the terrestrial story' is the end of the act of reading (we'll no longer be reading Amis then), but not necessarily the end of language. What follows is conceivably the language of death or the afterlife. In the meantime, new transformations of language are in order, the 'overpowering' discovery of 'a new way to write about modern life'.[9] According to this, then, Amis's talent is visibly 'new . . . modern'. Perhaps the 'new rhythms' (p. 70) that Richard is searching for? Despite the apocalyptic nature of Amis's writing, then, some other world, an after life, is envisaged as at least conceptually possible. The novel form will continue to mutate, to generate, in real time as it seeks to find a place in literary time.

Writing and sex have long been metaphorically linked, and perhaps somewhat obviously, Richard's creativity is sexual as well as literary, or rather, his impotence is both. The metaphor works both ways: his impotence is caused by literary envy, and his books are repeatedly described as offspring. Moreover, Richard is a 'marooned modernist' who 'didn't want to please the readers' (p. 170). In this he is quite different from Amis. Amis fans will be interested to note that for him writing is more a paternal contract: 'I feel about the reader the way I feel about my children'.[10] For Richard, '[i]f you had to settle on a one-word description of his stuff then you would almost certainly make do with *unreadable*' (p. 171). It is implied that Richard in the wake of the *Wake* [that is, James Joyce's *Finnegans Wake* (1939)], has missed the moment for unreadability.

There is an increasing likelihood that one might well have to settle for a one-word description of a writer. Amis has great fun with the temporal shift this involves, not unlike the shift of register occasioned by the backward direction of time in *Time's Arrow*.[11] Herein lies one of Amis's claims to literary status, for he is a stylist of some originality and many followers. One might note that 'style' is also related to the name and to the person, the identification of which is a troubled moment in Amis's fiction. The extent to which a style might be said to belong to an individual writer, with its inevitable intertextuality, renders problematic our organization of canons with their assumptions of propriety and value.

In *The Information*, style, like genre, is linked to a confused temporality. Richard is appalled by a disc jockey (Dub) who seems to think that one invents a slogan and then writes a book about it. Then there is Darko whose pizza is heated in the 'MW', where the time-saving device is abbreviated to more syllables than the word microwave. The danger, we are warned, seems to be of becoming like certain cosmologists with acronyms for the universe, who look back 'sixteen billion years' only to 'reach for catchphrases that were getting old six months ago' (p. 174). However, that has long been the lot of readers faced with the unreadable. Joyce wrote to his patroness in 1923, advocating the use of a new term to replace 'interior monologue':

> They [the reading public] cannot manage more than about one such phrase every six months – not for lack of intelligence but because they are in a hurry.[12]

This is the importance of a readership: the contemporary audience work in Amis's real time, but their reception can have an effect within literary time as well.

Amis's self-allusive, self-parodic narrators raise the question of literary value, the problem of judgement, for the work of Martin Amis. For instance, Amis's work is often situated in relation to canonical authors, such as his use of Shakespeare in *Money* (plot structure and characterization self-consciously borrowed from *Othello*). In *The Information*, ghosts of literature's GM Vauxhall Conference float through the working life of Richard Tull, a reviewer of biographies in a place where, '[i]f literature was the universal then all you'd ever get in here was space trash' (p. 424). Not only is a league table of literary value implied, but so is the issue of influence, of literary parentage. *The Information*, in its content, addresses the relationship between value and intertextuality by invoking plagiarism.

Richard thinks he has discovered a new poet, one Keith Horridge (Amis readers will immediately be alerted by the forename [that is, the allusion to Keith Talent in *London Fields*]), whose work excites Richard 'to seek out the pleasures, if any, of the literary middleman'. In the last batch to arrive, in their 'distinctive' (the word is used three times) envelope, clip and print, Horridge's first is 'Ever':

> In the Gnostic cosmogonies
> The demiurgi knead and mould
> A red Adam who cannot stand
> Alone (p. 422).

These lines make Richard consider him to be '"the real thing"' (p. 423).

Accompanying the poems is a note from Horridge concerning what he calls his "'newborns'" especially "'Woman'": "'[h]ere for the first time I cast off all influences and speak in my own voice'" (p.423). 'Woman' is pitiful self-pitying, and Richard recognizes that the lines from 'Ever' are lifted from some 'impregnably famous' (p.424) story by Borges. They are from 'The Circular Ruins' and the theme and some of the details of this scene in *The Information* are also reminiscent of Borges's tale, which is also about paternity, mortality and the impossibility of original creation.[13] Richard's cigarette recalls the fire that could not burn Borges's magician; Amis's waning sun, and afternoon moon is similar to Borges's 'vain light of afternoon'; Richard's informing 'soaring insomnias' (p.420) recall the magician's 'intolerable lucidity of insomnia';[14] and even the surname of the talentless (and son-less) Gwyn Barry (a heraldic term meaning divided by colours) forms an ironic comment on the magician's 'colourlessness'[15] of perception when his powers have waned.

One implication of 'The Circular Ruins' is that all creators (magicians, writers) are inventions of previous ones who in turn reinvent their predecessors. *The Information* values its own intertextual relation to Borges (among others). By placing itself in a tradition of canonic value, Amis's work asks that it be judged accordingly. Moreover, it asserts a distinction between intertextuality and plagiarism, one which can sometimes be notoriously difficult to define. Horridge has plagiarised Borges, Amis has been self-consciously intertextual.

Amis is presumably quite aware of the legal implications of intellectual property rights since his first novel, *The Rachel Papers* . . . was roughly used by Jacob Epstein in his *Wild Oats* [see pp.22, 185 note 14] and was also made into a shallow and pretentious film [see Bibliography, p.202]. This gravest of academic crimes is also the subject of some fear in Kingsley Amis's *Lucky Jim*.[16] The repeated metaphor of *The Information* – the novel as a child – helps demonstrate the complexity of the case: an author protects his published work by copyright, but one's child grows up as quite distinctive from the parent, even in competition with the parent. Martin Amis points out that he and Kingsley Amis are the only case of father and son writers whose work is coterminously 'out there' to be judged.[17] Literary canons become a paternal form of legal fiction.

Detecting Horridge's crime (Plagiarism: kidnap; seduction; literary theft) inspires Richard to adopt a similar charge against Gwyn Barry, so he writes an 'earlier version' of *Amelior*: a kind of plagiarism in itself. The bland *Amelior* wins so many readers because it does not challenge them; it is scrupulously inoffensive. Richard thinks that Gwyn has arrived at this method by following his idea of the development of fiction. That is to say, he thinks Gwyn has lifted his own idea.

As Richard puts it, in his unwritten *The History of Increasing Humiliation*, 'literature describes a descent': a decline in the status of fictional heroes.

'First, gods. Then demigods. Then . . . failed kings, failed heroes. Then the gentry. Then the middle-class . . . Then it was about you – . . . social realism. Then it was about *them*: lowlife. Villains. The ironic age' (p.435).

Only, this idea was earlier used by Tull's creator in his left-handed piece on his real-life hero, Saul Bellow, in the *London Review of Books* and then in *The Moronic Inferno*.

In thumbnail terms: the original protagonists of literature were gods; later, they were demigods; later still, they were kings, generals, fabulous lovers . . . ; eventually they turned into ordinary people. The twentieth century has been called an ironic age . . . Nowadays, our protagonists are a good deal more down the human scale than their creators (*Moronic Inferno*, p.5).

Distinctions between good and bad writing are broken down just as journalism has been the vehicle for an invited confusion between author and character. Richard's repetition of Amis's work has an ironic significance in the light of the context in which he uses it. The fact that Richard is here 'borrowing' from Amis's earlier non-fictional work is an interesting reversal of the plagiarism scenario. Furthermore, just as Richard is a fictional author, who repeats the work of an actual writer, so he invents a further fictional author in order to make the charge of plagiarism.

Having already told Gwyn a shamefaced lie, praising *Amelior*'s '"sheer originality"' (p.113), Richard contents himself with the thought that plagiary is a hazard 'that could sneak up on you, at [any] time' (p.425). Plagiarism, he tells a journalist, '"*always* comes out. It's just a matter of time"' (p.481). That is to say, its temporality is long-term; as with literary value, time will tell. Plagiarism becomes a necessary possibility because it can come at any time, and it will come. Literary parentage, influence, is not always determinable, but always necessary, and so illegitimacy is always in the offing. (Amis seems to say: the authentic and the stolen are monstrous twins not to be announced.)

The Information makes an interesting comment on the relation of plagiary to value, for plagiarism implies positive value in the copied text. It would be satisfying had *Amelior* been copied, but such 'trex' (p.43) is legally original. Horridge's theft is ignored – Richard silently dumps him – for he at least copied something that was good. By implying that Gwyn copied his idea, Richard suggests its positive value. By having Gwyn repeat his own work, Amis suggests the value of that.

An essay about literary value, canons and academic syllabi that focuses upon a particular writer implicitly values that writer, and in this instance the value is interesting because the writer is probably too contemporary to be canonized or academicized. Moreover, any claims for his 'inclusion' would not be motivated by biographical politics, by a desire for canons to be culturally representative. Amis is a white, middle-class Englishman, and his audience seems to be largely the same. Amis repeatedly answers the question of his target audience by saying that he writes for a version of his earlier self (a reply which may sustain the remarks of some of his detractors). As shown, *The Information* is not only about literary value, it is also about the conditions of reception of a work, including its own audience. That is to say, it implicitly recognizes that the two are linked. It is such self-conscious opening of the questions of value, genre and originality that makes *The Information* a suitable text for the concerns of contemporary literary studies.

Amis's conceptualization of the literary is thus complex. Although he speaks of 'talent', and implies a transcendent value, his notion of the literary is more than a formalist assumption. Amis's work goes beyond such formalism by openly engaging a generic crossover between the plots of popular fiction and serious writing, testing Nabokov's saying that style is morality. Whereas this essay argues the literary relevance of the content of Amis's novel, Amis clearly wants to be known as a stylist (and as I have indicated, his preoccupation with time makes him an interesting stylist). It also tests the notion of a division between popular and literary in its promotional aspect: the paperback covers of the early novels prominently suggest sex and drugs, and as shown, Amis's interviews and journalism have invited a certain obfuscation between writer and character, even to the extent where a fictional writer, Richard Tull, 'plagiarizes' his author's previous journalism. However, style and content cannot be so easily distinguished, for one of the most challenging aspects of Amis's work is its gift of a seductive story-telling ability to morally offensive characters, the best example of which remains John Self in *Money*. In that sense, such a character 'borrows' the author's style.

The Information asks that a concept of the literary – and hence of canons and syllabi – be directly related to a problematics of *writing*, that is, of language and style, of genre, and of the attendant institutions of literature. Amis seems to endorse the view (expressed also by Bloom) that it is generic or stylistic innovation that shapes canons. Such a view of literary history is at odds with a syllabus that attempts 'field coverage' not only chronologically and generically (in Gerald Graff's sense of the term) but also culturally.[18] One of the problems of Gwyn's bestseller is that it offends no-one [except, of course, Richard Tull!]. Ironically, it is precisely the *content* of *The Information* which raises this issue. This is important because it highlights the historical specificity of a work that explicitly expresses the concerns of academic criticism.

Amis's guarded promotion of intertextuality may be thought to be somewhat at odds with his invocation of the canon, for the indeterminable character of linguistic enmeshing may disrupt the clear delineation of a canon of great writers, to which the paternity metaphor used by Amis is quite appropriate (at least in Bloom's sense of the canon). However, such work as Amis's, which makes explicit a major concern of contemporary critical practice, is not simply a rearticulation or reflection of critical issues but a symptom of the extent to which fiction and criticism can do each others' jobs, and therefore indicative of changes in the institutional organization of literature.

Novels such as *The Information*, then, are part of a particular historical moment in the institutional development of a discipline of literary studies. The self-consciousness of much modernist and later fiction is both a form of self-criticism and a statement of criticism. The discipline's own self-consciousness about its modernity and social relevance are now the subject of a fiction that deliberately blurs academic/popular (literary and marketplace) distinctions. Furthermore, by asking the impossible question of its own value, Amis's work both invokes and disrupts canon-formation, be it on aesthetic or political agendas. The very notion of a canon, 'the canon-debate', is now a canonical text for literary studies.[19] □

Nash's essay suggests the significance of *The Information*'s concern with literary reputation, evaluation and endurance. It is one of the many ironies of Martin Amis's career that the novel which so directly engaged with these issues should also be the one which detracted from the higher esteem he had begun to earn with *Time's Arrow*. Throughout his writing life, Amis had shown a capacity to take punishment; but after the public bruising he had suffered with *The Information*, the question inevitably posed itself: what sort of novel would he write next?

CHAPTER TEN

Cops and Slobs: *Night Train* (1997) and *Heavy Water and Other Stories* (1998)

A MIS'S NEXT novel, *Night Train*, was a *tour de force*, a metaphysical thriller with a female narrator, a 'police' (not a 'policewoman') investigating an apparent suicide. But it received mixed reviews. In the *Independent on Sunday* of 28 September 1997, John Walsh suggested that the senior American novelist John Updike (1932–) was 'one of the few literary commentators that the America-loving Amis would go out of his way to impress'.[1] But, as Walsh pointed out, Updike was not impressed by *Night Train*. He acknowledged that he wanted to like the book 'because Martin Amis, for all his spectacular talents and fierce dedication, has received a lot of bad press lately . . . and because he is one of the few English writers of any era who has attempted to learn anything from the Americans'.[2] But he still ended up hating Amis's latest novel, and the rest of his review explained why:

■ [*Night Train*] . . . takes place in a nameless 'second-echelon American city' (p. 3) and, promisingly, is a takeoff on those [Dashiel] Hammett/ [Raymond] Chandler/[James M.] Cain 'tough-guy' detective stories behind noir films [that is, films such as *The Maltese Falcon* (1940), *The Big Sleep* (1943), *Double Indemnity* (1944)]. The hero, police detective Mike Hoolihan, is a heroine, a deep-voiced, 180lb, 5ft 10in former alcoholic, child-abused, Irish-American single woman in love with police work. 'I am a police' (p. 1) she announces at the outset, in the first of a number of American locutions new to this native speaker, and belts out her resumé in a typical burst of Amis lyricism:

In my time, I have come in on the aftermath of maybe a thousand suspicious deaths . . . So I've seen them all: [j]umpers, stumpers, dumpers, dunkers, bleeders, floaters, poppers, bursters. I have seen the bodies of bludgeoned one-year-olds. I have seen the bodies of gang-raped nonagenarians. I have seen bodies left dead so long that your only shot at a t.o.d. [time of death] is to weigh the maggots (p. 4).

This displays an excellent verve, holding out simultaneous hope of a thriller's bloody satisfactions and the subtler pleasures of postmodern irony, the transmutation of a lowdown genre in the manner of Umberto Eco['s *The Name of the Rose* (1980)] or Alain Robbe-Grillet's [*Les Gommes (The Erasers)* (1953)]. The puzzling crime in this: Jennifer Rockwell, a beautiful, intelligent, twentysomething, 5ft 10in, 140lb (no lightweight she) astronomer, is found sitting nude in a chair in her apartment, apparently a suicide. But, if so, she has shot herself three times in the mouth, and without apparent motive: she is widely admired, professionally successful, and happily mated with an associate professor of philosophy auspiciously named Trader Faulkner. Before her abrupt demise, they lived together for seven years, enjoyed a voracious sex life, and planned to marry and have children. Jennifer, furthermore, was the daughter of Colonel Tom Rockwell, a police higher-up who rescued our heroine Hoolihan from alcoholism some years ago . . .

The novel's style evinces the simple faith that repeating something magically deepens it . . . But the trouble . . . my trouble, the reviewer's trouble – with [*Night Train*] isn't the faux-demotic mannerisms or the heavy debt that Amis's Oz of an America owes to frequently cited cop shows on the telly but with the unmentionable way the plot proceeds. My problem is with the solution of the mystery and the point of the book.

Amis, beneath his banter, is a scowling, atrocity-minded author . . . In [*Night Train*] he makes us closely watch an autopsy and spotlights the void around us, not just the moral void, in which criminals 'fuck a baby and throw it over the wall' and 'chop up eighty-year-olds for laughs' (p. 84), but astronomical phenomena such as black holes, the missing dark matter, and the Bootes Void – 'more nothing than you could possibly imagine. It's a cavity 300 million light years deep' (p. 94). Jennifer Rockwell, all 140 luscious pounds of her, mentally dwelt among these crushing immensities: she thought that Stephen Hawking cracked the problem of black holes because he 'has been staring at death all his adult life' (p. 95). Within the astronomical equations, presumably, lies the clue. Detective Hoolihan, before going off on a self-destructive tear, speculates: 'I sometimes think that Jennifer Rockwell came from the future' (p. 147).

Young people, I was told last summer in Italy, are talking no longer about the postmodern but the post-human. To keep up with the future, they are going in for mutilation and artificial body parts. Amis writes out of a sensibility uncomfortably on the edge of the post-human. His characters strikingly lack the soulful, wilful warmth that he admires in Saul Bellow: they seem quick-moving automata, assembled of mostly disagreeable traits. His fiction lacks what the late Queenie [Q.D.] Leavis called 'positives'. As a mystery, [*Night Train*] suffers from a lack of minor characters even momentarily sympathetic enough to serve as red herrings. We can believe, initially at least, in Hoolihan's wonderfully slangy way of talking and her bluesy love of police work; we can't believe in anything about Jennifer Rockwell but her supposedly beautiful and now-vacated body. She, and [*Night Train*], become pure diagram, on a blackboard as flat as it is black.³ □

Updike's alarmed invocation of the 'post-human' suggests, of course, that he is applying humanist criteria to *Night Train* which may be inappropriate – though it is certainly possible to see Mike Hoolihan as a more sympathetic character than his review implies. The 'post-human' theme is echoed by the Booker prizewinning novelist Anita Brookner in her *Spectator* review of 27 September 1997:

■ The psychotic confidence of Martin Amis's new novel is no less worrying because its subject is psychotic confidence, of a kind which raises suspicions of irony. It may be post-modern. It is certainly post-human. There are few facts that are without disclaimers, few acts that are unambiguous. To read it is to undergo a temporary brain dysfunction . . .
Detective Mike Hoolihan . . . has to investigate the death of Jennifer Rockwell. Mike is a large, tough, slangy blonde with a damaged liver. Jennifer is the alpha female who works in the Department of Terrestrial Magnetism at the Institute of Physical Problems. But Mike is also Philip Marlowe [the private detective in Raymond Chandler's thrillers], with his not quite concealed aura of knightly chivalry. Mike goes down those mean streets into an explosion of brutal ellipses and aggressive abbreviations. What she finds out does nobody the slightest good and may even conceal the truth. But the truth is the most expendable commodity in a narrative which sets out to celebrate the demotic but ends up so out of hand that it is experienced as an assault on the reader's good faith.
Jennifer Rockwell is Mike Hoolihan's weakness, in that the two are exact opposites. While Mike was abused as a child and taken into care, Jennifer came from a loving family of mother, father, and brothers. While Mike was drying out in the Rockwells' spare bedroom Jennifer tiptoes in and reads to her. One night Mike gets a call to a suspicious death and finds Jennifer naked, on a chair, with a bullet in her head. It later transpires that there were three bullets, which would seem to rule out the possibility of suicide. When the body is opened up it is found to be in perfect order, with no sign of physical illness.
Certainly there are anomalies. There are traces of lithium [a drug used to control manic-depression] in the brain, but lithium has never been

prescribed by Jennifer's doctor. There is the lover who was last seen on the street looking 'distressed' (p. 54). There is the crazy female flatmate who was later removed to Canada. There is the worrying incident at the lab, where Jennifer falsified a computer in an apparently ludic episode which may have been caused by too much concentration on dark matter. There is the uneasy man whom she may have picked up at the Mallard Hotel. There is the wholesale obfuscation occasioned by Mike's police methods, which involve injustice, sentimental self-communings, and extreme economy with the truth. Above all there is the voice of the unreliable narrator, which is almost a mystery on its own.

Did Jennifer commit suicide because she had seen into the heart of a black hole? We are becoming used to novels which are Open University courses in astrophysics and chaos theory (no bad thing). Jennifer's work is mercifully never explained, but it seems to have left her as merry as a grig [an extravagantly lively person], apart from the incident with the computer. By the same token her lover may have been looking 'distressed' because on leaving Jennifer's apartment he had torn his jacket on the door handle. Jennifer's father . . . may have been a little too protective. The father is straight out of Chandler, as is the sinister atmosphere of the lawless city at night – except that this is a city almost totally deprived of its normal markers, as are sequential deduction and an unprejudiced perusal of the facts.

The conclusion, which is inconclusive, will satisfy no one. Even the red herrings are unconvincing. Even more alarming is the brutal, soft-headed behavior of the detective, who does not so much conduct the enquiry as make it up as she goes along. The case is declared closed just as the reader demands that it be handed over to someone more competent. It may be that the whole thing is parodic. Such games with verifiability are always exhausting, and if this is a game it is a subversive one.

There is another mystery here. The novel is written in a thorough-going American idiom and is roughly the same length as Saul Bellow's recent novella, *The Actual* (1997). It is even dedicated to Bellow and his wife Janis. The style may therefore be an attempt at homage, which is curiously off the mark. The point about Bellow's style is not merely that it is American but that it is Yiddish – but, as Philip Roth [the American novelist] would say, this is the Yiddish of Flaubert. Bellow meanders round the minds of those who do not readily or easily reproduce current usage. Amis, on the other hand, goes native so whole-heartedly that there is barely a trace of his literary origins. Streetwise, and without a trace of honest intention, *Night Train* will delight those with raised but skewed expectations. I found it frustrating, and all the more so because I expected more from an author whose dithyrambic [wild, passionate] narratives have so engaged me in the past.[4] □

The unfavourable concluding comparisons with Saul Bellow made by both Brookner and Updike could also be found in Russell Celyn Jones's review in the *Times*, which affirmed in its final paragraph that 'Amis had built his career out of twentieth-century American voices, principally Bellow's'; but whereas Bellow was 'inimitable as an archivist of the human condition', 'Amis is just not in that league . . . *Night Train* is a slick fast ride but it lacks soul'. Jones also considers the novel in relation to the genre of the police procedural, contending that 'there is something about Amis's voice that seems at odds with this genre', when he attributes to Hoolihan '[h]is mini-essays on the Big Bang and self-slaughter'.[5] A similar point is made by Sean O'Brien in the *Times Literary Supplement*, when he says that 'Amis seems uncertain of his relationship to the genre' and underlines its supposed seriousness too anxiously. He concludes that 'as a novella among other material in a collection, *Night Train* would be a striking curiosity, but as a thing in itself it must throw doubts on Amis's literary wisdom'.[6] Philip Oakes, in the *Literary Review*, thought it an effective 'pocket thriller' in which Amis used 'familiar techniques to arrive at his own discoveries', but that it had 'little to distinguish [it] from many other current runners . . . . . . Its weakness is that it does nothing different or better than what's being done already'.[7]

Natasha Walter, however, writing in the 'Women' section of the *Guardian*, felt that the novel did do something different and effective in Amis's *oeuvre* because, by writing in a female persona, he had released aspects of feeling that had not been evident in his previous work:

■ Already, critics are acting surprised that Amis has taken this step; Amis, the man's man, the writer the lads love, the guy whose heroines tend to be more tits'n'arse than thought and emotion.

You can't help wondering how on earth Martin Amis can take a woman's point of view on life. He's already had a go; his 1981 novel. [*Other People*] was told almost entirely from a female viewpoint, and it was probably his worst novel to date. It was telling that its beautiful heroine, Mary Lamb, was an amnesiac . . . [*Other People*] was about as convincing at depicting a woman's world as [*Take A Girl Like You*], the 1960 novel Kingsley Amis wrote from a female point of view. His heroine was also a beauty and, though not an amnesiac, she was quite silly enough to be one.

As a teenager, I remember reading [*Other People*] and [*Take A Girl Like You*] with a sort of fascinated horror. I knew Martin and Kingsley Amis were solidly important writers. And these novels showed how they believed women would think; maybe how they wanted women to think; maybe how all men wanted women to think. These dumb, beautiful, vulnerable women . . . weighed on me. How could intelligent men be guilty of such failures of imagination when it came to exploring a woman's point of view?

But that failure isn't the inevitable result of male writers speaking in female tones. Men can also create very good female narrators. From the very first paragraph of [*Night Train*] . . . you can see its narrator is hardly the stooge of a cynical writer. Mike Hoolihan has an independent, determined spring in her step. More than that, Amis has clearly found that writing from a woman's point of view has released unexpected emotion into his work. There is unfeigned sorrow behind this little thriller and a sense of direct intimacy Amis has not attempted before. It is as though by taking on a woman's voice, he has found a franker, less ironic world than in his other novels.

There is something almost shocking about watching a male writer feeling so easy in the guise of a woman. But it's hardly unknown. On the contrary. It's surprising how many of the finest moments in 19th and 20th century novels rest on just that somersault; a male writer, with no way of knowing first-hand what he is describing, suddenly leaps into a woman's world and taps a spring of real emotion . . . . . .

[I]n the late 20th century[, m]en's worlds and women's worlds have moved so much closer together [than in the nineteenth and early twentieth century] that when a male writer takes on a woman's voice, it doesn't have to sound terrifically different from his own voice. Detective Mike Hoolihan, with her black pants and her wisecracks, her confidence and her straightforward relationships with men, isn't always that far from Martin Amis's own experience.

But Amis is still crossing some sort of boundary in writing as a woman . . .[8] □

Adam Phillips, in the *London Review of Books*, agrees with Natasha Walter that the persona of Hoolihan allows Amis 'a broader register of feeling than is usual in his narrators' and acknowledges that Mike Hoolihan '(at long last) . . . "represents" the female voice in Amis's boyish fiction', but identifies her as 'Martin Amis in drag' and 'glaringly, . . . brashly literary'. But this is only one set of observations in an appreciative and insightful review that grasps something of the complexity and power of the novel:

■ Self-consciousness, as a threat and a promise (the furtive logic, the demonic secrecy people live by), has been [Amis's] great preoccupation, which makes suicide, especially the suicide of the nominally happy – the theme of *Night Train* – an obvious subject for him . . . Nothing makes people more other to us than their suicide. Nothing makes them seem both more and less the authors of their own lives. Every suicide, like every mid-life crisis, is a whodunnit. So after *The Information*, in its wake as it were, comes the far more troubled and troubling *Night Train*: a mock-thriller about a subject profoundly unmocked by its author. And one of Amis's most interesting books.

In a sense *Night Train* is two books, one of which could be called 'A Reply to My Critics' . . . on a first reading some of the least convincing parts [of the novel] are those in which Amis tries to confront, if that's the word, political correctness; or rather, his own much-vaunted lack of it . . . . . . 'Allow me to apologize in advance', . . . Mike Hoolihan . . . says very early on in the book, 'for the bad language, the diseased sarcasm, and the bigotry' (p. 4). *Night Train* tries to be partly about what there might be to apologise for . . . . . . Hoolihan . . . seems unusually cultured (i.e., Oxbridge-cultured) for a middle-aged American cop . . . Amis often makes [her] sound like a slangy, street-wise academic.

. . . In *Night Train* there is, in a sense, a character in drag called Martin Amis, who is the narrator of the book. Or, to put it another way, a character who is the opposite of the 'real' Martin Amis: 'I used to be something', the female cop Mike Hoolihan writes, 'but now I'm just another big blonde old broad' (p. 7). Hoolihan is so glaringly, so brashly literary that Amis makes us wonder what he's up to. Hoolihan is the writer of the book, a shrewd 'reader' of crime scenes, suicide notes and character; she solves crimes like a novelist writes a book ('I had to do this alone and in my own way. It's how I've always worked' (p. 45)); she makes umpteen literary allusions; she's even in a biography 'Discuss Group' (p. 5) . . . it is too obvious that Mike Hoolihan, however much (at long last) she 'represents' the female voice in Amis's boyish fiction – and she is, curiously, one of the most haunting narrators in Amis's work – does not sound like a female cop in Homicide in [an American city] (even though few of us have known any). A cop like Mike . . . would not, one imagines, write a book like *Night Train*, or 'apologize . . . for any inconsistencies in the tenses (hard to avoid, when writing about the recently dead)' and for the informalities in the dialogue presentation (p. 5). If there is a joke here, who is it on? And why does the writer have so much to apologise for? An apology, as Amis knows, is also a justification and an excuse. Like a suicide note, *Night Train* asks to be read more than once.

. . . the effect of [Amis's] often brilliant verbal delirium is to make things wordy and unreal, language warding off the experience it describes, whisking it away. So Hoolihan implausibly combines the thug and the poet . . . Hoolihan, as a device, as a shrewd and suspect invention, allows Amis a broader register of feeling than is usual in his narrators: some of it too deliberately assuaging of his critics but some of it extremely puzzling. And not in a trivially self-conscious way; partly because the novel is more subtle than Amis's previous books about the terrifying mislogic of self-consciousness. Hoolihan doesn't sound like she ought to sound, if she is what she says she is. What she . . . writes – the way she represents herself – doesn't tally with what she is. Just like the faultlessly happy – 'a kind of embarrassment of perfection' (p. 7) – suicide, Jennifer Rockwell: at once the double and the nemesis of the narrator . . .

. . . *Night Train* is at once a spoof of a detective novel: Hoolihan is investigating a crime that was solved when it was discovered, and for which the perpetrator cannot be punished, in which the punishment is the crime. And a metaphysical thriller about cause and effect: 'we all want a why for suicide' (p. 108), as Hoolihan says. And the novel makes much gruesomely amusing play with the fact that when it comes to suicide it's easy to get the who and the how, but the why is a big problem. So the question that the novel investigates – the 'crime' that a novelist might be better equipped to solve than a detective – is: what is character without motive? 'Suicides generate false data' (p. 70), Hoolihan informs us: '[a]s a subject for study, suicide is perhaps uniquely incoherent. And the act itself is without shape and without form' (p. 77). It makes a mockery, in other (more literary) words, of the expected satisfactions of narrative. Suicide violates our sense of an ending. And frantic to make sense of it, we are forced to go back to the beginning.[9] □

Phillips's review of *Night Train*, more sophisticated and perceptive than those of Updike or Brookner, is able to account for an unease that the novel arouses which they are unable to explain except as literary weakness because of the constricting critical categories to which they adhere (as novelists of a more conventional stamp than Amis, a certain degree of self-protection perhaps also determines their response). Phillips is also able to suggest why *Night Train* is likely to be reread and why it will probably attract, in future, further subtle and extended criticism – criticism which will certainly begin by consulting Phillips as an indispensable starting-point.

In 1998, Amis published *Heavy Water and Other Stories*, his first collection of short stories since *Einstein's Monsters*. Three of them were originally published in journals well before any of the stories in *Einstein's Monsters* were written – 'Denton's Death' (*Encounter*, 1976), the title story, 'Heavy Water' (*New Statesman*, 1978, though, according to Amis's own note, 'rewritten, 1997' (p. 153)); and 'Let Me Count the Times' (*Granta*, 1981). In the *Times* of 25 September 1998, Russell Celyn Jones, who had reviewed *Night Train* unfavourably, remarked that these three tales 'seem rather mothballed alongside the newer ones' but served to show 'Amis's maturation, and not only as the stylist he is primarily famed for being':

■ A cavalcade of sex-prose in ['Let Me Count the Times'] is displaced by an ironic review of the emotional consequences of extra-marital sex in ['State of England'], written in 1996 [and first published in the *New Yorker*] . . . . . . ['Heavy Water'] is set two years before the Labour Party were to be booted out of office for the next 18 years and purports to show the exhaustion of working class culture. There is something quite risible about the young Amis sounding off about the proletariat . . . and his comic hyperbole falls flat.

However, in ['State of England'], the best story in the collection, he regroups around the same theme armed with both a pitiless comedy and a compassion hitherto missing. His protagonist, Mal, is a culture-free untouchable reminiscent of Keith Talent in *London Fields*, who is attending his son's school sports day. He and his estranged wife talk to each other across the field by mobile phones, while the sun . . . sets on their textless, impoverished world. But there is redemption for Mal in the story, and when he gets beaten up by some opera-goers who discover him clamping their Range Rover, you can detect Amis switching empathies since the long-gone days of penning ['Heavy Water']. 'You know what it was like? A revolution in reverse . . . Two bum-crack cowboys scragged and cudgelled by the quality' (p. 69).

The class motif is reprised in the very fine story, ['The Coincidence of the Arts' (1997)]. In ['The Janitor on Mars' (1997)] he alights upon preoccupations aired in *Night Train*. What marred *Night Train* mars this foray into science fiction also. Reams of appropriated high-tech dialogues do not amount to character . . .

Amis's predominant technique is inversion. So poets in ['Career Move' (first published in the *New Yorker*, 1992)] earn millions in Hollywood while screenwriters have to contend with rejection slips from little magazines. These one-joke stories could easily run out of steam if it were not for his crackling prose propping up the whole enterprise – usually a parallel narrative structure working in counterpoint: background-foreground in constant mutation.[10] □

The inversion identified by Jones was also evident in his own and Natasha Walter's responses to *Heavy Water*. Where Jones had disliked *Night Train* and admired the stories in *Heavy Water* that did not resemble that flawed work, Walter had praised *Night Train* and found *Heavy Water* objectionable because it lacked the previous book's 'gentler look at life':

■ [I]n *Heavy Water*, Amis, again and again, serves up characters such as Denton [in 'Denton's Death'], 'an old tramp in a dirty room' (p. 32); Vernon [in 'Let Me Count the Times'], . . . a sad businessman who masturbates [']23.8 times a week' (p. 81); and Rodney [in 'The Coincidence of the Arts'], a bad painter whose pyjamas have remained unlaundered for 15 years. Why does Amis do it to himself? Why does he do it to us? Why do we have to keep sitting down with such antipathetic men? . . . [The] anti-hero [of 'State of England'] is a recognizable archetype. He's fat – of course; ugly – naturally; slobby – enormously so; and inarticulate, which almost goes without saying. But not quite without saying.

In fact, Amis revels in laying out quite how gross his protagonist is. Mal's not just fat; he's 'five feet nine in all directions' (p.35). He's not just slobby; he's sick-making – he remembers, in detail, eating over 100 burgers before a transatlantic flight and putting all the toilets on the plane out of order (pp.58–60). And he's not just inarticulate; he's breathtakingly inarticulate. 'Call Adam a cunt, but you couldn't call him corny' (p.39), goes one riff. 'The defence was crap and midfield created fuck-all' (p.43) goes another.

But when it all gets too much we suddenly move out of Big Mal's mind and into Martin Amis's, into his fluent sentences, his startling articulacy. So we find ourselves standing outside Big Mal and looking at him as he stands there – '[a]wkward, massively cuboid, flinching under a thin swipe of dark hair' (p.41) – and we quickly feel reassured that we aren't really going to be left alone with Big Mal. No, Amis will be there all the way, touching us on the elbow, showing us quite how unprepossessing his anti-hero is.

There is necessarily something patronizing in this desire of Amis's to set his protagonists up for us to snigger over. Why does he so rarely create a character he can respect, a story that isn't a bit of a joke; that isn't something he's already seen through and laughed at? I felt that he did make that experiment in *Night Train*, his only novel to suggest that a current of human sympathy might run between author and protagonist. But many readers didn't like that gentler look at life. Amis's usual expression – the fixed sneer – is what brings in the fans.

But let's get back to Big Mal, since he distils much of what's good and bad in Amis's work. Mal's story is a sad one; as a slobby, ugly, fat, inarticulate man the cards are stacked against him. He fails in his work, he fails in his marriage, he is even failing in the work that comes after that (clamping cars) and in the affair that takes the place of his marriage. He's running scared. Modern life scares him. Women scare him. Black people scare him. *Restaurants* even scare him. We catch him on school sports day where, naturally, his son loses his race and he himself loses the dads' race.

'State of England' is a big title for such a story; and Amis clearly thinks this is more than just the story of Big Mal; rather, this is the story of England – and especially of the English male. And it's a nasty story, Amis keeps telling us. It's about bad food and bad sex, about fear and failure.

Why does his vision sometimes appear a little thin and forced? . . . Is [Amis] pushing himself to his limits, as it were; is he daringly presenting Britain with a vivid and horrifying picture of itself? Or has Amis actually retreated from having to put himself and his own society on the line? By making his State of England stories – and although this is the only one called 'State of England', it's not the only one that could bear that title – centre on such crazily pathetic men, Amis makes sure that his readers never need to feel implicated in the tale. Oh sure, men might read them and wince a little over the protagonists' pornographic imaginations; and anyone might read them and wince at the protagonists' taste in television and junk food. But as Amis pushes his characters deeper and deeper into the dirt, ridiculing their accents and bodies, their social ineptitude and myriad failures, their wounded faces and their impotence – well, his readers begin to feel more and more comfortable. You know these tales aren't about you, not really; and though you can sit down and spend an hour playing some game with them, you know that, in the end, it is exactly that: a game.[11] □

The sharply contrasting responses of Walter and Jones to *Heavy Water* demonstrate the continued power of Martin Amis's fiction to provoke vigorous controversy and debate – and, as Walter's attack demonstrates, intelligent hostile criticism of his work can have as much and sometimes more to offer than intelligent praise. A critic who wanted to offer a detailed close reading of *Heavy Water*, as Rachel Falconer did of *Einstein's Monsters* (pp. 87–96), might well start from Walter's proposition that more than one of the stories could be called 'State of England'; and Walter's perceptive strictures should not be ignored by anyone who wished to produce a serious positive account of Amis's fiction as a whole.

As yet, of course, Amis's fiction is an unfinished whole: there is still, one hopes, much more to come. A memoir is promised for the millennium, but this excursion into autobiography is unlikely to divert him from fiction for long. And while it is impossible to predict what kind of fiction he might produce next, one thing is certain: it will be exciting. But what can be said of Amis's achievement to date?

In an interview in 1990, George Steiner – the critic whose verdict Amis feared when he started *Time's Arrow* – proposed an interesting criterion for literary judgement: 'I wonder what book you have in your pocket when things go very, very wrong, or – an even harsher test in some ways – are ecstatically wonderful.'[12] It is unlikely that much of Martin Amis would be to Steiner's taste, and his verdict on *Time's Arrow* has not been made public. But when, to use the central metaphor of Amis's eighth novel, the information comes at night – the information about mortality, decay, suffering, failure, and the atrocities perpetrated by that intelligent, cruel, flesh-eating species that is our own[13] – then one could do worse than have the fiction of Martin Amis by one's side: its complex cartography of our lower depths, its vivid mapping of our traumas and transgressions, can serve as a guide and a stay. And its anatomy of the abyss does not preclude, as in Samson's letter to Kim Talent at the end of *London Fields*, glimpses of possibility that are the more dazzling for being hard-won from all that goes wrong in time.

NOTES

INTRODUCTION

1 For an account of the hostile criticism of Dickens in the nineteenth and twentieth centuries, and some key examples, see Nicolas Tredell, ed., *Charles Dickens: 'Great Expectations'*, Icon Readers' Guides series (Cambridge: Icon Books, 2000), chapters one and two.

2 See Tredell (2000), p. 8.

3 Even in his own time, however, Dickens was not wholly immune to, for example, pro-feminist criticism. Kate Flint points out that John Stuart Mill wrote to his wife in 1865 about coming across a copy of *Bleak House* by '[t]hat creature Dickens' in the London Library, taking it home and reading it, and finding that Dickens 'has the vulgar impudence in this thing to ridicule the rights of women'. Quoted Flint, *Dickens*, Harvester New Reading series (Brighton: Harvester, 1986), p. 122.

4 Sara Mills, 'Working with Sexism: What Can Feminist Text Analysis Do?', in Peter Verdonck and Jean Jacques Weber, eds., *Twentieth-Century Fiction: From Text to Context*, Interface series (London and New York: Routledge, 1995), pp. 206–19.

5 Anthony Quinn, 'The Investment', *Independent Magazine* (25 March 1995), p. 34.

6 Jonathan Wilson, 'A Very English Story', *The New Yorker* (6 March 1995), pp. 105–6.

7 Wilson (1995), p. 106.

8 James Diedrick, *Understanding Martin Amis*, Understanding Contemporary British Literature series (Columbia, South Carolina: University of South Carolina Press, 1995), p. 5.

9 Kevin Byrne, 'The Two Amises [a radio conversation]', *Listener*, 92:2368 (15 August 1974), p. 220.

10 Wilson (1995), p. 106.

11 Charles Michener, 'Britain's Brat of Letters: Who *is* Martin Amis, and why is everybody saying such terrible things about him?', *Esquire*, 107 (January 1987), p. 109.

12 Wilson (1995), p. 106.

13 '[F]ourteen schools' is the figure given by both Diedrick (1995), p. 3, and David Hawkes, 'Martin Amis (1949–)', in George Stade and Carol Howard, eds., *British Writers: Supplement IV* (New York: Charles Scribner's Sons, 1997), p. 25; 'thirteen schools' is the figure given by David Thomson, 'Martin Amis (25 August 1949–)', in Merritt Moseley, ed., *British Novelists Since 1960: Second Series, Dictionary of Literary Biography*: vol. 194 (Detroit, Michigan: Gale Research, 1997), p. 8.

14 See Martin Amis, 'Expelled', in *Visiting Mrs Nabokov* (1994), pp. 186–88.

15 Martin Amis, in Ann Thwaite, ed., *My Oxford*, My [Cambridge/LSE/Drama School, etc.] series (London: Robson Books, 1977), p. 213.

16 *Sunday Times* (5 July 1998), Section 1, p. 36.

CHAPTER ONE

1 Peter Prince, 'Out of Afrika', *New Statesman*, 86:2226 (16 November 1973), p. 744.

2 Peter Ackroyd, 'Highway of Good Intentions', *Spectator*, 231:7587 (24 November 1973), p. 674.

3 'Martin Amis', in John Haffenden, *Novelists in Interview* (London and New York: Methuen, 1985), pp. 9–10.

4 Susan Morrison, 'The Wit and the Fury of Martin Amis', *Rolling Stone*, 578 (17 May 1990), p. 101.

5 Jonathan Swift, *The Poems of Jonathan Swift*, Harold Williams, ed. (London: Oxford University Press, 1958), p. 597.

6 [*Diedrick's Note:*] Amis acknowledged the autobiographical matrix of *The Rachel Papers* in an interview [Michener (1987), p. 110.] [*Editor's Note:*] In fact, the reference to the autobiographical aspect of *The Rachel Papers* seems to occur on p. 111 of the Michener interview, where the following exchange takes place: [Michener:] 'Why was there never any thought about sending you to boarding school or trying to get you ready for Oxford?'/ [Martin Amis:] 'I don't know. My parents were always sort of loose about that sort of stuff. Somehow, in all the shuffling about, it never occurred to them that I would have to know Latin, for example, in order to be considered for Oxford. But suddenly it just came to me, and I did a crash education in one year, studying Latin and poetry, which I really took to, especially the Romantics. *The Rachel Papers* was about that year'.

7 Kingsley Amis, *Lucky Jim* (Harmondsworth: Penguin, 1961), p. 140.

8 Diedrick (1995), pp. 20–6, 27, 28, 30–1.

9 Hawkes (1997), p. 27.

10 Hawkes (1997), p. 28.

11 Alfred Tennyson, *Poems and Plays*, T. Herbert Warren, ed., revised and enlarged by Frederick Page (London, Oxford, New York: Oxford University Press, 1971), p. 90.

12 Hawkes (1997), pp. 28–29.

13 Richard Brown, 'Postmodern Americas in the Fiction of Angela Carter, Martin Amis and Ian McEwan', in Ann Massa and Alistair Stead, eds., *Forked Tongues: Comparing Twentieth-Century British and American Literature* (London and New York: Longman, 1994), p. 99.

14 See Martin Amis, 'A Tale of Two Novels', *Observer* (19 October 1980), p. 26; Jacob Epstein's letter under almost the same heading (26 October 1980), p. 32; and, for a detailed account, 'The Epstein Papers: Writing a Second First Novel', Chapter 3 in Thomas Mallon, *Stolen Words: Forays into the Origins and Ravages of Plagiarism* (New York: Ticknor and Fields, 1989), pp. 89–143.

15 Kingsley Amis's second novel was *That Uncertain Feeling* (London: Victor Gollancz, 1955).

CHAPTER TWO

1 See 'What's "Dark Secrets?"', *Sunday Times* (3 April 1977), p. 35.

2 See Betty Radice, *Who's Who in the Ancient World* (Harmondsworth: Penguin, 1973), pp. 163 (Menippus), 191 (Petronius), 155 (Lucian).

3 John Mellors, 'Raw Breakfast', *The Listener*, 30:2430 (30 October 1975), p. 582.

4 Elaine Feinstein, *New Statesman*, 90:2326 (17 October 1975), p. 480.

5 Peter Ackroyd, 'Tirades', *Spectator*, 25:7686 (18 October 1975), pp. 510–11.

6 Brown (1994), p. 99.

7 Brown (1994), pp. 99–100.

8 Neil Powell, 'What Life Is: The Novels of Martin Amis', *PN Review* 20, 7:6 (1981), pp. 43–44.

9 Anon., 'Many Voices', *Times Literary Supplement*, 3760 (29 March 1974), p. 346.

10 Mikhail Bakhtin, *Problems of Dosteovski's Poetics*, trans. R. W. Rotsel (Ann Arbor: Ardis, 1973), p. 94.

11 Bakhtin (1973), p. 94.

12 Bakhtin (1973), p. 94.

13 Diedrick (1995), pp. 32, 33–8, 39.

14 Hawkes (1997), p. 30.

CHAPTER THREE

1 See Blake Morrison, *The Movement: English Poetry and Fiction of the 1950s* (Oxford and New York: Oxford University Press, 1980).

2 Blake Morrison, 'Into Nastiness', *Times Literary Supplement*, 3967 (14 April 1978), p. 405.

3 Paul Ableman, 'Sub-texts', *Spectator*, 240:2815 (15 April 1978), pp. 23–24.

4 Diedrick (1995), p. 40.

5 [*Diedrick's Note:*] For Kingsley Amis's relationship to Larkin, see Kingsley Amis, *Memoirs* (New York: Summit, 1991), pp. 51–64. In a 1993 interview, Philip Amis remembers being deeply offended when *Success* appeared; he clearly assumed that he was the only 'Philip' alluded to in the dedication [whereas, Diedrick suggests, the dedication also alludes to Philip Larkin]: 'You could say I was the taller one who got his come-uppance in the end . . . But that's simplistic. It was probably about Martin and someone else, a friend, say. I happen to be taller than Martin but there the resemblance ends. When he dedicated the book to me I was outraged, but it's water off a duck's back now'. Andrew Billen, 'On a Whimsical Carousel Ride Back to Boyhood', *Observer Review* (28 November 1993), p. 8.

6 [*Diedrick's Note:*] See Martin Amis, 'Philip Larkin 1922–1985', [in] *Visiting Mrs Nabokov and Other Excursions* (New York: Harmony, 1994), [pp. 201–6]; 'Don Juan in Hull', *New Yorker* (12 July 1993), pp. 74–82.

7 Philip Larkin, 'This Be the Verse', in Anthony Thwaite, ed, *Collected Poems*, revised edn (London and Boston: The Marvell Press and Faber and Faber, 1990), p. 180.

8 Martin Amis, 'The Sublime and the Ridiculous: Nabokov's Black Farces', in Peter Quennell, ed., *Vladimir Nabokov, His Life, His Work, His World: A Tribute* (New York: William Morrow, 1980), p. 76.

9 Martin Amis, '*Lolita* Reconsidered', *Atlantic*, 270:3 (September 1992), p. 111.

10 Diedrick confuses Greg and Terry four times in this paragraph, which inadvertently emphasises his earlier point that the two characters are 'doubles'. See Diedrick (1995), pp. 40, 43, 44.

11 Graham Fuller, 'Yob Action', *Village Voice* (1 December 1987), p. 66.

12 Diedrick (1995), pp. 42, 43–4, 45–7.

13 Powell (1981), p. 42.

14 Thom Gunn, 'Elvis Presley', *The Sense of Movement* (London: Faber and Faber, 1957), p. 31.

15 Powell (1981), pp. 44–5.

CHAPTER FOUR

1 Allan Massie, *The Novel Today: A Critical Guide to the British Novel 1970–1989* (London and New York: Longman in association with the British Council, 1990), p. 47.
2 Victoria Glendinning, 'Lamb's Tale from Amis', *Listener*, 105:2702 (5 March 1981), p. 319.
3 Glendinning (1981), p. 320.
4 Glendinning (1981), p. 319.
5 Alan Hollinghurst, 'Opening Eyes', *New Statesman*, 101:2608 (13 March 1981), p. 21.
6 John Sutherland, 'Making Strange', *London Review of Books*, 3:5 (19 March–1 April 1981), p. 21. This issue bears on the front cover a large close-up photograph of Martin Amis looking soulful and drowsy.
7 Craig Raine, 'A Martian Sends a Postcard Home' (Oxford; New York; Toronto; Melbourne: Oxford University Press, 1979), pp. 1–2.
8 Kingsley Amis, *Ending Up* (London: Jonathan Cape, 1974), p. 23.
9 Christopher Reid, 'Baldanders', *New Statesman*, 95:2443 (13 January 1978), p. 52.
10 See Craig Raine, *The Onion, Memory* (Oxford and New York: Oxford University Press, 1978), pp. 2–8.
11 Blake Morrison 'In the Astronomical Present', *Times Literary Supplement*, 4066 (6 March 1981), p. 247.
12 Paul Ableman, 'Fairies and Violence', *Spectator*, 246:7967 (21 March 1981), p. 22.
13 Craig Raine's 'A Martian Sends a Postcard Home' first appeared in the *New Statesman*, 94:2440/2441 (23 and 30 December 1977), p. 891. It was reprinted, along with a reprint of Reid's 'Baldanders', in the *New Statesman*, 95: (20 October 1978), p. 520, under a short piece by James Fenton, 'Of the Martian School', which announced that he had awarded the Prudence Farmer Prize, for a poem published in the *New Statesman*, to 'A Martian . . . ' but had decided to create a second prize for Reid's 'Baldanders' – hence, perhaps, the conjunction of these two poems in Blake Morrison's review of *Other People*.
14 Haffenden (1985), pp. 17–18.
15 Martin Amis, 'Point of View', *New Statesman*, 98:2543 (14 December 1979), p. 954.
16 Diedrick (1995), p. 55.
17 Diedrick (1995), p. 57.
18 Samuel Taylor Coleridge, *The Collected Works of Samuel Taylor Coleridge*, James Engell and W. Jackson Bate, eds. (Princeton: Princeton University Press, 1983), vol. 7, part 2, p. 7.
19 Morrison (1990), p. 98.
20 In Sartre's play *Huis Clos*, Garcin, one of the three characters trapped together in Hell, comes to the conclusion that 'l'enfer, c'est les Autres' ['Hell is other people']. See Sartre, *Huis Clos* suivi de *Les Mouches* (Paris: Gallimard, 1976), p. 92.
21 Patrick McGrath, 'Martin Amis', in Betty Sussler, ed, *Bomb Interviews* (San Francisco: City Lights Books, 1992), p. 192.
22 Sartre (1976), p. 94.
23 Haffenden (1985), p. 18.
24 Brian Finney, 'Narrative and Narrated Homicides in Martin Amis's *Other People* and *London Fields*', *Critique: Studies in Contemporary Fiction*, 37:1 (Fall 1995), pp. 3, 4–7, 8.
25 Massie (1990), p. 47.

CHAPTER FIVE

1 Richard Todd, 'The Intrusive Author in British Postmodernist Fiction: The Cases of Alasdair Gray and Martin Amis', in Matei Calinescu and Douwe Fokkema, eds., *Exploring Postmodernism: Selected Papers Presented at a Workshop on Postmodernism at the XIth International Comparative Literature Congress, Paris, 20–24 August 1985*, Utrecht Publications in General and Comparative Literature vol. 23 (Amsterdam/Philadelphia: John Benjamins, 1987; 1990), p. 123.
2 'Self's the Man', Larkin (1990), pp. 117–8.
3 [*Editor's Note:*] For a discussion of the names in *Money*, see Leonard R.N. Ashley, '"Names Are Awfully Important": The Onomastics of Satirical Comment in Martin Amis'[s] *Money: A Suicide Note*', *Literary Onomastics Studies*, 14 (1987), pp. 1–48.
4 Eric Korn, 'Frazzled Yob-Gene Lag-Jag', *Times Literary Supplement*, 4253 (5 October 1984), p. 1119.
5 Brown (1994), pp. 100–1.
6 'Bernard Bergonzi', in Nicolas Tredell, *Conversations with Critics* (Manchester: Carcanet, 1994), pp. 101–2.
7 William Shakespeare, *The Complete Works*, Stanley Wells, Gary Taylor, John Jowett, William Montgomery, eds. (Oxford: Oxford University Press, 1988), p. 848.
8 Haffenden (1985), pp. 3, 4–5, 6, 7, 11, 12, 13–14, 21–2, 23–4.
9 Kingsley Amis, 'A Bookshop Idyll', in Philip Larkin, ed., *The Oxford Book of Twentieth-*

NOTES

Century *English Verse* (Oxford: Oxford University Press, 1978), pp. 527–8. This quotation, p. 528.

10 Karl Miller, *Doubles: Studies in Literary History*, corrected edn (Oxford; New York: Oxford University Press, 1987), pp. 411–4.

11 Todd (1990), p. 123.

12 Todd (1990), p. 124.

13 Todd (1990), p. 125.

14 Todd (1990), p. 131.

15 Miller (1987), p. 409.

16 Korn (1984), p. 1119.

17 Shakespeare (1998), p. 998.

18 Todd (1990), pp. 131, 132–5.

19 Todd (1990), p. 135.

20 Miller (1985), p. 411.

21 Todd (1990), p. 136.

22 Laura L. Doan, '"Sexy Greedy Is the late Eighties": Power Systems in Amis's *Money* and Churchill's *Serious Money*', *The Minnesota Review: A Journal of Committed Writing*, 34–5 (Spring 1990), p. 69.

23 Haffenden (1985), p. 5.

24 Benoîte Groult, 'Les Portiers de Nuit', trans. Elissa Gelfand, in Elaine Marks and Isabelle de Courtivron, eds., *New French Feminisms* (New York: Schocken, 1981), p. 72.

25 Suzanne Kappeler, *The Pornography of Representation* (Minneapolis: University of Minneapolis Press, 1986), p. 50.

26 Doan (1990), pp. 70–1, 72–4, 74–5, 78, 79.

27 Not all the praise came from men, however. The novelist Emma Tennant (1937–) concluded a laudatory review of *Money*: '[i]n this world impoverished by money [Martin Amis] has discovered an extraordinary verbal richness' ('Seriously Rich', *Literary Review*, 77 (November 1984), p. 45).

CHAPTER SIX

1 William Rose Benét, ed, *The Reader's Encyclopedia*, 2nd edn (London: Book Club Associates, 1977), p. 1071.

2 David Profumo, 'Interview: David Profumo drops in on Martin Amis', *Literary Review*, 107 (May 1987), pp. 41–2.

3 Adam Mars-Jones, *Venus Envy*, Chatto Counterblasts series (London: Chatto and Windus, 1990), p. 8.

4 Mars-Jones (1990), p. 1.

5 Mars-Jones (1990), p. 2.

6 Mars-Jones (1990), p. 11–17.

7 M. M. Bakhtin, 'Forms of Time and of the Chronotope in the Novel: Notes toward a Historical Poetics' (1937–38), in Michael

Holquist, ed., trans. Caryl Emerson and Michael Holquist, *The Dialogic Imagination: Four Essays* (Austin: University of Texas Press, 1981), p. 84.

8 Rachel Falconer, 'Bakhtin's Chronotope and the Contemporary Short Story', *South Atlantic Quarterly*, 97:3–4 (Summer-Fall 1998), p. 706.

9 Falconer (1998), p. 707.

10 Jorge Luis Borges, 'The Garden of Forking Paths', trans. Donald A. Yates, in Donald A. Yates and James E. Irby, eds., *Labyrinths: Selected Stories and Other Writings* (Harmondsworth: Penguin, 1970), p. 51.

11 [*Falconer's Note* – *but her page reference is incorrect:*] Elizabeth Deeds Ermarth, *Sequel to History: Postmodernism and the Crisis of Representational Time* (Princeton: Princeton University Press, 1992), p. 20.

12 [*Falconer's Note:*] Critics who have traced romance roots in short fiction include Propp, Bettelheim, Bierce, Canby, Marcus, May, and Rohrberger, while those who have identified the genre's realist affinities include Baldwin, Barzini, and Fitzgerald; see the annotated bibliography in *The New Short Story Theories*, ed. Charles E. May (Athens, Ohio: Ohio University Press, 1994), pp. 312–37.

13 Fredric Jameson, *Postmodernism, or, The Cultural Logic of Late Capitalism* (London: Verso, 1991).

14 [*Falconer's Note:*] See Italo Calvino, 'Lightness', in *Six Memos for the Next Millennium*[: *The Charles Eliot Norton Lectures 1985–86*, trans. Patrick Creagh (London: Vintage, 1996 [1988]), pp.]3–29.

15 Falconer (1998), pp. 708–11, 712–17, 718–20.

CHAPTER SEVEN

1 *Times* (22 September 1989), p. 1. The six shortlisted authors were Margaret Atwood, *Cat's Eye*; John Banville, *The Book of Evidence*; Sybille Bedford, *An Unsentimental Education*; Kazuo Ishiguro, *The Remains of the Day* (the eventual winner); James Kelman, *Disaffection*; and Rose Tremain, *Restoration*.

2 Melvyn Bragg, 'A Novel Experience', *Sunday Times* (17 December 1989), Section C, p. 1.

3 Jane Ellison, 'Battle Fields', *Guardian* (12 October 1989), p. 21.

4 See the *Times* (27 October 1989), p. 24.

5 Anon., 'News', *Times Literary Supplement* 4524, *Liber* section (15 December 1989), p. 13.

187

6 David Lodge, 'The Novelist Today: Still at the Crossroads?', in Malcolm Bradbury and Judy Cooke, eds., *New Writing* (London: Minerva in association with the British Council, 1992), p.208.

7 Ellison (1989), p.21.

8 Penny Smith, 'Hell Innit: The Millennium in Alasdair Gray's *Lanark*, Martin Amis's *London Fields*, and Shena Mackay's *Dunedin*', *Essays and Studies*, 48 (1995), p.115.

9 D.H. Lawrence, *Women in Love* (Harmondsworth: Penguin, 1960), p.36.

10 See Doan, p.79.

11 Smith (1995), pp.120–3.

12 Bernard Levin, 'Forgetfulness of Things Past', *Sunday Times* (8 March 1981), p.43.

13 Charles Trueheart, 'Through a Mirror, Darkly', *Washington Post* (26 November 1991), p.B2.

14 Jean Baudrillard, *Simulations*, trans. Paul Foss, Paul Patton, Philip Beitchman (New York: Sémiotexte, 1983), p.11.

15 Melvyn Bragg, *The South Bank Show* (*Martin Amis*) (London Weekend Television, 1989).

16 Bragg, *South Bank Show* (1989).

17 Graham Fuller, 'Murder He Wrote: Martin Amis's Killing Fields', *Village Voice* (24 April 1989), p.75.

18 Bellante, Carl and John, 'Unlike Father, Like Son: An Interview with Martin Amis', *Bloomsbury Review*, 12:2 (March 1992), p.5.

19 Finney (1995), pp.8–15.

20 Roland Barthes, 'The Death of the Author', in Stephen Heath, ed. and trans., *Image-Music-Text* (New York: Hill and Wang, 1977), p.146.

21 Mick Imlah, 'A Dart in the Heart', *Times Literary Supplement* (29 September 1989), p.1051. The bound volume of the *Times Index: January–December 1989* (Reading: Research Publications, 1990), p.21, gives an incorrect date of 'SEPT 5' for this issue.

22 [*Holmes's Note:*] Imlah rightly concludes that Samson 'has the personal thinness of a weak invention: his Americanness, for example, is registered by one reference to a "faucet" in nearly 500 pages' (Imlah (1989)), p.1051.

23 Luc Sante, 'Cheat's Tale', *The New Republic* (30 April 1990), p.46.

24 Mark MacLeod, 'Apocalyptic Metafiction in Four British Novels', Diss[ertation], Lakehead University (1993), p.115.

25 Bette Pesetsky, 'Lust Among the Ruins', *New York Times Book Review* (4 March 1990), p.42.

26 Fredric Jameson, *Postmodernism, or, The Cultural Logic of Late Capitalism* (Durham, N.C.: Duke University Press, 1991), p.x.

27 MacLeod (1993), p.113.

28 Linda Hutcheon, *A Poetics of Postmodernism: History, Theory, Fiction* (New York and London: Routledge, 1988), pp.207–8.

29 Hutcheon (1988), p.26.

30 Pesetsky (1990), p.42.

31 Jean-François Lyotard, *The Postmodern Condition: A Report on Knowledge*, trans. Geoff Bennington and Brian Massumi (Minneapolis: University of Minnesota Press, 1984), p.xxiv.

32 Frederick Holmes, 'The Death of the Author as Cultural Critique in *London Fields*', in Ricardo Miguel Alfonso, ed., *Powerless Fictions? Ethics, Cultural Critique, and American Fiction in the Age of Postmodernism* (Amsterdam – Atlanta, Georgia: Editions Rodopi B.V., 1996), pp.53–61.

33 Peter Stokes, 'Martin Amis and the Postmodern Suicide: Tracing the Postnuclear Narrative at the Fin de Millennium', *Critique: Studies in Contemporary Fiction*, 38 (1997), pp.305–6.

34 Will Self, 'An Interview with Martin Amis', *The Mississippi Review*, 21:3 (Summer 1993), p.150.

35 Self (1993), p.149.

36 George Szamuely, 'Something Amiss with Martin', *National Review*, 42:10 (28 May 1990), p.47.

37 Self (1993), p.149.

38 Michel Foucault, 'What Is an Author?', Paul Rabinow, ed., *The Foucault Reader*, ed. Paul Rabinow (New York: Pantheon, 1984), p.120.

39 Graham Fuller, 'The Prose and Cons of Martin Amis', *Interview* (May 1995), p.125.

40 Stokes (1997), pp.306–11.

CHAPTER EIGHT

1 See George Steiner, *Language and Silence: Essays 1958–1966*. 2nd edn. with new Preface by the author (London: Faber, 1985), and 'George Steiner', in Tredell (1994), pp.75–93.

2 'Martin Amis interviewed by Christopher Bigsby', in Bradbury and Cooke (1992), p.173.

3 Eleanor Wachtel, 'Eleanor Wachtel with Martin Amis: *Interview*', *Malahat Review*, 114 (March 1996), p.47.

4 Frank Kermode, 'In reverse', *London Review of Books* 13:17 (12 September 1991), p.11.

5 M. John Harrison, 'Speeding to cradle from

grave', *Times Literary Supplement*, 4614 (20 September 1991), p. 21.

6 For a discussion of the shortlisted novels, see 'Six characters in search of a Booker', *Sunday Times* (29 September 1991), Section 7, pp. 10–11.

7 Roger Scruton, 'International Books of the Year', *Times Literary Supplement*, 4628 (13 December 1991), p. 12.

8 Donald E. Morse, 'Overcoming Time: "The Present of Things Past" in History and Fiction', in Donald E. Morse, ed., *The Delegated Intellect: Emersonian Essays on Literature, Science and Art in Honor of Don Gifford*, American University Studies Series XXIV, American Literature, vol. 57 (New York, Washington DC/Baltimore, 1995), p. 203.

9 Morse's other example is Sean O'Faolain's *And Again?* (1979; Harmondsworth: Penguin, 1982).

10 Morse (1995), p. 205.

11 J. T. Fraser, 'Human Temporality in a Nowless Universe', *Time and Society*, 1:2 (1992), p. 167.

12 David H. Hirsch, *The Deconstruction of Literature: Criticism after Auschwitz* (Hanover, New Hampshire and London, UK: University Press of New England, 1991), p. 158.

13 *The Tower and the Abyss*, quoted in Hirsch (1991), p. 159.

14 Dr. Allodi quoted in Don Gifford, *The Farther Shore* (New York: Atlantic Monthly Press, 1990), p. 202.

15 Hirsch (1991), pp. 152–3.

16 Hirsch (1991), p. 152. [*Morse's Note:*] Hirsch cites as his source: 'Terrence Des Pres's brilliant chapter, "The Excremental Assault", in *The Survivor: An Anatomy of Life in the Death Camps* (New York: Oxford University Press, 1976).'

17 [*Morse's Note:*] 'Lords of lies and trash' is a variant on the traditional title and picture of Satan as 'Lord of Lies' whom Dante pictures as trapped at the bottom of hell in the frozen cesspool formed by all the rivers of the world dumping their sewage (that is, their crap and trash) down into hell.

18 Friedmann (1990), p. 88, quoted in Fraser (1992), pp. 159–73.

19 [*Morse's Note:*] The final revelation is specific about the direction of time's arrow, but it is not the first or only revelation. In the final weeks of the baby's life, the narrator attempts to understand what happened and finds many unanswered questions; 'questions of time: certain durations' (p. 172). There were also hints earlier in paintings he observed in the Metropolitan Museum of Art in New York

(p. 95).

20 [*Morse's Note:*] Stephen Donaldson, *Epic Fantasy in the Modern World* (Kent, Ohio: Kent State University Libraries, 1986), no page no.

21 Kurt Vonnegut, *Slaughterhouse-Five* (New York: Dell, 1970), pp. 54–5.

22 Hayden White, *The Content of the Form: Narrative Discourse and Historical Representation* (Baltimore and London: The Johns Hopkins University Press, 1987), p. 57.

23 [*Morse's Note:*] Adorno actually spoke of lyric poetry, rather than poetry in general. Later he added: 'I have no wish to soften the saying that to write lyric poetry after Auschwitz is barbaric; it expresses in negative form the impulse which inspires committed literature. The questions asked by a character in Sartre's play *Morts Sans Sépulture* (1946), "[i]s there any meaning in life when men exist who beat people until the bones break in their bodies?", is also the question whether any art now has a right to exist; whether intellectual regression is not inherent in the concept of committed literature because of the regression of society . . . ' (Theodor Adorno, 'Commitment', *Aesthetics and Politics* (1965), trans. Francis MacDonagh, in Dennis Walder, ed., *Literature and the Modern World* (London: Oxford University Press, 1990)), p. 95.

24 Hirsch (1991), p. 158.

25 [*Morse's Note:*] Adorno rightly objected to ' . . . victims [being] used to create something, works of art, that are thrown to the consumption of a world which destroyed them. The so-called artistic representation of the sheer physical pain of people beaten to the ground by rifle-butts contains, however remotely, the power to elicit enjoyment out of it. The moral of this art, not to forget for a single instant, slithers into the abyss of its opposite' (Adorno (1990)), p. 96. Diving head-long into that abyss, however, is an advertized discussion 'Humor and the Holocaust' at a recent international scholarly conference.

26 [*Morse's Note:*] 'The fourth dimension is the native medium of evil. Villains traditionally love the night because it obscures their deeds; but no darkness obscures things as effectively as time' (Robert Grudin, *Time and the Art of Living* (New York: Ticknor and Fields, 1988)), p. 82.

27 Morse (1995), pp. 208–10, 211, 212–15, 216–18.

28 Richard Wolin, '*Schindler's List* and the Politics of Remembrance', *In These Times* (21 March 1994), pp. 28–31.

29 Vladimir Nabokov, *Lectures on Literature*, Fredson Bowers ed. (San Diego: HBJ, 1980), p. 3.

30 Robert Jay Lifton and Eric Markusen, *The Genocidal Mentality Nazi Holocaust and Nuclear Threat* (New York: Basic Books, 1990), p. 196.

31 [*Easterbrook's Note:*] *Schloss Hartheim* is a 'killing hospital' or 'killing center'. Converted 'nursing homes, mental hospitals, or prisons' (Lifton (1990), p. 164), the killing centers 'were run by physicians, usually psychiatrists' (p. 164); as *'pre-genocidal* institutions' (p. 166), they were mere studies in the art of butchery.

32 [*Easterbrook's Note:*] Between March and June 1944, over 450,000 Hungarian Jews were gassed at Auschwitz alone. Estimates of the total number of Jews murdered at Auschwitz vary widely, from 1.1 to 3 million, although most historians say the smaller number is probably correct. During the period of extermination, beginning with forced-labour camps in 1937 and ending with the German surrender in 1945, some 5.1 to 5.9 million Jews were killed, an astonishing two-thirds of European Jewry and 40 percent worldwide. Auschwitz was liberated on 27 January 1945.

33 [*Easterbrook's Note:*] The implicit source of this architectonic [construction] is quantum theory. As the Nobel laureate Richard Feynman notes: '[i]n all the laws of physics that we have found so far there does not seem to be any distinction between past and future' ([Richard Feynman, 'The Distinction of Past and Future', *The Treasury of Physics* (Boston: Little, Brown, 1991), p. 148]). Physics conceives temporality as *mere* order rather than *meaningful* order.

34 Lifton (1990), p. 13.

35 Lifton (1990), p. 197.

36 [Compare] Lifton (1990), p. 148.

37 [*Editor's Note:*] For further discussion of the names in *Time's Arrow*, see Phil Joffe, 'Language Damage: Names and Naming in Martin Amis's *Time's Arrow*', *Nomina Africana: Journal of the Names Society of Southern Africa*, 9:2 (October 1995), pp. 1–10.

38 Lifton (1990), p. 148.

39 Lifton (1990), p. 106; see also pp. 102–4 and 196–7.

40 [*Easterbrook's Note:*] Such as Rudolf Hoss; for details on the physician's greed and whining, see [George J. Annas and Michael A. Grodin, eds., *The Nazi Doctors and the Nuremberg Codes* (New York: Oxford University Press, 1992).]

41 [*Editor's Note:*] Flaubert wrote in 1857, in a letter to Mlle. Leroyer de Chantepie: 'An artist must be in his work like God in creation, invisible and all-powerful; he should be everywhere felt, but nowhere seen'. Trans. Francis Steegmuller, in Richard Ellmann and Charles Feidelson, Jr., eds., *The Modern Tradition: Backgrounds of Modern Literature* (New York: Oxford University Press, 1965), p. 132.

42 Neil Easterbrook, '"I know that it is to do with trash and shit, and that it is wrong in time": Narrative Reversal in Martin Amis'[s] *Time's Arrow*', *Conference of College Teachers of English*, 55 (1995), pp. 52–4, 55–6, 57–9.

43 See Anthony Thorlby, ed, *The Penguin Companion to Literature: Europe*, revised edn (London: Allen Lane, The Penguin Press, 1971), p. 173.

44 [*Menke's Note:*] In his ['Afterword'] to the novel, Amis acknowledges the influence of 'a certain paragraph – a famous one – by Kurt Vonnegut' (p. 168): the passage of *Slaughterhouse-Five* (1969) in which Billy Pilgrim, unmoored in time, watches a late movie about World War II 'backwards, then forwards, again' (Vonnegut (1991)), p. 53.

45 A.S. Eddington, *The Nature of the Physical World: Gifford Lectures 1927* (Cambridge: Cambridge University Press, 1928), p. 68.

46 [*Menke's Note:*] For another discussion of Amis's use of *The Nazi Doctors*, with different examples from Lifton, see Diedrick (1995), pp. 165–68. As Diedrick comments, 'virtually every aspect of *Time's Arrow* – historical setting, plot, characterization, even language – is informed by *The Nazi Doctors*'; his concession that there are 'many more parallels than those discussed here' (p. 173, n22) must apply to my discussion as well. [*Editor's Note:*] See also Easterbrook's discussion in this Guide (pp. 134–41).

47 Robert Jay Lifton, *The Nazi Doctors: Medical Killing and the Psychology of Genocide* (New York: Basic Books, 1986), p. 425.

48 Lifton (1986), p. 418.

49 Lifton (1986), p. 427.

50 Lifton (1986), p. 30.

51 [*Menke's Note:*] In fact the second law of thermodynamics does not declare that entropy cannot decrease in a closed system, merely that the probability that it will decrease is mathematically infinitesimal.

52 Eddington (1928), p. 74.

53 Eddington (1928), p. 68.

54 Eddington (1928), p. 69.

55 [Menke's Note:] For an exploration of time's arrow in a more recent popular scientific work, see [Stephen W.] Hawking, *A Brief History of Time: From the Big Bang to Black Holes* (Toronto: Bantam, 1988), pp. 143–53. Here Hawking investigates the relationship between the thermodynamic and psychological arrows explored by Eddington and the cosmological arrow that marks the direction of time according to the universe's expansion.
56 Eddington (1928), p. 51.
57 Gillian Beer, 'Eddington and the Idiom of Modernism', in Henry Krips, J. E. McGuire, Trevor Melia, eds., *Science, Rhetoric, and Reason* (Pittsburgh: University of Pittsburgh Press, 1995), pp. 295–315.
58 Eddington (1928), p. 51.
59 Eddington (1928), p. 51.
60 Brian McHale, *Postmodernist Fiction* (New York: Methuen, 1991), p. 10.
61 Eric Charles White, 'Negentropy, Noise, and Emancipatory Thought', in N. Katherine Hayles, ed., *Chaos and Order: Complex Dynamics in Literature and Science* (Chicago: University of Chicago Press, 1991), p. 263.
62 McHale (1991), pp. 84–96; Amy J. Elias, 'Defining Spatial History in Postmodernist Historical Novels', in Theo D'haen and Hans Bertens, eds., *Narrative Turns and Minor Genres in Postmodernism*, Postmodern Studies 11 (Amsterdam: Rodopi, 1995), pp. 105–14.
63 J[ames] Clerk Maxwell, *Theory of Heat* (New York: Appleton, 1872), p. 308.
64 Maxwell (1872), pp. 308–9.
65 Richard Menke, 'Narrative Reversals and the Thermodynamics of History in Martin Amis's *Time's Arrow*', *MFS: Modern Fiction Studies*, 44 (1998), pp. 959–75, 976–77.

CHAPTER NINE

1 Adam Mars-Jones, 'Looking on the Blight Side', *Times Literary Supplement*, 4799 (24 March 1995), p. 19.
2 Quoted on back cover of first UK hardback edition of *The Information*. No source given.
3 'Trex', originally the brand-name of a type of cooking fat, and used in a way which alludes to this at one point in *The Information* ('slapping some slice of trex on to a frying pan' (p. 444)), is a recurrent term in the novel to mean junk or rubbish, mainly but not exclusively of a literary or subliterary kind – see pp. 43, 75, 133, 138, 156, 171, 214, 289, 319, 421.
4 Julian Loose, 'Satisfaction', *London Review of Books*, 17:9 (11 May 1995), pp. 9–10.

5 [Nash's Note:] Martin Amis, interviewed by Melvyn Bragg on the South Bank Show, London Weekend Television (19 March 1995).
6 Sally Vincent, 'In the Boy, Find the Man', *The Guardian Weekend Section* (18 March 1995), pp. 12–23.
7 Harold Bloom, *The Western Canon: The Books and Schools of the Ages* (London: Macmillan, 1994), pp. 30, 32.
8 Jacques Derrida, '"This Strange Institution Called Literature": An Interview with Jacques Derrida', in Derek Attridge ed., *Acts of Literature* (New York: Routledge, 1992), p. 42.
9 [Nash's Note:] Saul Bellow, backcover blurb for *The Information*.
10 Vincent (1995), p. 23.
11 See Maya Slater, 'Problems When Time Moves Backwards: Martin Amis's *Time's Arrow*', *English: The Journal of the English Association*, 42:173 (Summer 1993), pp. 141–53.
12 [Nash's Note:] To Harriet Shaw Weaver, 19 November 1923, in Richard Ellmann, ed., *Letters of James Joyce*, vol. 3 (London: Faber, 1966), p. 83.
13 Borges, 'The Circular Ruins', trans. James E. Irby, in Borges (1970), p. 75.
14 Borges (1970), p. 74.
15 Borges (1970), p. 76.
16 [Nash's Note:] For the points about Epstein and *Lucky Jim* I am indebted to Don Nichol, 'Rewriting Plagiarism', *Angelaki*, 1:2 (Winter 1993/94), pp. 13–23.
17 Bryan Appleyard, 'Balancing the Books: Martin Amis's Mid-Life Crisis', *Sunday Times Magazine* (19 March 1995), pp. 30–8.
18 See Gerald Graff, *Professing Literature* (Chicago and London: University of Chicago Press, 1987), pp. 6–9.
19 John Nash, 'Fiction May Be A Legal Paternity: Martin Amis's *The Information*', *English: The Journal of the English Association*, 45:183 (Autumn 1996), pp. 213–24.

CHAPTER TEN

1 *Independent on Sunday* (28 September 1997), Section 2, p. 5. Amis has written about Updike in *The Moronic Inferno*, pp. 155–9, and *Visiting Mrs Nabokov*, pp. 47–59.
2 John Updike, 'It's a Fair Cop', *Sunday Times Books* (21 September 1997), Section 8, p. 1.
3 Updike (1997), pp. 1–2. It should be noted that this review contains a number of misquotations from *Night Train*: on p. 1, 'weigh the maggots' is rendered 'size the maggots', and on p. 2, 'fuck' is rendered 'f***' (perhaps

for reasons of decorum), 'eighty-year olds' as 'eight-year olds' and 'has been staring' as 'had been staring'.

4 Anita Brookner, 'Farewell, My Lovely', *Spectator*, 279:8826 (27 September 1997), pp. 36–37.

5 Russell Celyn Jones, 'Unable to Do the Locomotion', *Times*, 18 September 1997, p. 42.

6 Sean O'Brien, 'Choo-Choo Time', *Times Literary Supplement*, 4929 (19 September 1997), p. 22.

7 Philip Oakes, 'Bloody and For Real', *Literary Review*, 232 (October 1977), p. 50.

8 Natasha Walter, 'The Gender Benders', *Guardian* (29 July 1997), pp. 4–5.

9 Adam Phillips, 'Cloud Cover', *London Review of Books*, 19:20 (16 October 1997), pp. 3, 6.

10 Russell Celyn Jones, 'Not Such Light Reading', *Times* (24 September 1998), p. 40.

11 Natasha Walter, 'Fat Men, Thin Lives', *New Statesman* (25 September 1998), pp. 81, 82.

12 Tredell (1994), p. 80.

13 Compare Jean-Paul Sartre, *Critique de la raison dialectique précédée de Question de méthode:*

Tome I: Théorie des ensembles pratiques. Bibliothèque des Idées series. Paris: Editions Gallimard, 1960, p. 208. 'Rien, en effet – ni les grands fauves ni les microbes – ne peut être plus terrible pour l'homme qu'une espèce intelligente, carnassière, cruelle, qui saurait comprendre et déjouer l'intelligence humaine et dont la fin serait précisément la destruction de l'homme. Cette espèce, c'est évidemment la nôtre se saisissant par tout homme chez les autres dans le milieu de la rareté.' 'Nothing, neither microbes nor the Lords of the Jungle, can be more terrible for man than an intelligent, cruel, flesh-eating species, capable of understanding and outwitting human intelligence, and whose prime aim lies in the destruction of man. This species is obviously our own, comprehending itself in each individual through the intermediary of others in an environment dominated by scarcity' (trans. Philip Thody, in his *Sartre: A Biographical Introduction*, Leaders of Modern Thought series (London: Studio Vista, 1971), p. 123).

SELECT BIBLIOGRAPHY

Novels
(Details of first UK editions, followed by details of editions quoted in this Guide, where these are different from the first UK editions.)

The Rachel Papers. London: Jonathan Cape, 1973. Harmondsworth: Penguin, 1984.
Dead Babies. London: Jonathan Cape, 1975. London: Penguin, 1984. [Also Published as *Dark Secrets*. London: Triad/Panther Books, 1977.]
Success. London: Jonathan Cape, 1978. London: Penguin, 1985.
Other People: A Mystery Story. London: Jonathan Cape, 1981.
Money: A Suicide Note. London: Jonathan Cape, 1984. London: Penguin, 1985.
London Fields. London: Jonathan Cape, 1989. London: Penguin, 1990.
Time's Arrow or The Nature of the Offence. London: Jonathan Cape, 1991. London: Penguin Books in association with Jonathan Cape, 1992.
The Information. London: Flamingo, 1995.
Night Train. London: Jonathan Cape, 1997. London: Vintage, 1998.

Short Stories
Einstein's Monsters. London: Jonathan Cape, 1987.
Heavy Water and Other Stories. London: Jonathan Cape, 1998.

Poem
'Point of View'. *New Statesman*, 98:2543 (14 December 1979), p. 954.

Non-fiction
Books
Invasion of the Space Invaders. London: Hutchinson, 1982.
The Moronic Inferno And Other Visits to America. London: Jonathan Cape, 1986.
Visiting Mrs Nabokov and Other Excursions. London: Jonathan Cape, 1993. London: Penguin, 1994.

Articles
'Martin Amis', in Ann Thwaite, ed. *My Oxford*. My [Cambridge/LSE/Drama School, etc.] series. London: Robson Books, 1977, pp. 201–13.
'The Sublime and the Ridiculous: Nabokov's Black Farces', in Peter Quennell, ed. *Vladimir Nabokov: His Life, His Work, His World: A Tribute*. New York: William Morrow, 1980, pp. 73–87.
'A Tale of Two Novels', *Observer* (19 October 1980), p. 26 (on Jacob Epstein's alleged plagiarism, in his novel *Wild Oats* (London: Alison Press, Secker and Warburg, 1980), of *The Rachel Papers*. See also Epstein's reply under the same heading (26 October 1980), p. 32, and Mallon (1989) below).
'Lolita Reconsidered'. *Atlantic* 270.3 (September 1992), pp. 109–20.
'Don Juan in Hull'. *New Yorker* (12 July 1993), pp. 74–82.

Interviews

These are arranged in order of year of appearance, rather than in alphabetical order of author/interviewer, to make it easier, where appropriate, to link particular interviews with specific Amis novels or short story collections.

1974

Byrne, Kevin. 'The Two Amises [a radio conversation]'. *Listener*, 92:2368 (15 August 1974), pp.219–20.

1984

Haffenden, John. 'Domestic Burlesque: Interview: John Haffenden Talks to Martin Amis'. *Literary Review incorporating Quarto*, 76 (October 1984), pp. 31–38. (Reprinted, with a slightly amended introduction, in 1985 – see next entry.)

1985

Haffenden, John, ed. *Novelists in Interview*. London: Methuen, 1985, pp.1–24.

1987

Michener, Charles. 'Britain's Brat of Letters: Who *Is* Martin Amis, and Why Is Everybody Saying Such Terrible Things about Him?'. *Esquire*, 107 (January 1987), pp.108–11.

Hebert, Hugh. 'Messages From the Other Side'. *Guardian* (25 April 1987), p.11.

Profumo, David. 'Interview: David Profumo Drops in on Martin Amis'. *Literary Review*, 107 (May 1987), pp. 41–42. (*Einstein's Monsters.*)

1989

Ritchie, Harry. 'The Greening of Martin Amis'. *Sunday Times* (10 September 1989), Section G, pp.8–9.

Taylor, Paul. 'Waiting for the End'. *Independent* (16 September 1989), p.32.

1990

Morrison, Susan. 'The Wit and the Fury of Martin Amis'. *Rolling Stone*, 578 (17 May 1990), pp.95–102.

1991

Lawson, Mark. 'The Amis Babies'. *Independent Magazine* (7 September 1991), pp.42–44.

Wood, James. 'The Literary Lip of Ladbroke Grove'. *Weekend Guardian* (7–8 September 1991), pp.12–14.

Trueheart, Charles. 'Through a Mirror, Darkly'. *Washington Post* (26 November 1991), Section B, pp.1–2.

Hoare, Philip. 'Martin Amis'. *Details* (November 1991), pp.132–3.

1992

Bellante, Carl and John. 'Unlike Father, Like Son: An Interview with Martin Amis'. *Bloomsbury Review*, 12:2 (March 1992), p.5.

Bigsby, Christopher. 'Martin Amis interviewed by Christopher Bigsby', in Malcolm Bradbury and Judy Cooke, eds. *New Writing*. London: Minerva in association with the British Council, 1992, pp. 169–84.

McGrath, Patrick. 'Martin Amis', in Betty Sussler, ed. *Bomb Interviews*. San Francisco: City Lights Books, 1992, pp. 187–97.

1993

Self, Will. 'An Interview with Martin Amis'. *Mississippi Review* 21:3 (Summer 1993), pp. 143–69.

1995

Wilson, Jonathan. 'A Very English Story'. *New Yorker* (6 March 1995), pp. 96–106.

Vincent, Sally. 'In the Boy, Find the Man'. *Guardian Weekend* (18 March 1995), pp. 12–23.

Appleyard, Bryan. 'Smart Mart'. *Sunday Times Magazine* (19 March 1995), pp. 30–33, 35–36, 38.

Quinn, Anthony. 'The Investment'. *Independent Magazine* (25 March 1995), pp. 34–37.

Self, Will. 'Something Amiss in Amis Country'. *Esquire: British Edition* (April 1995), pp. 70–76.

Kaplan, James. 'Tennis with Amis'. *New York Magazine* (29 May 1995), pp. 38–43.

Fuller, Graham. 'The Prose and Cons of Martin Amis'. *Interview* (May 1995), pp. 122–25.

Shnayerson, Michael. 'Famous Amis'. *Vanity Fair* (May 1995), pp. 132–40, 160–62.

1996

Wachtel, Eleanor. 'Eleanor Wachtel with Martin Amis: Interview'. *Malahat Review*, 114 (March 1996), pp. 43–58.

'Success, Money, Happy?'. *Observer Review* (12 October 1996), p. 5.

1997

Cowley, Jason. '"There Is a Kind of Mean Spiritedness of Which I Am the Focus"'. *Times* (4 August 1997), p. 15.

1998

Moss, Stephen. 'After the Storm'. *Guardian Weekend* (3 October 1998), pp. 22–4, 26.

Books devoted to Martin Amis

Diedrick, James. *Understanding Martin Amis*. Understanding Contemporary British Literature series. Columbia: University of South Carolina Press, 1995. (All Amis's novels from *The Rachel Papers* to *The Information*; *Einstein's Monsters*.)

Books with key discussions of the fiction of Martin Amis
(main novels discussed in brackets at the end of each entry)

Mallon, Thomas. *Stolen Words: Forays into the Origins and Ravages of Plagiarism.* New York: Ticknor and Fields, 1989. Chapter 3, 'The Epstein Papers: Writing a Second First Novel', pp. 89–143, discusses Jacob Epstein's alleged plagiarism of *The Rachel Papers* in his novel *Wild Oats* (1980). See also: Nichol, Don. 'Rewriting Plagiarism'. *Angelaki*, 1:2 (Winter 1993/94), pp. 13–23.

Massie, Allan. *The Novel Today: A Critical Guide to the British Novel 1970–1989.* London and New York: Longman in association with the British Council, 1990, pp. 46–8. (*The Rachel Papers, Dead Babies, Success, Other People, Money.*)

Miller, Karl. *Doubles: Studies in Literary History.* Corrected edn. Oxford and New York: Oxford University Press, 1987, pp. 409–15. (*Success, Other People, Money.*)

Taylor, D.J. *A Vain Conceit: British Fiction in the 1980s.* London: Bloomsbury, 1989, pp. 103–6. (*Money.*)

Essays that focus wholly on Martin Amis
Essays which cover two or more Martin Amis novels/short story collections (where it is not clear from the essay title, Amis titles discussed are in brackets at the end of each entry).

Alexander, Victoria N. 'Martin Amis: Between the Influences of Bellow and Nabokov'. *Antioch Review*, 52:4 (Fall 1994), pp. 580–90. (*Money; London Fields.*)

Caputo, Nicoletta. 'L'Etica della Forma: Strategie di Straniamento in *Other People: A Mystery Story* (1981) e *Time's Arrow* (1991) di Martin Amis [The Ethics of Form: Strategies of Estrangement in Martin Amis's *Other People: A Mystery Story* (1981) and *Time's Arrow* (1991)]'. *Confronto Letterario: Quaderni del Dipartimento di Lingue e Letterature Straniere Moderne dell'Universita di Paviae*, 21:23 (May 1995), pp. 73–104.

Finney, Brian. 'Narrative and Narrated Homicides in Martin Amis's *Other People* and *London Fields*'. *Critique: Studies in Contemporary Fiction*, 37:1 (Fall 1995), pp. 3–15.

Hawkes, David. 'Martin Amis (1949–)', in George Stade and Carol Howard, eds. *British Writers: Supplement IV.* New York: Charles Scribner's Sons, 1997, pp. 25–44. (All Amis's novels up to *The Information; Einstein's Monsters.*)

Moyle, David. 'Beyond the Black Hole: The Emergence of Science Fiction in the Recent Work of Martin Amis'. *Extrapolation: A Journey of Science Fiction and Fantasy*, 36:4 (Winter 1995), pp. 305–15. ('Martin Amis' Bibliography on MLA Database gives an incorrect first page no. of 304.) (Moyle states that it 'is difficult to ascertain' whether Martin Amis 'was inspired by his father's interest in . . . science fiction . . . or whether he was, or is, an "addict" of the genre' (p. 305). As chapter six of this Guide (p. 81) shows, however, Amis, according to his interview with David Profumo, was both a science fiction reader and, under a pseudonym, a reviewer of works in that genre.) (*Einstein's Monsters, London Fields, Time's Arrow.*)

Padhi, Shanti. 'Bed and Bedlam: The Hard-Core Extravaganzas of Martin Amis'. *Literary Half-Yearly* (Mysore, India), 23:1 (January 1982), pp. 36–42. (*The Rachel Papers, Dead Babies.*)

Powell, Neil. 'What Life Is: The Novels of Martin Amis'. *PN Review* 20, 7:6 (1981), pp. 42–5. (*The Rachel Papers, Dead Babies, Success.*)

Stokes, Peter. 'Martin Amis and the Postmodern Suicide: Tracing the Postnuclear Narrative at the Fin de Millennium'. *Critique: Studies in Contemporary Fiction* (1997), 38, pp. 300–11. (*Money; London Fields.*)

Thomson, David. 'Martin Amis (1949–)', in Merritt Moseley, ed. *British Novelists Since 1960: Second Series. Dictionary of Literary Biography*, vol. 194. A Bruccoli Clark Layman Book. Detroit, Washington DC; London: Gale Research, 1998, pp. 7–18. (All Amis's novels up to *The Information; Night Train* is listed in the Bibliography (p. 7) but not discussed; *Einstein's Monsters.*)

Essays that focus partly on Martin Amis

Titles of specific Amis novels discussions, and page references to main mentions within each essay, are given after each essay title.

Bernard, Catherine. 'Dismembering/Remembering Mimesis: Martin Amis, Graham Swift', in Theo D'haen and Hans Bertens, eds. *British Postmodern Fiction*. Postmodern Studies series no. 7. Amsterdam – Atlanta GA: Rodopi Press, 1993, pp. 121–44. (*Money*, pp. 125–6, 137–8; *London Fields*, pp. 124–5, 129–31, 137–44; *Time's Arrow*, pp. 133–4.)

Brown, Richard. 'Postmodern Americas in the Fiction of Angela Carter, Martin Amis and Ian McEwan', in Ana Massa and Alistair Stead, eds. *Forked Tongues: Comparing Twentieth-Century British and American Literature*. London and New York: Longman, 1994, pp. 97–103. (*The Rachel Papers*, pp. 98–9; *Dead Babies*, pp. 99–100; *Money*, pp. 100–1; *London Fields*, pp. 101–3; *Time's Arrow*, p. 103.)

Gilman, Sander L. 'Love + Marriage = Death', in Thomas Foster, Carol Siegel, Ellen E. Berry, eds. *Sex Positives: The Cultural Politics of Dissident Sexualities*. New York: New York University Press, 1997, pp. 197–224. (*The Rachel Papers*, pp. 216–17; *The Information*, pp. 217–19.)

Kemp, Peter. 'British Fiction of the 1980s', in Bradbury and Cooke (1992), pp. 216–28. (*Money*, p. 222; *London Fields*, pp. 222–3.)

Lodge, David. 'The Novelist Today: Still at the Crossroads?', in Bradbury and Cooke (1992), pp. 203–15. (*Success*, p. 210; *Money*, pp. 208, 210; *London Fields*, p. 208.)

Robson, Ian. 'Faking Emotion: Sentimentality in Modern Literature', Essay no. 7 in Digby Anderson and Peter Mullen, eds. *Faking It: The Sentimentalisation of Modern Society*. London: Social Affairs Unit, pp. 119–36. (*London Fields*, pp. 131–3; *The Information*, p. 133.)

On *Money*

Ashley, Leonard R.N. '"Names Are Awfully Important": The Onomastics of Satirical Comment in Martin Amis'[s] *Money: A Suicide Note*'. *Literary Onomastics Studies*, 14 (1987), pp. 1–48.

Doan, Laura L. '"Sexy Greedy Is the Late Eighties": Power Systems in Amis's Money and Churchill's *Serious Money*'. *The Minnesota Review: A Journal of Committed Writing*, 34–35 (Spring 1990), pp. 69–80.

Pacard-Huguet, Josiane. 'De La Fiction Pornographique A L'Errance Litteraire: *Money* de Martin Amis [From Pornographic Fiction to Literary Roving: Martin Amis's *Money*]'. *Etudes Anglaises*, 50:2 (April–June 1997), pp. 244–56.

Todd, Richard. 'The Intrusive Author in British Postmodernist Fiction: The Cases of Alasdair Gray and Martin Amis', in Matei Calinescu and Douwe Fokkema, eds. *Exploring Postmodernism*. Utrecht Publications in General and Comparative Literature series vol. 23. Amsterdam/Philadelphia: John Benjamins, 1987, pp. 123–37.

On *Einstein's Monsters*

Falconer, Rachel. 'Bakhtin's Chronotope and the Contemporary Short Story'. *South Atlantic Quarterly*, 97:3–4 (Summer–Fall 1998), pp. 699–732.

Mars-Jones, Adam. *Venus Envy*. Chatto Counterblasts series. London: Chatto and Windus, 1990, especially pp. 2–19.

On *London Fields*

Bernard, Catherine. '*London Fields* de Martin Amis: La Mimesis Revisitée [Martin Amis's *London Fields*: Mimesis Revisited]'. *Etudes Britanniques Contemporaines: Revue de la Société d'Etudes Anglaises Contemporaines*, 1 (December 1992), pp. 1–15.

Holmes, Frederick. 'The Death of the Author as Cultural Critique in London Fields', in Ricardo Miguel Alfonso, ed. *Powerless Fictions? Ethics, Cultural Critique, and American Fiction in the Age of Postmodernism*. Amsterdam – Atlanta GA: Editions Rodopi B.V., 1996, pp. 53–62.

Mills, Sara. 'Working with Sexism: What Can Feminist Text Analysis Do?', in Peter Verdonk and Jean Jacques Weber, eds. *Twentieth-Century Fiction: From Text to Context*, Interface series. London and New York: Routledge, 1995, pp. 206–19.

Smith, Penny. 'Hell Innit: The Millennium in Alasdair Gray's *Lanark*, Martin Amis's *London Fields*, and Shena Mackay's *Dunedin*. *Essays and Studies*, 48 (1995), pp. 115–28.

On *Time's Arrow*

Easterbrook, Neil. 'I Know That It Is To Do with Trash and Shit, and That It Is Wrong in Time: Narrative Reversal in Martin Amis'[s] *Time's Arrow*'. *Conference of College Teachers of English Studies*, 55 (1995), pp. 52–61.

Joffe, Phil. 'Language Damage: Names and Naming in Martin Amis's *Time's Arrow*'. *Nomina Africana: Journal of the Names Society of Southern Africa*, 9:2 (October 1995), pp. 1–10.

Joffe, Phil. 'Martin Amis'[s] *Time's Arrow* and Christopher Hope's *Serenity House*. After Such Transgressions, What Reconciliation?', in Hermann Wittenberg and Loes Nas, eds. *Auetsa 96: Proceedings of the Conference of the Association of University English Teachers of South Africa*. University of the Western Cape, 30 June–July 1996: Volume 1: Southern African Studies.

Bellville, South Africa: University of Western Cape Press, 1996, pp. 200–12. (The discussion of *Time's Arrow* here is to some extent the same as in the Joffe essay above.)

Marta, Jan. 'Postmodernizing the Literature-and-Medicine Canon: Self-Conscious Narration, Unruly Texts, and the *Viae Ruptae* of Narrative Medicine'. *Literature and Medicine*, 16:1 (Spring 1997), pp. 43–69. (The Bibliography on the MLA Database gives the incorrect volume no. of 6.)

Menke, Richard. 'Narrative Reversals and the Thermodynamics of History in Martin Amis's *Time's Arrow*'. *MFS: Modern Fiction Studies*, 44 (1998), pp. 959–80.

Morse, Donald E. 'Overcoming Time: "The Present of Things Past" in History and Fiction' in Donald E. Morse, ed. *The Delegated Intellect: Emersonian Essays on Literature, Science and Art in Honor of Don Gifford*. American University Studies, Series XXIV, American Literature, vol. 57. New York: Peter Lang, 1995, pp. 203–23.

Slater, Maya. 'Problems When Time Moves Backwards: Martin Amis's *Time's Arrow*'. *English: The Journal of the English Association*, 42:173 (Summer 1993), pp. 141–52.

On *The Information*

Howard, Gerald. 'Slouching Towards Grubnet: The Author in the Age of Publicity'. *Review of Contemporary Fiction*, 16:1 (Spring 1996), pp. 44–53.

Nash, John. 'Fiction May Be A Legal Paternity: Martin Amis's *The Information*'. *English: The Journal of the English Association*, 45:133 (Autumn 1996), pp. 213–24.

Reviews of and other press comment on Martin Amis's novels

The Rachel Papers

Ackroyd, Peter. 'Highway of Good Intentions'. *Spectator*, 231: 7587 (24 November 1973), p. 674.

Prince, Peter. 'Out of Afrika'. *New Statesman*, 86:2226 (16 November 1973), p. 744.

Dead Babies

Ackroyd, Peter. 'Tirades'. *Spectator*, 25:7686 (18 October 1975), pp. 510–1.

Feinstein, Elaine. 'Killing Time'. *New Statesman*, 90:2326 (17 October 1975), pp. 479–80 (*Dead Babies* discussed on p. 480.)

Mellors, John. 'Raw Breakfast'. *Listener*, 30:2430 (30 October 1975), p. 582.

Success

Ableman, Paul. 'Sub-texts'. *Spectator*, 240:2815 (15 April 1978), pp. 23–4.

Morrison, Blake. 'Into Nastiness', *Times Literary Supplement*, 3967 (14 April 1978), p. 405.

Other People

Ableman, Paul. 'Fairies and Violence'. *Spectator*, 246:7967 (21 March 1981), p. 22.

Glendinning, Victoria. 'Lamb's Tale from Amis'. *Listener*, 105:2702 (5 March 1981), p.319.

Hollinghurst, Alan. 'Opening Eyes'. *New Statesman*, 101:2608 (13 March 1981), p.21.

Levin, Bernard. 'Forgetfulness of Things Past'. *Sunday Times* (8 March 1981), p.43.

Morrison, Blake. 'In the Astronomical Present'. *Times Literary Supplement*, 4066 (6 March 1981), p.247.

Sutherland, John. 'Making Strange'. *London Review of Books*, 3:5 (19 March–1 April 1981), p.21.

Money

Korn, Eric. 'Frazzled Yob-Gene Lag-Jag'. *Times Literary Supplement*, 4253 (5 October 1984), p.1119.

Tennant, Emma. 'Seriously Rich'. *Literary Review*, 77 (November 1984), pp.44–5.

London Fields

Fuller, Graham. 'Murder He Wrote: Martin Amis's *Killing Fields*'. *Village Voice* (24 April 1989), p.75.

Imlah, Mick. 'A Dart in the Heart'. *Times Literary Supplement*, 4513 (29 September–5 October 1989), p.1051. (The bound volume of the *Times Index: January–December 1989* (Reading: Research Publications, 1990), p.21, gives an incorrect date of 'SEPT 5' for this issue.)

Pesetsky, Bette. 'Lust Among The Ruins'. *New York Times Book Review* (4 March 1990), p.42.

Sante, Luc. 'Cheat's Tale'. *New Republic* (30 April 1990), p.46.

Szamuely, George. 'Something Amiss with Martin'. *National Review*, 42:10 (28 May 1990), pp.46–8.

London Fields and The Booker Prize

Anon. 'News'. *Times Literary Supplement*, 4524, *Liber* section (15 December 1989), p.13.

Bragg, Melvyn. 'A Novel Experience'. *Sunday Times* (17 December 1989), Section C, pp.1–2.

Ellison, Jane. 'Battle Fields'. *Guardian* (12 October 1989), p.21.

Howard, Philip. 'Booker Jury Omits Famous Authors'. *Times* (22 September 1989), p.1.

Lodge, David. 'The Novelist Today: Still at the Crossroads', in Bradbury and Cooke (1992), p.208.

Time's Arrow

Anon. 'Six Characters in Search of a Booker'. *Sunday Times* (29 September 1991), Section 7, pp.10–11.

Harrison, M. John. 'Speeding to Cradle from Grave'. *Times Literary Supplement*, 4614 (20 September 1991), p.21.

Kermode, Frank. 'In Reverse'. *London Review of Books*, 13:17 (12 September 1991), p.11.

Koenig, Rhoda. 'Holocaust Chic'. *New York Magazine* (21 October 1991), pp.117–8.

Scruton, Roger. 'International Books of the Year'. *Times Literary Supplement*, 4628 (13 December 1991), p.12.

Taylor, D.J. 'Backward Steps'. *New Statesman and Society* (27 September 1991), p.55.

The Information

Howard, Gerald. 'Slouching towards Grubnet: The Author in the Age of Publicity'. *Review of Contemporary Fiction*, 16:1 (Spring 1996), pp.44–53.

Loose, Julian. 'Satisfaction'. *London Review of Books* (11 May 1995), pp.9–10.

Mars-Jones, Adam. 'Looking on the Blight Side'. *Times Literary Supplement*, 4799 (24 March 1995), pp.19–20.

Nash, Gerald. 'Fiction May Be a Legal Paternity: Martin Amis's *The Information*'. *English: The Journal of the English Association*, 45:183, pp.213–24. ('Martin Amis' Bibliography on MLA Database gives an incorrect part no. of 133.)

Comment on Amis's advance for *The Information* (see also 'Interviews' section above, entries for 1995–98)

Anon. '"I'm Looking for Money. Give Me Some. Go On. Do It"'. *Sunday Times* (8 January 1995), Section 3, p.3.

Grove, Valerie. 'How Amis Signed Up the Demon King [the American literary agent Andrew Wylie]'. *Times* (13 January 1995), p.15.

Hillmore, Peter. 'A Novel Way of Making a Fortune'. *Observer Review* (15 January 1995), p.6.

Jones, Nicolette. 'An Advance Taken Amiss'. *Times* (13 January 1995), p.32.

Jones, Nicolette. 'The Selling of Martin Amis'. *Bookseller*, 4648 (20 January 1995), pp.10–11.

Lezard, Nicholas. 'Counting the Cost of Martin's Money'. *Independent* (11 January 1995), p.24.

Tonkin, Boyd. 'Better Rich than Read'. *Independent* (18 December 1996), p.13.

Young, Toby. 'The Amis and Means'. *Guardian* (13 January 1995), p.4.

Night Train

Brookner, Anita. 'Farewell, My Lovely'. *Spectator*, 279:8826 (27 September 1997), pp.36–7.

Jones, Russell Celyn. 'Unable to Do the Locomotion'. *Times* (18 September 1997), p.42.

Oakes, Philip. 'Bloody and For Real'. *Literary Review*, 232 (October 1997), p.50.

O'Brien, Sean. 'Choo-Choo Time'. *Times Literary Supplement*, 4929 (19 September 1997), p.22.

Phillips, Adam. 'Cloud Cover'. *London Review of Books*, 19:20 (16 October 1997), pp.3, 6–7.

Updike, John. 'It's a Fair Cop'. *Sunday Times Books* (21 September 1997), Section 8, pp.1–2.

Walsh, John. 'Where Did All the Book Editors Go?'. *Independent on Sunday* (28 September 1997), Section 2, p. 5.

Walter, Natasha. 'The Gender Benders'. *Guardian* (29 July 1997), pp. 4–5.

Heavy Water and Other Stories

Jones, Russell Celyn. 'Not Such Light Reading'. *Times* (24 September 1998), p. 40.

Walter, Natasha. 'Fat Men, Thin Lives'. *New Statesman* (no volume or part no) (25 September 1998), pp. 81–2.

Film

The Rachel Papers (1989). Written and directed by Damian Harris, with Dexter Fletcher as Charles Highway, Ione Skye as Rachel Noyce [*sic*], Jonathan Pryce as Norman and Michael Gambon as Dr Knowd. A moderately entertaining comedy of adolescence which wholly lacks the hard edge of the original novel.

An article in the *Sunday Times* of 23 August 1998 (Section 1, p. 7a) announced that over the next twelve months, Hollywood was set to film four of Amis's novels – *Dead Babies, Money, London Fields* and *The Information*, 'despite [Amis's] reputation as Britain's most "unfilmable" author'. According to the *Times* of 17 June 1999, p. 39, director Nicolas Roeg has signed to film *Night Train*.

Websites

'The Martin Amis Web'
http://martinamis.albion.edu

A valuable site, established by James Diedrick, the author of *Understanding Martin Amis*. It includes interviews, selected reviews, criticism, biography, bibliographies and a filmography.

The address of the associated 'Martin Amis Discussion' is
http://amisdiscussion.albion.edu

ACKNOWLEDGEMENTS

The editor and publisher wish to thank the following for their permission to reprint copyright material: Methuen (for material from 'Martin Amis', in *Novelists in Interview*); University of South Carolina Press (for material from *Understanding Martin Amis*); Charles Scribner's Sons (for material from 'Martin Amis (1949–)', in *British Writers: Supplement IV*); Longman (for material from 'Postmodern Americas in the Fiction of Angela Carter, Martin Amis and Ian McEwan', in *Forked Tongues: Comparing Twentieth-Century British and American Literature*); *The Spectator* (for material from 'Tirades', 'Sub-texts', and 'Farewell, my lovely'); *PN Review* (for material from 'What Life is: The Novels of Martin Amis'); *Times Literary Supplement* (for material from 'Into Nastiness', 'In the Astronomical Present', 'Frazzled Yob-Gene Lag-Jag', and 'Looking on the Blight Side'); *Critique: Studies in Contemporary Fiction* (for material from 'Narrative and Narrated Homicides in Martin Amis's *Other People* and *London Fields*', and 'Martin Amis and the Postmodern Suicide: Tracing the Postnuclear Narrative at the Fin de Millennium'); Oxford University Press (for material from *Doubles: Studies in Literary History*); John Benjamins (for material from 'The Intrusive Author in British Postmodernist Fiction: The Cases of Alasdair Gray and Martin Amis', in *Exploring Postmodernism*); *The Minnesota Review* (for material from '"Sexy Greedy Is the Late Eighties": Power Systems in Amis's *Money* and Churchill's *Serious Money*'); *Literary Review* (for material from 'Interview: David Profumo Drops in on Martin Amis'); Chatto and Windus (for material from *Venus Envy*); *South Atlantic Quarterly* (for material from 'Bakhtin's Chronotope and the Contemporary Short Story'); *The Guardian* (for material from 'Battle Fields', and 'The Gender Benders'); *Essays and Studies* (for material from 'Hell Innit: The Millennium in Alasdair Gray's *Lanark*, Martin Amis's *London Fields*, and Shena Mackay's *Dunedin*'); Editions Rodopi (for material from 'The Death of the Author as Cultural Critique in *London Fields*', in *Powerless Fictions? Ethics, Cultural Critique, and American Fiction in the Age of Postmodernism*); Peter Lang (for material from 'Overcoming Time: "The Present of Things Past" in History and Fiction', in *The Delegated Intellect*); *Conference of College Teachers of English* (for material from '"I know that it is to do with trash and shit, and that it is wrong in time": Narrative Reversal in Martin Amis's *Time's Arrow*'); *MFS: Modern Fiction Studies* (for material from 'Narrative Reversals and the Thermodynamics of History in Martin Amis's *Time's Arrow*'); *London Review of Books* (for material from 'Satisfaction', and 'Cloud Cover'); *English: The Journal of the English Association* (for material from 'Fiction May Be a Legal Paternity: Martin Amis's *The Information*'); *Sunday Times* (for material from 'It's a Fair Cop'); *New Statesman* (for material from 'Fat Men, Thin Lives').

There are instances where we have been unable to trace or contact copyright holders before our printing deadline. If notified, the publisher will be pleased to acknowledge the use of copyright material.

The editor is most grateful to his wife, Angela Tredell, and to her colleagues in East Sussex County Library service, especially Carol Russell, for their speed and efficiency in obtaining copies of the many books and essays consulted in the preparation of this Guide. Another of her colleagues, Tina Smith, very kindly provided transport for bulky batches of the *Literary Review*.

Nicolas Tredell teaches courses in literature, art history, cultural and film studies, and information technology and society for the University of Sussex. He has contributed widely to journals in the UK and USA and his recent books include *Uncancelled Challenge: The Work of Raymond Williams; The Critical Decade: Culture in Crisis; Conversations with Critics* and *Caute's Confrontations: The Novels of David Caute*. His study of the novelist B. S. Johnson, *Fighting Fictions*, appears this year (2000). He is Consultant Editor for the Icon Readers' Guides series and has edited Icon Guides to *The Great Gatsby, Great Expectations*, 'Heart of Darkness', and *The Sound and the Fury/As I Lay Dying*.

INDEX

Ableman, Paul 11, 36–7, 47
Ackroyd, Peter 14, 25–6
Adorno, Andy 27, 28, 31, 32
Adorno, Theodor 133, 144, 189 n23, n25
America 21, 22, 23, 24, 26–7, 58–9
Amis, Kingsley 8–9, 10
    on Amis, Martin 50, 86
    'A Bookshop Idyll' 66–7
    Ending Up 45
    Larkin 185 n5
    Lucky Jim 18, 19, 20, 169
    New Maps of Hell 81
    One Fat Englishman 71
    Take A Girl Like You 177–8
Amis, Martin
    on Amis, Kingsley 8–9, 71
    life/work 7–8, 9, 81, 154, 166
    and main characters 57–8
    marriages/children 9–10
    in *Money* 9, 57, 59–60, 63, 65–6, 71, 76–7
    status 7, 183
Amis, Philip 38, 185 n5
anal humour 18–19
    see also coprocentrism
anti-hero 159–60, 181–2
apocalypse 89, 119, 124, 125
Arendt, Hannah 134, 140
art
    history 147–8
    victimisation 189 n23, n25
Asprey, Mark 104, 105, 106, 107–8, 119, 123
astronomy 158–9, 161, 174
Auschwitz 133, 134, 138–9, 145, 146, 190 n32
author 10, 68, 110, 123–4, 159
    Dead Babies 30, 33
    death of 110–11, 124
    intrusive 11, 55, 73–4

Bakhtin, Mikhail 29, 30, 32, 87
Ballard, J. G. 81
Barry, Gwyn 155, 156–7, 160, 169, 172
Barthes, Roland 110–11
Baudrillard, Jean 106, 108
Beer, Gillian 149
Bellamy, Edward 81
Bellow, Saul 63, 65, 68, 170, 174, 176
Bennett, Arnold 42–3
Bergonzi, Bernard 11, 60–1
Bigsby, Christopher 126
Bloom, Harold 8, 165, 166, 171–2
bodily functions 24, 32, 44

Booker Prize 11, 97, 98
Borges, Jorge Luis 87, 169
Bradbury, Malcolm 69–70
Bradley, A. C. 62
Bragg, Melvyn 97
Brookner, Anita 11, 175–6
Brown, Richard 10, 11, 21–2, 26–7, 58
'Bujak and the Strong Force' 85, 86, 88–9
Buzhardt, Marvell 26, 27, 28, 30, 31

canon 163–4, 166, 169, 172
'Career Move' 181
Celan, Paul 140–1
characters 57–8, 112, 174–5
    doubling 146, 155–6
    plot 61–2
    women 66–7, 108–9, 118, 157, 159, 177–8
chess games 66, 72
chronotope 87, 95
Churchill, Caryl 74, 77, 79
city life 36, 37, 158
class 78, 79, 181
Clausius, Rudolf 148
Clinch, Guy 104, 107, 111, 114–15
'The Coincidence of the Arts' 181
Coldstream, Giles 28, 32
Coleridge, Samuel Taylor 49
commodification 116, 117
confidence 62, 68
consumerism 63
contemporaneity 42, 43
coprocentrism 129, 131, 139, 143–4

Dead Babies 9, 23, 32
    Ackroyd 25–6
    America 23, 24, 26–7
    author 30, 33
    Brown 26–7
    Diedrick 29–33
    Feinstein 24–5
    Hawkes 33
    irony 29, 42
    Korn 58
    literary allusions 27–8
    Mellors 23–4
    names 27, 31–2
    pornography 29
    Powell 27–9
    sentimentality 24, 25
defamiliarisation 49, 51, 136–7
dehumanisation 129–30
'Denton's Death' 180, 181
Derrida, Jacques 166
destruction 46, 47–8, 51, 102
Dickens, Charles 18, 38, 184 n1, n3
Diderot, Denis 29, 30

Diedrick, James 8, 10, 14
  Dead Babies 29–33
  Other People: A Mystery Story 48–9
  The Rachel Papers 16–19
  Success 38–41
Doan, Laura L. 11, 74–9
Donaldson, Stephen 132
doubling
  characters 146, 155–6
  Money 67
  and orphan 11, 66, 67, 69, 70
  postmodern parody 117
  psychological 137–8, 146
  reader/narrative 136, 146
  Success 38

Easterbrook, Neil 11, 134–40
Eco, Umberto 174
Eddington, A.S. 141, 142, 149, 150
Einstein's Monsters 10, 11, 80
  Falconer 87–96
  irony 84–5
  military analogies 86–7
  narrators 86, 94–5, 96
  Profumo 80–3
Ellison, Jane 97, 99
entropy 142, 148–9, 150
Epstein, Jacob 22, 169
Ermarth, Elizabeth 92–4
evil 133, 134, 140, 189 n26

Falconer, Rachel 11, 87–96, 183
Feinstein, Elaine 11, 24–5, 33
feminism 64, 74–5, 83
Finney, Brian 11, 49–54, 103–10
Foucault, Michel 124
Fowles, John 69–70
Fraser, J.T. 129
Freud, Sigmund 139–40
Friendly, Tod 136, 141–2
Fuller, Graham 41, 124

Gay, Enola 102, 108
Gee, Maggie 97, 98
gender relations 74–5, 77
Genette, Gérard 137
genres 87, 174
Glendinning, Victoria 44
Golding, William 45
Goodney, Fielding 59, 60, 61–2, 65, 71, 75
Gray, Alasdair 69, 70, 73–4, 99–100
The Guardian 97
Gunn, Thom 43

Haffenden, John 10, 11, 15, 47–8, 61–6
Harrison, M. John 127

Hawkes, David 10, 19–21, 33
'Heavy Water' 180–1
Heavy Water and Other Stories 8, 10, 12, 180–3
Heidegger, Martin 125
hell 50, 53, 103
Hide, Amy 47, 50, 52
Highway, Charles 13–14, 15, 19, 20, 57–8
Hirsch, David H. 129–30
history 142, 147–8, 151–2
Hogg, James 74
Hollinghurst, Alan 44
Holmes, Frederick 11, 110–18
Holocaust 126, 127, 139, 143–4
holocaust imagery 85, 100
Hoolihan, Mike 173, 175–6, 177, 178, 179
Horridge, Keith 168
humour, black 109–10
Hutcheon, Linda 117
Huxley, Aldous 81

Imlah, Mick 112
'The Immortals' 82–3, 88, 94–5
impotence
  Dead Babies 32
  The Information 157–8, 160, 162, 167
  Time's Arrow 132, 138, 146–7
Independent on Sunday 173
The Information 8, 10
  astronomy 158–9, 161
  impotence 157–8, 160, 162, 167
  intertextuality 167, 169, 172
  Mars-Jones 154–9
  names 154, 169
  narrator 155
  Nash 163–72
  satire 156–7
  self-consciousness 172
  style 168
  women characters 157, 159
'Insight at Flame Lake' 82, 86, 88, 90–2
intertextuality
  The Information 167, 169, 172
  London Fields 105, 112
  The Rachel Papers 16
  Success 38
interviews 7–8
  Bigsby 126
  Haffenden 10, 11, 15, 47–8, 61–6
  Wachtel 126–7
The Invasion of the Space Invaders 73
irony
  Dead Babies 29, 42
  Einstein's Monsters 84–5
  Night Train 174
  time 162
  Time's Arrow 128, 131, 145–6

Jameson, Fredric 95, 116
'The Janitor on Mars' 181
Jones, Russell Celyn 11, 12, 177, 180

Kafka, Franz 18, 81
Kahler, Erich 129
Kappeler, Suzanne 78
Keats, John 17, 68, 115
Kermode, Frank 127
Korn, Eric 11, 55–8, 71

Lamb, Mary 45–6, 49, 52
Larkin, Philip 38, 56, 185 n5
Lawrence, D.H. 101
Leavis, Q.D. 175
'Let Me Count the Times' 180, 181
Lifton, Robert J. 11, 126, 134, 141, 146, 151
The Listener 23–4, 44
literary allusions
    Dead Babies 27–8
    London Fields 109
    Money 65, 68, 71–2
    Night Train 179
    The Rachel Papers 17–18
Literary Review 80
literature
    character's use of 15, 17, 20–1
    history 142, 151–2
    pornography 42
    value 164–5, 170–1
'The Little Puppy That Could' 81–2, 84, 85, 87–8, 92–4
Lodge, David 98
London Fields 10, 115–16
    apocalypse 81, 100–1, 111, 125
    Booker shortlist 11, 97
    Finney 103–10
    Holmes 110–18
    intertextuality 105, 112
    literary allusions 109
    misogyny 101, 117
    murder 103–4
    names 112, 162
    narrator 98, 101
    parody 115–16
    plagiarism 119–20
    plot 105–6
    self-reflexiveness 112–13, 165
    sexism 7, 97, 99
    Smith 99–103
    Stokes 118–25
    women characters 108–9, 118
London Review of Books 159, 170, 178
Loose, Julian 11, 159–63
Lyotard, Jean-François 117

McEwan, Ian 47, 83
McHale, Brian 149–50
Mackay, Shena 99–100
McKendrick, Alexander 9
MacLeod, Mark 116
Manson, Charles 23
Mars-Jones, Adam 11, 83–7, 154–9
Marshall, Skip 28
Martian techniques 44, 45, 48, 51, 58, 73, 161
Massie, Allan 44, 54
Maxwell, James Clerk 152–3
Mellors, John 11, 23–4
Melville, Herman 68
Mengele, Josef 134, 135, 144
Menippus 23–4, 25, 29, 30, 31, 32
Menke, Richard 11, 141–53
metafiction 50, 98, 109, 110, 112
Michener, Charles 8
Miller, Karl 11, 66–9, 70
Mills, Sara 7
mimesis/diegesis 141
misogyny 67, 78, 101, 117
money 63, 78–9
Money
    Americans 58–9
    Amis, Martin 9, 57, 59–60, 63, 65–6, 71, 76–7, 165
    Bellow 68
    Bergonzi 60–1
    class 78, 79
    Doan 74–9
    doubling 67
    Korn 11, 55–8
    literary allusions 65, 68, 71–2
    morality 63–4
    names 56, 59, 60, 75
    narrator 55
    parody 68
    satire 62
    self-reflexiveness 70, 72–3
    sexism 78, 79
    Shakespeare 65, 168
    Tennant 187 n27
    Todd 69–73
    women characters 66–7
morality 63–4
The Moronic Inferno 58–9, 170
Morris, William 81
Morrison, Blake 11, 34–6, 44–7
Morse, Donald E. 11, 127–33
murder 49, 103–4

Nabokov, Vladimir 38–9, 81, 134
names
    Dead Babies 27, 31–2

The Information 154, 169
London Fields 112
Martianism 45
Money 56, 59, 60, 75
The Rachel Papers 16–17
Time's Arrow 136, 138
narrative 136, 142–3, 146
narrator 39–40, 49, 110, 155, 176
  Einstein's Monsters 86, 94–5, 96
  The Information 155
  London Fields 98, 101
  Money 55, 57
  Night Train 173, 179
  Other People: A Mystery Story 49–50
  Time's Arrow 128
Nash, John 11, 163–72
Nazi doctors 129–30, 132–3, 137–8, 146, 151
negentropy 151
New Statesman 9, 13, 45, 48
Night Train 8, 10, 11, 12
  astronomy 174
  irony 174
  literary allusions 179
  narrator 173, 179
  parody 173–4, 180
  Phillips 178–80
  self-consciousness 178
  Updike 173–5
  Walter 177–8
  women characters 177–8

Oakes, Philip 177
O'Brien, Sean 177
The Observer 9–10, 81
Onan 66, 67
orphan/double 11, 66, 67, 69, 70
Orwell, George 65, 81
Othello 65, 168
Other People: A Mystery Story 9, 11
  destruction 46, 47–8, 51
  Diedrick 48–9
  Finney 49–54
  Massie 44
  Morrison 44–7
  narrator 49–50
  women's viewpoint 67, 177

parody 19, 68, 115–16, 173–4, 180
Parry, Diana 27, 28
Pesetsky, Bette 114, 117
Phillips, Adam 12, 178–80
plagiarism 22, 119–20, 169–70
plot 61–2, 105–6
pornography 29, 42, 64, 67, 76, 99, 113–14
post-holocaust 84, 87–8
post-human 174–5

postmodernism 11
  commodification 116
  intrusive author 73–4
  parody 117
  rhythmic time 93
  simulation 106, 108
  unbildungsroman 141
Powell, Neil 11, 27–9, 41–3
Prince 46, 48, 50, 52–3
Prince, Peter 11, 13–14
Profumo, David 11, 80–3
psychic numbing 28, 137–8

quantum theory 190 n33
Quinn, Anthony 7

Rabelais, François 24
The Rachel Papers 9, 13, 16, 184 n6
  adolescence 14–15, 20
  America 21, 22
  Diedrick, James 16–19
  Hawkes 19–21
  literary allusions 17–18
  names 16–17
  parody 19
  self-consciousness 16, 18
Raine, Craig 44, 45, 46, 48, 69, 186 n13
readers 96, 110, 164, 168
  narrative 136, 146
  reversals 129, 133
Reid, Christopher 45, 46
responsibility 127, 139
Riding, Gregory 34–5
Riding, Terry 34–5
Robbe-Grillet, Alain 174
Rockwell, Jennifer 174, 175–6, 180
Roth, Philip 159, 176

Sade, Marquis de 31, 33
Sante, Luc 112–13
Sartre, Jean-Paul 50, 53, 192 n13
satire 32, 62, 156–7
  see also Menippus
Schell, Jonathan 80
schizophrenia 90–2, 129
Scruton, Roger 11, 127
Self, John 56, 59–60
  and Amis, Martin 63, 65, 72
  narrator 55, 57
  as orphan 70–1
  suicide attempt 69
  as victim 65–6, 74–5
  women 78
  word usage 75–6
self-consciousness 16, 18, 172, 178
self-destruction 47–8, 101–2

self-disapproval 67
self-plagiarism 170
self-referentiality 165
self-reflexiveness 16, 70, 72–3, 112–13, 165
sentimentality 24, 25, 35–6
sex 78–9, 84, 167
sexism 7, 78, 79, 97, 99
sexual inversion 81
similes 163
simulation 106, 108
Six, Nicola 98, 101–2, 104–5, 111–12, 117–18, 120
Smith, Penny 11, 99–103
Smith, Roxeanne 28
sodomy 101–2, 104
The Spectator 14, 25–6
'State of England' 180, 181, 182–3
Steinem, Gloria 64
Steiner, George 126, 183
Stokes, Peter 11, 118–25
Street, Selina 56, 70, 76, 78
style
    Jones 180
    Loose 159, 161, 163
    Mars-Jones 85–6, 155, 159
    Nash 167, 168
    Walter 182
Success 9, 35–6, 38, 39–40
    Diedrick 38–41
    Morrison 34–6
    Powell 41–3
Sutherland, John 44
Swift, Jonathan 17, 18, 19, 32, 34

Talent, Keith 104, 106–7, 111, 113–14, 120–1, 162
Talent, Kim 106, 123
Tennant, Emma 187 n27
thermodynamics 11, 148–53
'Thinkability' 80, 85
time 148, 165
    consciousness 149–50
    end of 89, 94–5
    ethics 140
    evil 189 n26
    irony 162
    postmodernism 93

psychic 139–40
'The Time Disease' 80–1, 86, 87, 89
time reversal 89, 128
The Times 97, 177, 180
time's arrow 149–50, 189 n19
Time's Arrow 10, 11, 89
    Easterbrook 134–40
    Holocaust 100, 126, 139, 143–4
    impotence 132, 138, 146–7
    irony 128, 131, 145–6
    Menke 141–53
    Morse 127–33
    names 136, 138
    narrator 128
Times Literary Supplement 9, 34, 44, 97–8, 127, 154, 177
Todd, Richard 11, 55, 58, 69–73
Tull, Gina 157, 158
Tull, Richard 155, 156–7, 159–60, 162
Twain, Martina 56, 60, 62, 67, 70, 72

Unverdorben, Odilo 128–33, 134–8, 146
Updike, John 11, 159, 173–5

victimisation 40, 49, 65–6, 74–5, 123, 189 n23, n25
Villiers, Quentin 27, 28, 30, 31, 33
Vonnegut, Kurt 132, 190 n44

Wachtel, Eleanor 126–7
Walsh, John 173
Walter, Natasha 11, 12, 177–8, 181–3
Whitehead, Keith 28, 30, 32
Wilson, Jonathan 8
Winterson, Jeanette 99
women 40, 66–7, 78, 99, 118, 177
women characters
    The Information 157, 159
    London Fields 108–9, 118
    Money 66–7
    Night Train 177–8
Woolf, Virginia 82
Wordsworth, William 49
writing 99, 167, 171–2

Young, Samson 98, 101, 103–4, 106–8, 117, 119, 121–3

Printed in the United States
40273LVS00002B/100